VIOLENT PHENOMENA: 21 ESSAYS ON TRANSLATION

EDITED BY

VIOLENT PHENOMENA

21 ESSAYS ON TRANSLATION

KAVITA BHANOT
JEREMY TIANG

TILTED AXIS PRESS

CONTENTS

INTRODUCTION

Kavita Bhanot & Jeremy Tiang

In the summer of 2020, in the midst of a pandemic, a large, joyful group of protestors pulled slave trader Edward Colston from his plinth on Colston Avenue, rolled him through the city, and threw him into Bristol Harbour. Four of the protestors were later found not guilty in a court of law, prompting the Conservative MP Scott Benton to tweet, 'Are we now a nation which ignores violent acts of criminal damage?'

In *The Wretched of the Earth*, Frantz Fanon asserts that 'decolonisation is always a violent phenomenon'[1]. He continues: 'Colonialism is not a thinking machine, nor a body endowed with reasoning faculties. It is violence in its natural state, and it will only yield when confronted with greater violence.' And indeed, the activists protesting the Colston statue had tried non-violent means, with years of petitions and lobbying.

The toppling, when it came, was a concrete act of collective impatience, a refusal to wait any longer. This anthology represents a similar spirit of defiance and resistance, drawing upon the work, discussions, and struggle of numerous writers and translators over many years, only a small fraction of whose voices are represented here. We have sought to put together a cross-section of a much larger conversation, with a growing number of translators and writers acknowledging that translation is a fundamentally political act, something Aaron Robertson alludes to with his mischievous comparison of 'the good translator and the good civic actor'.

Like all literature, translation is produced by labour, and is therefore affected by the material conditions of societies and systems. As Yogesh

[1] Or at least he does in Constance Farrington's 1963 translation. In Richard Philcox's 2004 rendition, 'un phénomène violent' becomes 'a violent event', but we found Farrington's phrasing more resonant – thus illustrating the importance of translation choices!

Maitreya writes: 'Literature in any world language, with translation being one of its facets, has always been a reflection of the dominant community.' So it shouldn't be surprising to find life's inequalities present here too – not only in the text but also the circumstances surrounding the production and marketing of it. We need to name these dynamics and hierarchies, rather than treating literature as an abstract entity untouched by real world structures.

Campaigns to improve the working conditions and stature of translators often focus on incremental change, which is inadequate. On their own, even calls for diversity and inclusion *within* translation can be tokenistic, a way of preventing or containing the violence of *real* change, maintaining a comfortable (for some) status quo. Whilst we should certainly be paying attention to who translates and what is translated, especially in a field dominated by middle-class whiteness, we also have to consider ideology and perspective, to ask how a text is translated, why it is being translated, who it is translated for, how the translation industry upholds existing hierarchies. In other words, we have to consider the harm inherent to translation itself.

Translation is often, in Khairani Barokka's phrase, an act of 'colonial extractivism' that presumes a 'right of access to information'. Many within the Anglophone literary world have an impulse to learn about other cultures and languages that arises from a sense of being 'above' the world and wanting to grasp it, leading to an acquisitive approach to translation. This can be traced back to an imperial mindset; Western interest in literature in 'other' languages was motivated by a desire or need to better understand their colonies and colonised subjects – to rule, dominate, and exploit. Such translations disseminated this 'knowledge' more widely in the West. As Edward Said says in *Orientalism*:

> On the one hand, Orientalism acquired the Orient as literally and as widely as possible; on the other, it domesticated this knowledge to the West, filtering it through regulatory codes, classifications, specimen cases, periodical reviews, dictionaries, grammars, commentaries, editions, translations, all of which together formed a simulacrum of the Orient and reproduced it materially in the West, for the West.

Translation can inhabit a similar role today. The Indonesian translator Tiffany Tsao notes in an interview a 'dispiriting' trend on the part of Western readers, whose 'consumption of Indonesian literature so far is tied up with how much it can teach them about local culture, history, food, feel, etc. Ultimately, literature isn't a tourist guidebook.'[2] At a more institutional level, a translation grant offered by a US university articulates its interest in 'developments outside the historical West', as an 'inquiry into epistemologies and paradigms emerging from societies and spaces beyond the West'. Such phrasing is common, but this seemingly benign 'curiosity' can be questioned as an assertion of power. 'Doesn't translation act also as unconditional access, as surveillance, as an expanding force of the global capitalist market of literature?' writes Mona Kareem in her essay.

This imperialist mindset tends to play out within translations themselves. The dominant framing of literary translation suggests that it exists on a spectrum between 'domestication' and 'foreignisation'.

The first approach, in which cultural and linguistic 'difference' is absorbed and assimilated, is referred to by Shushan Avagyan as 'the illusory dictates of the translator's invisibility, the concomitant domestication of the foreign text and replacement of difference' turning translation into 'an act of ideological violence, in which its aim is to bring back a cultural other as the recognizable and the familiar'. This attitude can be traced back to translators such as Richard Burton, who writes in his foreword to *The Book of the Thousand Nights and One Night* (subtitled "a plain and literal translation of the Arabian Nights' Entertainments"):

> Holding that the translator's glory is to add something to his native tongue[...] I have carefully Englished the picturesque turns and novel expressions of the original in all their outlandishness[....] I have carefully sought out the English equivalent of every Arabic word, however low it may be or "shocking" to ears polite...not exaggerating the vulgarities and the indecencies which, indeed, can hardly be exaggerated.

[2] Tiffany Tsao interviewed by Whitney McIntosh, *Liminal*, 16 November 2020

Lest we imagine Burton's idea of translation as 'adding to the native tongue' is an antiquated one, a 2010 anthology of translated work was titled *Making The World Legible*, making one wonder who the presumed reader of this book might be – someone *outside* 'the world'?

The second approach of 'foreignising' – maintaining difference to keep the text 'exotic' – is exemplified by Sawad Hussain's description of publishers insisting on 'a desert scene' for her book cover. Lawrence Venuti presents this as a more enlightened method than domesticating:

> A translated text should be the site where a different culture emerges, where a reader gets a glimpse of a cultural other, and resistancy, a translation strategy based on an aesthetic of discontinuity, can best preserve that difference, that otherness, by reminding the reader of the gains and losses in the translation process and the unbridgeable gaps between cultures.[3]

While a refusal to domesticate might seem admirable, Venuti's framing is one of fetishising and othering. The main problem with the domesticating/ foreignising framework, is that it defines translation strategy in terms of difference from a presumed normality. In this paradigm, the 'mainstream' perspective is presumed to be a neutral, stable centre – such as the 'mythical white reader' of Anton Hur's essay – against which all translations must be measured.

Given the longstanding, ongoing relationship between translation and colonialism, while we were putting this anthology together, we found ourselves asking if there was a contradiction inherent in the very idea of decolonising translation. ('What will we talk about next? Decolonising Colonialism?' asks Ayesha Manazir Siddiqi.)

It's tempting to draw a parallel in response to ongoing colonial domination: colonial nations once set forth from centres of power to extract labour and resources from elsewhere, their ships returning laden with rare spices. Now the colonised are in a position to say: We are no longer willing to be your spice; we are asserting our own stories, sailing our own ships. But the structures that have formed us, that this anthology has emerged from, are bigger and more powerful than individuals.

---

[3] Lawrence Venuti, *The Translator's Invisibility*

Setting out to put together an anthology of essays by translators across the world – searching for, gathering together, presenting these 'world' voices (that some may choose to see as representing regions, nations, races, religions, languages and struggles) – felt undeniably colonial at times. This anthology is located within Anglophone structures of publishing and funding; likewise, its editors are limited by the voices (via English) that we could 'access' and bring together (and even here, in this framing, in the use of the word 'access', the effort to make these voices 'accessible', we see glimpses of the colonial legacy we have inherited).

Meanwhile as editors, via different yet overlapping circumstances,[4] we have been formed through colonisation and continuing colonial structures of whiteness in ways that we cannot even comprehend. We can't claim that we're not colonial or that we could ever fully decolonise ourselves (as well as inhabiting other supremacies of race and gender, religion and caste, class and anti-blackness). The decolonial struggle for self-assertion falls too often and too easily into a binary, which doesn't account for ongoing layers of power and dominance.

Across these essays we see different strategies employed to resist traditional perceptions of translation and the translator, including questioning the idea of 'good' translation, claiming and producing 'bad' translation, or, echoing Glissant's call for the right to opacity, refusing to translate at all. M. NourbeSe Philip and Barbara Ofosu-Somuah analyse how a dystranslation of Philip's poem *Zong!* came to be 'yet another site of unapologetic colonial claiming', while Elisa Taber speaks of how her translation practice includes untranslating Guaraní terms. Eric Fishman notes in the afterword to his translation of Monchoachi, 'it's obvious that Creole is, at the least, resistant' to accepting 'the status of a language' – a further complication to any kind of translation attempt. Hamid Roslan also discusses a Creole – Singlish, 'hewed from the Chinese, Malay and English' – and its role in his 'faithless act of translation'.

Other contributors, by contrast, focus on how translation can make visible the hitherto unseen. Yogesh Maitreya writes about translating

[4] Kavita Bhanot's parents are from Punjab, India while she was born and brought up in Britain. Jeremy Tiang was born and raised in Singapore just over a decade after independence.

Nagraj Manjule's poetry from Marathi into English, seeing himself in the language for the first time and articulating and communicating this presence to the rest of the world. This is also important to Haitian writer René Depestre who, in Kaiama L. Glover's words, 'has long been preoccupied with the power differential that places him on the margins of a world order he has worked passionately to upset'. Meanwhile, an absence of translation can feel like erasure. As Sofia Rehman says, 'Who knew a blank page could feel so oppressive.'

Above all, this book is a challenge to inherited assumptions about translators and translations being neutral, making the case that every aspect of translation is political. Strikingly, and going against the stereotype of the 'objective' translator, none of these essays are dispassionate. From Eluned Gramich's conversations with her mother to Layla Benitz-James's culture shock in Spain, there is a strong personal element to most of them; we can't extricate ourselves from the worlds we translate from or into, even if we want to. These are accounts of translators in the thick of it, so enmeshed in the cultures and languages they are translating between, that neutrality is neither possible nor desirable. Madhu Kaza, whose contribution 'Not a Good Fit' charts her tangled heritage language journey, articulates this idea clearly in the seminal *Kitchen Table Translation:*

> [T]ranslation can be an intimate act, and many of us use our translation skills in non-professional as well as professional capacities. Some of us, when we translate, call on our family (rather than colleagues) to help us with challenging passages or words. Some second generation, diasporic and indigenous writers who speak (or partly speak) an ancestral language at home might find the discourse of mastery fraught, especially when access to a language has been lost through historical violence and dislocation. And some of us experience translation all the time in our bodies, names, homes, movements and daily lives even if we are not translating from one text to another.

Gitanjali Patel and Nariman Youssef explore the complicated relationship that the diaspora has (or doesn't have) to 'heritage' languages, a sometimes fraught association that we also see in Onaiza

Drabu's learning of Kashmiri as an adult 'through a lot of luck, a little bit of effort and a rage inside me', and Sandra Tamele's 'absence of a mother tongue [leaving] a void inside me that I tried to fill by learning foreign languages'. Amid such linguistic complexity, simplistic ideas about only translating into one's 'native tongue' are inadequate, as amply shown in Lúcia Collischonn's essay.

Even as many of these essays draw from personal experience, they are ultimately about systems. While individual efforts and experiences are important, real change, fundamental change, takes place at the level of structures, and in order to shift these, we first need to see them clearly. Oppressive systems must be dismantled rather than negotiated, in order for new possibilities to emerge, for us to even imagine something else.

Broadcaster and historian David Olusoga, who gave evidence in the Colston trial, later said, 'The toppling of the statue and the passionate defence made in court[...] makes [a] deliberate policy of historical myopia now an impossibility.' There is a similar need to address structural inequalities and historical myopia in the publishing and translation worlds because business as usual is no longer possible. We hope this anthology will contribute to that conversation. Colonialism is violence, and it is difficult to see how decolonising could be anything other than a violent disruption.

1. ALL THE VIOLENCE IT MAY CARRY ON ITS BACK*: A CONVERSATION ABOUT LITERARY TRANSLATION

Gitanjali Patel & Nariman Youssef

* The phrase 'all the violence it may carry on its back' is used in relation to translation by Madhu Kaza in her Editor's Note to *Kitchen Table Translation*, a major source of inspiration for the authors.

London 2019: *You're at a drinks reception after a literary translation event and find yourself talking to two colleagues. It's unclear whether they are talking to you. Their body language seems to suggest you're in the conversation, although you haven't been addressed yet.* Heritage languages. *Your ears prick up. Here we go. They must be about to ask your name, no doubt they are keen to hear about your...* Natural translators. *You blush, it's rare to receive compliments from white colleagues. And what's in a name, anyway?* Raw talent. *Does raw mean good? Surely they're not suggesting all 'heritage' speakers have...* Need to nurture that. *Wait, what?* No pride in their heritage. *You start edging slowly away from the conversation. Your colleagues barely notice.*

Words have the power to distort and misrepresent, to blind us to the unarticulated, to the wilfully or accidentally obscured. Sometimes, our stories are left untold for fear that they would crack, splinter, and break under the pressure of the moulds available for the telling. Or because the words we have at our disposal would leave large swathes of our experiences in the dark. But words also have the power to reimagine and reconfigure. At the very least, they can illuminate some of the hidden corners of our lived experience. Audre Lorde writes: 'The quality of light by which we scrutinize our lives has direct bearing upon the product which we live, and upon the changes which we hope to bring about through those lives'. Let the stories come as they are then, cracks and all. Perhaps that's how just the right quality of light gets in.

* * *

The idea of being a professional translator seems strange when it's a seamless part of what you've always done from a young age – back and forth between home (family members) and the world (school, university, doctors, shops, public transport).

One day my mum claimed she wasn't fluent in any of the four languages she speaks and I haven't stopped thinking about it since.

As someone who has been writing fiction and poetry in English for over a decade, I first became interested in translation three years ago when I developed a passion for drawing on my Chinese heritage and literary roots to inform my writing. I had been practicing code-switching in many ways already as a writer of the Chinese diaspora, so translation felt like a natural extension of my writing journey.

Even now, I worry that much of the interest in my work as a translator has to do with the novelty of a Black person who somehow stumbled into the field.

I am a writer as well as a translator, which I like to think means I approach language with a lot of intention. I would even go so far as to say that I approach it with more intention than white writers and translators, if only because my claims of mastery over it are always tenuous, always being called into question.

I debuted at the same time as a white translator in the same competition. The white translator kept getting books to translate. I was given nothing.

At some point I started to remove my nationality from my bio and CV. It had become clear to me that the fact that I hadn't been born in an English-speaking country was hurting my chances of finding work as a literary translator, and in English-language publishing more broadly.

You're usually one of a few non-white faces amongst translator communities – and others who are not white tend to be from more privileged backgrounds.

I was brought up reading Enid Blyton, despite not setting foot in the UK till I was eighteen.

Sometimes, I feel too foreign for this home. Sometimes, this home feels too foreign for me.

* * *

The world of Anglo-Atalantic literary translation has, for a long time, been dominated by a number of assumptions about who translators are and what translation is about. Translators are presumed to be white. Their

English that of the educated middle classes. Their modes of expression and creative processes primarily and unequivocally rooted in the language and tradition into which they translate. They come to learn and read 'other' languages out of curiosity about the 'outside' world. Translation is a bridge between two distinct cultures. Literatures are gateways into foreign lands. Translators cross the bridge, step through the gateway and bring back whatever treasures they can carry. Some things might get lost on the way.

These assumptions still dominate the way translation is thought of and talked about in 'most mainstream literary spheres'. We are centring, in this essay, the experiences of translators for whom such mainstream is not enough.

* * *

Whenever someone asks what my first language is, they get a speech about colonialism and its aftereffects. I'm sorry, did you think that was a simple question?

Read Jeremy Tiang's piece 'The world is not enough'.

Not all languages are equal. Some take up more space in the world and in our imaginations than others. For English users who have no other language, or none until school or university, it may not be clear how ubiquitous English is, even for those who never use it. Meanwhile, those who come to English as a lingua franca, a language of the world, might never think of it as *also* a private language. It may be hard to imagine what it's like to live in a world 'where all instructions, all the lyrics of all the stupidest possible songs, all the menus' are in the language you uncomplicatedly call your own. Olga Tocarczuk, not without some irony, posits this lack of a private language to hide behind as a reason to feel overexposed. But it is also a source and signifier of power: the ability to choose when and if you ever want to step outside the comfort of your own tongue.

I am often praised for translating into a non-native tongue, and told by translators that they wish their second language could be as good as my English. What they don't seem to understand is that English holds a different global status from other languages, and that English wasn't just some kind of hobby I picked up by choice, but my language of instruction.

Translators are often assumed, or told, to translate into their 'native tongue' or 'first language'. A simplistic rule that not only implicitly prescribes certain parameters of quality—which imprison a lot of translation into the blandest form of literary English—but also presupposes a very specific and narrow relationship to languages in general. A relationship that privileges language-learning on a foundation of monolingualism, discounting the phenomena of migration and the experiences of migrants. One that renders the majority world—where colonial languages prevail—invisible.

The most benign of responses to my source language are the most humiliating. 'Oh! Wow! Really? Interesting!' An awkward two-second silence and ten vigorous nods later, the next line is almost always, 'Your English must be very good!' That is usually the moment of a thousand deaths.

Not everyone comes to the languages and literatures of 'others' out of a conscious move beyond themselves. Reading in multiple languages does not have to be an act of generosity or curiosity; some of us have existed with multiplicity all our lives.

I grew up bilingual and can't relate when people say translation is a bridge. How can it be, when for me both languages reside in the same place?

Data published by Nielsen Book highlights a Eurocentric focus in terms of translators' source languages in the UK.

Because the anglophone literary translation world, especially in the UK, is so disproportionately concerned with European literatures —under-standably more so in the wake of Brexit—everything else is relegated to a separate sphere, which is seen as less literary, more othered, altogether inferior, labeled 'heritage', 'community' or 'minority'.

The experience of grappling with, translating from, your heritage language can be intense and emotional; you have a different relationship to the language – this is something that a non-heritage language translator perhaps can't relate to.

A 2020 Higher Education Policy Institute report defines 'heritage languages' as 'those spoken by a minority community, often learned at home or in Saturday schools'.

Translators who work with 'heritage' languages are rarely part of mainstream literary translation conversations. And those who are invited in can be seen to be doing the service of bringing in 'outsider' voices. If a white translator works from a minoritised language, their work is seen to be especially generous, selfless, or adventurous. The same does not apply if the translator is a heritage user of the language they translate from. Then, they are seen as not having had much of a choice. They are seen as examples of raw talent over delicate craft.

You feel as if the language that you're translating from is in your bones, your blood, your veins. It's deep inside you. But you still feel insecure that you learnt the language in the home, you didn't learn it in a thorough and formal way – for example, through a university course, through grammar, linguistics, literature.

Translators of colour who translate out of minoritised languages are often assumed to be a heritage speaker of that language. If they're not, they face a constant demand to explain themselves. In fact, if you're a translator who looks like you or someone in your family could have been born off the island, as it were, whatever language(s) you translate from, you're constantly called upon to explain yourself: have you considered translating from your heritage language? Or, so you're translating from the language of your childhood? (Unsaid: so you haven't studied it like *real* literary translators do.)

I am treated like an exotic creature when people see that I am brown and fluent in French. The questions and comments I get asked in return are insulting and thinly conceal a wonderment that, as a person of colour, I had access to learning a foreign language at all.

The reality is that many translators of colour do not have a 'heritage language', or may be estranged from it as a result of colonial legacies, conflict, or assimilation pressures. Our mother's tongue may be different to our father's and it's possible we know neither. Yet we are expected to, because 'heritage' is code for non-European, and functions as a perpetual reminder that we don't belong.

I have been asked why I don't study Black languages, as though that category means anything of substance. Black people exist all over the world. We come from several languages, and have had several languages forced upon us. What language is not a Black language, at this point?

A 2017 Authors Guild survey in the US compiled data from 205 literary translators and found:
→ 83% of translators were white, 6.5% Hispanic or Latinx, 1.5% Black/African American, 1.5% Asian American and 1% Native American.
→ 'the most common languages were French, Spanish, German, and Italian, followed by Portuguese, Russian, Chinese, Catalan, and Japanese.'

The field is often described as too white, lacking diversity, not representative of the communities surrounding it. A common response is to call for 'more diversity' and lament that translators of colour are 'hard to find'. Attention is then immediately turned to short-term solutions, such as creating pathways to train and mentor new translators to come into the industry. Without considering how those new translators would find a place for themselves in the field as it is.

After a translation reading, an established translator approached me to say he noticed my accent and wanted to advise me to get a co-translator who is a native speaker of English.

The 2019 UK Publishers Association Workforce Survey, based on data from over 57 publishing houses and 12,700 employees, found:
→ 86% of respondents identified as white
→ 90% straight
→ 69% female
→ 93% non-disabled;
→ a 'significant lack of class diversity: 20% of respondents had attended a fee-paying school (3 times the UK average)'

Diversity calls are problematic in a number of ways. They lump us all into two groups: white and 'non-white', homogenising 'the diverse' into a box that can be ticked by inviting one person of a non-white hue to a panel and calling it diverse. By talking about 'diversity' as the divergence from the norm, existing translators of colour are erased, engaged with as group representatives, not individuals. Newcomers are othered before they have even entered the room.

I can always tell when I'm only in a room as the diversity garnish because someone realised at the last minute that their guest list was all white.

For the 2020 Warwick Prize for Women in Translation there were 132 titles entered for the prize in 34 languages, which, as stated on the website, was a 'substantial increase' from the last three years. Of the 132 titles, there were:
→ 99 titles from Europe
→ 29 titles from Asia and Africa combined
→ 5 titles of the 132 were written by Black women
→ 11 of the 111 translators are translators of colour

Numbers are an easy distraction; the number of languages on a prize list (the further from Europe they sound like they are, the better), the number of people of colour on a panel or committee—both are seen to accomplish 'diversity' and signal 'progress'. But these numbers don't equate to making space for minoritised translators, writers, styles, languages, and Englishes, in all the different ways these may deviate from what is considered the norm. What these 'diversity' efforts do is create an illusion of inclusivity that in reality consists of a few, small spaces for us to squeeze into, shape ourselves

On the 2021 International Booker Longlist, the only translator of colour was Chen Zeping, who appears as co-translator.

by, shiny ourselves for. Power hierarchies prevail. Existing structures are kept intact.

Earlier this year, a colleague of mine remarked that I was the first Black translator he had ever met. I can't help but wonder whether this is by design. Communities, networks, entire industries are structured in such a way that isolates a segment of us and makes us feel that we have to navigate all this alone.

Read Kavita Bhanot, "Decolonise, not Diversify" and Brian Friel's *Translations*.

'Promoting diversity', 'celebrating multilingualism', 'nurturing minority talent', 'championing international voices' are all things that can be done without acknowledging or challenging underlying structures. Without facing how the practice of translation itself centers whiteness and westernness, and how it defaults to reflecting and replicating colonial patterns. English is a colonial language. The work of anglophone translators—venturing out and bringing back, only understanding others by making them in their image—follows the routes of colonial acquisition. English is also a global language. The literatures written in English often grapple with its imperial legacies. Why can't literary translation do the same? How can translators work with this larger-than-life language without acknowledging all the violence it may carry?

To untrained ears, English was the only language spoken in my family growing up. But underneath the violently enforced 'standard' English I think of as a veneer, our true language was African American Vernacular English, a variation on the English that was brutalized into my bloodline in the place of anything I would have been able to call a mother tongue. AAVE repurposes imperial English and ruptures its constraints. It's dynamic. It's warm. It's evocative. It is the closest thing I have to something I can call my language.

Read Kaiama L. Glover's '"Blackness" in French: On Translation, Haiti and the Matter of Race'.

Colonial acquisition has its rules and conventions. What is brought over is made to fit into the predetermined spaces of labs, libraries and museums, its difference accentuated but its foreignness contained. These rules and conventions have been internalised by many in the West who are allowed to go through life with uncontested identities. Their curiosity about what lies beyond the realms of their own identities remains trapped within a scale of otherness: too foreign on one end, not foreign enough on the other. We see this in the exoticising sparkle around 'discovering' literature from places that have little representation in the anglophone literary sphere, as long as they contain the expected degree of foreignness; no more, no less.

The agent said, 'give me a story more typically Indian, you know. Caste. Women's stuff. Poverty.'

During the Publishing Panel at the 2020 British Centre for Literary Translation Summer School,

For many anglophone publishers, stories from the Global South have to fit certain narratives and writing styles. Often 'fluency' is the main cri-

one publisher described how their process started with checking the translation has 'got the kind of fluency we would be looking for'.

terion used to assess the quality of a translation. Concepts of fluency shift our focus to the target language and the norms of its most standard form, the one with the highest capital: 'This is what works in English'. Whose English? Ethical concerns are seen to stand in opposition to formal elements, rather than pathways to new forms of experimentation: 'That would sound odd in English'. What if that which sounds odd to one person evokes familiarity for another?

While I pride myself on reading widely across different languages, I had never realised how much of what I was choosing to read in those languages was restricted by what had already been translated and 'accepted' by the West.

Read Madhu Kaza's Editor's Note to *Kitchen Table Translation*.

Migrating across linguistic and cultural borders means the translated text faces the same challenges as the migrant person in a new land: lack of belonging, pressure to assimilate, threats of erasure. It depends on where the text is migrating from. Some may find it easier to enter, easier to blend in. Other texts are held at the border and forced to prove their worth.

An agent I was working with told me there was a publisher interested in acquiring a book I'd translated a sample of, but that they refused to work with me because I was not a native speaker. Another publisher praised the same sample for how fluent it was, especially considering 'she's not a native speaker'.

The 2015 Writing the Future report highlighted that a Black, Asian or minority ethnic writer's 'best chance of publication' was to write on themes such as 'racism, colonialism or post-colonialism, as if these were the primary concerns of all BAME people'.

The anglophone literary translation border force are the gatekeepers of the industry, deciding which texts, which translators make it through. They define the scope of a 'good' text, what will 'work' in translation, what will sell, whose English. They define the reader. They interrogate the text at the border. And as translators, we are often made to choose between internalising the gatekeepers' terms and conditions and sending the text 'back home'.

I've been an immigrant my whole life, and I will often find myself listing reasons why I belong in this country as much as the next person. I go through the same mental process with literary translation. I tell myself I have to be better than *or I won't be allowed to stay, in the same way as immigrants are made to feel they have to be exceptional, either in terms of their skills or their suffering—otherwise, what are they doing here anyway?*

According to a 2020 Spread The Word report, 'the idea of the core reader as a white, middle-class older woman (sardonically referred to as "Susan" by several of [the report's] respondents) remains dominant [and] while publishers would like to publish more writers of colour, they believe it is too commercially risky to do so.'

The consequences of having a homogenous group at the port of entry is that a dominant, mainstream perspective is centred, actively encouraged, protected. Anxiety about the 'foreign', the 'different', is packaged as economic viability. These stories and the characters in them are seen as 'unrelatable', without spelling out exactly *to whom.*

I'm self-conscious of how much I have to prove myself, as an outsider in a Eurocentric field. What kinds of risks am I not taking or choices am I not making as a translator for the sake of proving my 'normalcy'?

The assumed readers that publishers cater for are undemanding and risk averse. These are readers who want things to make sense, instead of wanting to make sense of things, who want to journey into another world that is identical to the one they have already imagined. Demands are made on behalf of these 'core readers' with little interrogation of the underlying assumptions about who they are and who else is being excluded as a result. There will always be a 'for whom' question. The only ethical choice, then, is to be conscious of the question and to respond to it with intent.

I can't imagine that many of the white translators I know feel the same debt to the source language, the same desire to do it justice. Because that indebtedness comes, I think, from my own experiences of having my English(es) mocked, disparaged, invaded, misappropriated, co-opted, used for personal gain, and stamped out. I do not want to reenact that violence on another language.

When translation is done well, daringly, it can broaden perspectives, shift paradigms, challenge assumptions. But it doesn't carry inherent value in its own right. An ethical approach to translation requires understanding enough about linguistic power hierarchies to take chances on destabilising dominant forms of English, to deny those forms the unquestioned privilege of making the whole world in their image.

I am fascinated by the ability of translation to inform, add to, and expand the target language. In my translation practice, I try to work towards ways of translating that push against the Western gaze and decolonize translation practices.

Read Édouard Glissant on the 'right to opacity' and Khairani Barokka's 'Translation of/as Absence, Sanctuary, Weapon'.

Because power breeds entitlement, unquestioningly accepting and benefiting from the supremacy of a standardised English leads to the belief that anything can, and should, be translated. Untranslatability is not a temporary barrier to be broken into but a fundamental right. Understanding this is the cornerstone of translation as a reflective practice that involves ongoing learning and humility.

In an interview with Veronica Esposito, Yasmine Seale responds to a question about her background with this creative ideal: 'Where I am from and where I live may be less important here than the more private, complex biographies of eye and ear'.

The tendency to view 'otherness' as a challenge or a threat, to be neutralised with 'fluent' translation, rests on the many assumptions about who translates literature and for whom, and enables those assumptions to seep into every aspect of the translation experience. A more 'diverse' translation cadre will not seamlessly lead to a more diverse translation practice. Not while translators are measured by their ability to fall in line with a fluency imperative that implicitly privileges the dominant language and pits ethics against creativity as opposing forces. Only by continuing to shine the light on the power dynamics inherent in the ways we translate and the ways we talk about translation—until questioning the norms of the practice becomes the norm—will the private, complex, layered subjectivities of translators find spaces to flourish.

POSTSCRIPT

Writing this piece has been tremendously difficult. Somewhat surprising given that when we – the co-authors – first met, it was precisely over the themes of this essay that we bonded. But back then it was our secret conversation. We enjoyed the uncomplicated relief of being able to discuss things we didn't discuss with many others. Then the questions we were asking ourselves became public ones. And the answers that were being thrown around them seemed hasty and incomplete. A deeper engagement is needed – we know that much. We were never quite sure if it was as much about literary translation as it was about our place in the professional worlds we chose.

When we reached out to colleagues to share their experiences, we were struck by their generosity, honesty and willingness to trust two (in some cases) strangers with their personal stories. We realised that similar conversations were happening at the same time as ours, focussed on different themes in different but related ways. And it is precisely those conversations that we want to keep going.

For sharing their experiences (via the interspersed quotes, and in many more not included in the final version), our sincerest thank you to Aaron Robertson, Anton Hur, Bruna Dantas Lobato, Edwige-Renée Dro, Jen Wei Ting, Jeremy Tiang, Julia Sanches, Kavita Bhanot, Kavitha Karuum, Khairani Barokka, Kólá Túbòsún, Naima Rashid, Paige Aniyah Morris, Somrita Urni Ganguly, and Yilin Wang.

BIBLIOGRAPHY

'2017 Authors Guild Survey of Literary Translators' Working Conditions: A Summary', report published by *The Authors Guild,* 2017: www.authorsguild.org/wp-content/uploads/2017/12/2017-Authors-Guild-Survey-of-Literary-Translators-Working-Conditions.pdf

Porter Anderson, 'Nielsen Reports Translated Literature in the UK Grew 5.5 Percent in 2018', *Publishing Perspectives*, 2019: publishingperspectives.com/2019/03/nielsen-reports-translated-literature-in-uk-grows-5-percent-in-2018-booker

Porter Anderson, 'The UK's International Booker Prize 2020: The Longlist is Announced', *Publishing Perspectives,* 2020: publishingperspectives.com/2020/02/international-booker-prize-2020-longlist-is-announced

Khairani Barokka, 'Translation of/as Absence, Sanctuary, Weapon', *The Poetry Review,* 108:2, 2018: poetrysociety.org.uk/translation-of-as-absence

Kavita Bhanot, 'Decolonise, not Diversify', *Media Diversified,* 2015: mediadiversified.org/2015/12/30/is-diversity-is-only-for-white-people

Megan Bowler, 'A Languages Crisis?', report published by the Higher Education Policy Institute, 2020: www.hepi.ac.uk/wp-content/uploads/2020/01/HEPI_A-Languages-Crisis_Report-123-FINAL.pdf

'Diversity Survey of the Publishing Workforce 2019', report published by *The Publishers Association,* 2019: www.publishers.org.uk/publications/diversity-survey-of-the-publishing-workforce-2019

Veronica Esposito, '"Wild Irreverence": A conversation about Arabic Translation with Yasmine Seale', *World Literature Today,* 2020: www.worldliteraturetoday.org/blog/interviews/wild-irreverence-conversation-about-arabic-translation-yasmine-seale-veronica

Édouard Glissant, 'For Opacity', *Poetics of Relation*, trans. Betsy Wing, Ann Arbor: The University of Michigan Press, 1997: www.jackie-inhalt.net/reh/bilder/edouard-glissant-for-opacity.pdf

Kaiama L. Glover, '"Blackness" in French: On Translation, Haiti, and the Matter of Race', *L'Esprit Créateur*, John Hopkins University Press, 59:2, 2019: muse.jhu.edu/article/728220

Madhu Kaza, 'Editor's Note', *Kitchen Table Translation: An Aster(ix) Anthology*, Blue Sketch Press, 2017.

Audre Lorde, 'Poetry Is Not a Luxury', *Sister Outsider*, Penguin Books, 2019.

'Publishers Panel', *British Centre for Literary Translation*, Summer School, 2020: www.youtube.com/watch?v=aHCmWtb8jyU

'Re:Thinking "Diversity" in Publishing', report published by *Spread The Word*, 2020: www.spreadtheword.org.uk/wp-content/uploads/2020/06/Rethinking_diversity_in-publishing_WEB.pdf

Jeremy Tiang, 'The World is Not Enough', *Asymptote*: www.asymptotejournal.com/special-feature/jeremy-tiang-the-world-is-not-enough

Olga Tocarczuk, *Flights*, trans. Jennifer Croft, Fitzcarraldo Editions, 2017.

The Warwick Prize for Women in Translation, list of eligible titles, 2020: warwick.ac.uk/fac/cross_fac/women-intranslation/hp-contents/warwick_prize_for_women_in_translation_2020_-_eligible_submissions_.pdf

'Writing the Future Report: Black and Asian Authors Publishers in the Market Place', report published by *Spread The Word*, 2015: www.spreadtheword.org.uk/writing-the-future

2. "BLACKNESS" IN FRENCH: ON TRANSLATION, HAITI, AND THE MATTER OF RACE

Kaiama L. Glover

> The basic grammar of blackness is often [...] lost in translation.
> —Brent Edwards, *The Practice of Diaspora*[1]

In this article, I reflect on the stakes and the practice of translating into English an Afro-diasporic text written in French. More specifically, I address the imbricated layers of translation involved in bringing renowned Haitian author René Depestre's prize-winning 1988 novel *Hadriana dans tous mes rêves* first to the space of metropolitan France and, subsequently, to an anglophone reading public. Reflecting on the translation of this particular work provides an opportunity to consider the various challenges that inhere in translating Haiti, both metaphorically/culturally and literally/linguistically, to a world largely primed for its degradation.[2] A close look at *Hadriana* compels us to examine the stakes of translating, in particular, to a global readership that most often views Haiti through the lens of irrevocable, demeaningly racialized difference. What is entailed in 'carrying over'[3] meaning from a Haitian context to a non-Haitian, Euro-francophone audience and, from there, to an Afro-anglophone world? What is the task of the translator within this racially hierarchized transatlantic space?

In thinking through these questions, I have taken as my point of departure writer and translator John Keene's call for more substantive reflection on race across diverse cultural frameworks. Keene argues that to translate 'blackness' in its various iterations and geo-cultural contexts might serve to make plain the contingency of race as lived experience and, further, to push against homogenizing, U.S.-centric conceptions of what blackness represents. "Were more black voices translated," posits Keene, "we would have a clearer sense of the connections and commonalities, as well as the differences across the African Diaspora, and better understand an array of regional, national, and hemispheric issues."[4] Indeed, while there exists great continuity among the many sites of Africa and its diasporas, there is no such thing as a global 'Black experience.' Diverse and divergent colonial and postcolonial histories have produced heterogeneous Black geographies, epistemologies, cultures, and languages, rendering Black peoples in many ways illegible to one another.

It is within this broad context that I consider the geo-cultural site-symbol that is Haiti, a place whose 'blackness' continues to be seen as uniquely pathological. It must be said: Haiti is 'Black' in a special kind of way. Although as foundationally Afro-diasporic as its Caribbean neighbors, Haiti has been long disparaged by the particular racialized denigration of its popular religion. The idiosyncrasy of Haiti's 'blackness' has everything to do with degrading perceptions and representations of Vodou. A clear case of what Haitian anthropologist Michel-Rolph Trouillot identifies as the deployment of culture to euphemize the idea of race, North Atlantic discourse concerning Haiti consistently casts the island nation as fundamentally stunted by its Afro-spiritual practices. Insofar as theories of cultural difference equate more and less transparently with theories of race, the stigmatization of Vodou as cultural practice is unequivocally racial.

Haiti thus presents a high-stakes example of 'blackness' in need of translation. But not just any kind. Haiti needs translation as a potential tool/site of articulation, that is, as "a process of linking or connecting across gaps" (Edwards 11), of facilitating "the recognition of necessary heterogeneity and diversity," so as to produce "a conception of 'identity' which lives with and through, not despite, difference."[5] Translating *Hadriana* was, for me, such a potential "discourse of diaspora" (Edwards 12), a destigmatizing effort that might place an alternative narrative of Haitian Vodou into circulation in the Global North. Following Keene, I have understood translating Haitian literature from French into English as a means, however modest, of creating space for an expanded notion of blackness within the African diaspora.

Haiti's persistent denigration in globally circulating narratives of perceived political dysfunction and socio-economic despair makes this task of translating the "Black Republic" very much a matter of ethics. As Tejaswini Niranjana has argued convincingly, "[i]n a postcolonial context the problematic of translation becomes a significant site for raising questions of representation, power, and historicity."[6] In order to grasp fully the significance of this claim, it is important to begin by thinking about the means via which writers from the so-called Global South present themselves for circulation outside of their local context, presenting their 'foreignness' for appreciation and, ultimately, consumption on familiar terms.

VODOU AND HAITI IN A GLOBAL FRAME

> What is a book anyway? It is a product, a commercial item. I write in order to be read, in order to sell to the people around me. But if they cannot read, my book is worth nothing. It is a commercial product which is going to stay here, insulted by dust.[7]
>
> —René Philoctète

In 1946, nineteen-year-old Haitian poet and student revolutionary René Depestre left his homeland in the wake of a national political transformation he had been instrumental in effecting. Depestre spent the subsequent thirty years of his life engaged in militant socialist activism throughout Western and Eastern Europe, South America, and the Caribbean, including twenty years in Cold War Cuba, all the while prolifically writing poetry and political essays. He currently resides in Lézignan-Corbières, in the Aude region of southern France. Throughout these lifelong peregrinations, Depestre has sought to reach an audience situated well beyond the space of his native land. Be it in his capacity as poet, novelist, or political essayist, he has written consistently for a public situated primarily outside of Haiti, presenting his island to another—an Other—global space. In this respect, Depestre has long been preoccupied with the power differential that places him on the margins of a world order he has worked passionately to upset. He has understood that staging his desired intervention requires a sustained practice of cultural translation.

Depestre's extra-insular aspirations are as readily apparent in his poetry and prose fiction as they are in his political writings, and *Hadriana* is no exception. Steeped in the so-called marvelous real, *Hadriana dans tous mes rêves* foregrounds the fantastical and the erotic within a frame that opens onto the Atlantic world from a decidedly Haitian perspective. Upon its publication, *Hadriana* sold almost 200,000 copies and won several awards, including the prestigious Prix Renaudot.[8] But as Colin Dayan has brought to light, the popular success of the novel in many ways reflected and revealed the racialized projections and exoticist desires of the French reading public. Reviewers in France encouraged readers to "let themselves go," to immerse themselves in "the land of zombies," and to embrace the "deflowerings, aphrodisiac emanations, sexual exploits, forbidden ecstasies" and "irresistible sorcery" of the Haitian folk.[9]

Despite—or, perhaps, given—the terms of the novel's acclaim in France, *Hadriana* has been the subject of sustained critique in academic circles. Where French reviewers and award-givers rejoiced in the escapist fantasies permitted by Depestre's tropical narrative, North Atlantic Caribbeanist scholars have accused the author of exploiting Haitian culture as an exotic commodity for European consumption.[10] Although it is certainly true that many postcolonial writers choose or are compelled to live in the Global North while continuing to write about their home countries, the fact that Depestre distanced himself from socialism as of the late 1970s and ultimately retired to the French countryside has left him particularly vulnerable to critical interrogation involving questions of authenticity and political engagement.

It is the case that *Hadriana dans tous mes rêves* tells a Haitian story to a non-Haitian audience; the novel is marked linguistically, structurally, and narratively by efforts to translate Haiti (in)to a wider francophone space. Published in France by the prestigious Éditions Gallimard, *Hadriana* necessarily belongs to the fraught category of "world literature," a network of literary works that is ultimately embedded within the canons and hierarchies created by European imperial nation-states. Explicit elements of the novel make plain Depestre's attentiveness, at least in part, to a non-Haitian readership. Take, for instance, the extensive "Glossaire des termes haïtiens (Langue créole)" placed as an appendix to the narrative. Although the vast majority of the glossed words in this addendum relate to Vodou and so belong to a Haitian Creole lexicon, Depestre has rendered them orthographically in French. Also worth noting is Depestre's strategic deployment of epigraphs throughout the novel. His opening citation presents lines from a poem by French Surrealist René Char and is followed immediately by an allusion to French Surrealist intellectual André Breton's 1937 novel *L'amour fou*. Subsequent sections and chapters of *Hadriana* are framed by the words of James Joyce, Kateb Yacine, Victor Hugo, Johann Wolfgang von Gœthe, and Sophocles. Depestre makes use of these epigraphs to situate his novel, subtly yet insistently, within a predominantly European canon. He is clearly concerned both with *Hadriana*'s linguistic legibility and with the novel's positioning vis-à-vis the "regimes of value"[11] that consecrate the literary on a global scale.

This is the context within which Depestre has been subject to disapproval—critiqued for his perceived consent to, if not collusion with, the racist and ethnocentric "fetishisation of cultural otherness" (Huggan 10) mobilized by former and current imperial centers of the North Atlantic to circumscribe and exploit the Global South. It is a critical response that is bound up in anxieties regarding what theorist Graham Huggan has labeled "the postcolonial exotic." Huggan's concept outlines the recuperative tendencies of the Western literary institution—its capacity to absorb and domesticate difference as it consumes it. Indeed, postcolonial writers are often called upon to translate their foreignness for institutions, industries, and consumers situated primarily in the North Atlantic. Doing so is a tricky enterprise. Independent of an author's purpose or desire, a text can be easily co-opted "as an exotic good, not so different in its packaging from all of the other colonial exotica making its way into the metropole."[12] Postcolonial writers thus are caught within something of a bind. How does one represent Global South culture without sensationalizing it, reifying existing racial stereotypes, or censoring its idiosyncrasies in the interest of rendering it more palatable to a world that denies its value(s)?

How does one present non-Western culture to the West for consumption (comprehension, consideration) without betraying that culture in the process?

There is a fine line, it is true, between opening a window onto an "Other(ed)" culture and "staging racial and ethnic stereotypes" for commercial gain (Watts 11). This is arguably the line Depestre walks in *Hadriana dans tous mes rêves*. In chronicling the adventures of a pretty French girl who gets turned into a zombie, Depestre admittedly does not shy away from representing the pathologies of Haitian Vodou. He incorporates the unsavory dimensions of Haiti's religious practices, and he invites an interrogation of Vodou's ambivalence with regard to matters of race and gender. By including such over-the-top elements as evil sorcerers, sex-crazed human butterfly hybrids, and, yes, zombies, he risks affirming Western stereotypes about Afro-diasporic religion. By the same token, however, Depestre takes care to portray the intricacies of Vodou as epistemology, aesthetic, and faith.

At about the midpoint of the novel, for example, Depestre's narrator-protagonist Patrick Altamont (a character whose biography maps almost perfectly onto Depestre's own) presents a veritable anthropological treatise on the zombie myth in Haitian and global history. Titled "Prolegomena to a Dead-End Essay," the long passage lays out nine "propositions" that address the intersections between North Atlantic racism, global capitalism, and the philosophical purchase of Haitian cultural expression. Here and elsewhere in the novel,[13] Depestre's overtly outward-facing authorial gestures demand that Haitian Vodou be taken seriously as knowledge-system and worldview.[14] His narrator's thoughtful meditations on the mechanisms and philosophies of Haitian spirituality counterbalance and contextualize the more titillating portrayals of Vodou in the novel. The passages in which he explicates the intricacies of the zombie's juridical and legislative embeddedness in Haitian society, for example, or his staging of Vodou and Catholic rituals as equally valid and valued in the Jacmelian community, establish Vodou's complexity and real social legitimacy. Moreover, just as Depestre unabashedly represents Vodou's erotic investments, its preoccupation with blood and death, its hyper-valuation of whiteness, and its misogynist tendencies, he also gives us its practices of healing, its nourishment of the communal, and its insistence on joy and possibility.[15] To his reader, then, the responsibility for recognizing that a similarly fundamental duality informs the teachings and practices of every one of this world's most sanctioned global faiths.

PACKAGING HADRIANA: *THE TASKS OF THE TRANSLATOR*

> The dynamics of translation in a Caribbean frame must be inscribed within the region's histories and their afterlives; and these dynamics tend to suggest inequality and friction more than any senses of free flow and equivalence.
>
> —Charles Forsdick, "Translation in the Caribbean, the Caribbean in Translation"[16]

If Depestre's novel offered a translation of Afro-Haitian culture to a non-Haitian, francophone audience in the late 1980s, leaning as it did right into the whirl of complexities surrounding the global image of Haitian Vodou, my translation of *Hadriana* proposed carrying both Haiti's culture and language(s) across to a new target-reading public thirty years later. As an African-American woman of Caribbean descent, I kept foremost in mind three specific engagements in realizing this task: first, translating responsibly within the maelstrom of existing narratives about Haiti and 'blackness'/Vodou; second, translating to and for a desired Afro-diasporic readership; and third, remaining attentive to the 'packaging' of my translation.

The translator of Haitian literature must keep in mind "the politics of translating and the ethnocentric violence that sometimes accompanies it."[17] If done successfully, translating the work of postcolonial Black writers reveals "the range and complexity of black lives" on a global scale (Keene). If not, there can be more and less direct consequences regarding global policies toward peoples in 'Black' nations. Failures of cultural translation create hierarchies of value wherein 'lesser' cultures are mis-read as lacking or deficient—and subsequently are deemed worthy or not of protection from harm. As Huggan has convincingly noted, insofar as translation functions within a global market that tends to commodify difference, "the exoticist production of otherness [...] may serve conflicting ideological interests, providing the rationale for projects of *rapprochement* and reconciliation, but legitimizing just as easily the need for plunder and violent conquest" (Huggan 13). The case of Haiti provides a stark instance of the ways in which translation informs the discourses that determine which Black lives matter and, relatedly, the success or failure of policies and practices that have an explicit impact on those lives.

The power differential between Haiti and those (putatively post-)imperialist nation-states of Europe and North America that have been so imbricated in Haiti's social, political, and artistic institutions makes the question of translation less one of "the unequal power relations between languages" (Bassnett 343) and more one of the unequal power relations between cultures. Insofar as the majority of Haitian literature is translated into English from French, concern with the subjugation of a minority language is not 'the problem.' Rather, the concern is the subjugation of a racial and cultural "minority position" (Bassnett 341). In this position, Haiti and Haitians are assumed to be at once excessively legible (as in, transparent and simplistically two-dimensional) and absolutely *il*legible (as in, incomprehensible and 'other'). The most pernicious and obvious of these assumptions hinge on the matter of race. Exceptional and absolute, Haiti's 'blackness'—again, a 'blackness' fundamentally linked to Vodou—marks its every interaction with the world beyond its borders.

As postcolonialist cultural theorist Stuart Hall rightly argues, it is crucial not only to identify ways in which "economic structures are relevant to racial divisions," but also to consider "how the two are theoretically connected."[18] The first task is to attend to "the specificity of those social formations which exhibit distinctive racial or ethnic characteristics," what Hall names "this 'something else'" that *translates* backward and forward between the social/racial and the economic (Hall, "Race" 20, emphasis mine). Vodou is an instance of "this 'something else.'" It is an ostensibly "extra economic" (Hall, "Race" 20) factor that has a significant impact on Haiti's legibility to the outside world—a cipher through which the nation's political and economic struggles have been read, especially in the United States. As I have written about elsewhere, Vodou has been aggressively fashioned and thus widely perceived as an obstacle to Haiti's development.[19] Across various media and in myriad geocultural spaces, "no religion has been subject to more maligning and misinterpretation from outsiders over the past century."[20] From aid organizations, to the news media, to the Hollywood film industry, "the threatening spectacle of Vodou"—or "voodoo," in its so-called U.S.-American "translation"—is consistently deployed "by outsiders to signal the backwardness and indolence that they feel best describe Haitian history."[21] Further, ever since the word "voodoo" came into wide use in an English lexicon, the label has served to disparage Haitians. It has been used to evoke evil and brutality, sexual excess and depravity, and has had significant purchase in U.S. mediatizations of Haiti's supposed ungovernability and propensity for disaster.

The translation of Haitian Vodou into "voodoo" in English has been a highly politicized matter for the past several decades. Since 2011, Haitian and Haitianist scholars and practitioners of Vodou, spearheaded by historian Kate Ramsey and in conjunction with KOSANBA, a scholarly association dedicated to the study of Haitian Vodou, have petitioned various prominent media institutions to dissociate the term "voodoo" from Haitian spiritual practices by adjusting their stylesheets. To date, while the Policy and Standards Division of the Library of Congress has amended its subject heading to reflect the seriousness of getting these terms right, the Associated Press and numerous national U.S. publications have shown a marked indifference to the long-historical force of this malapropism. This insensitivity to the power of the term is regrettable, and it has been an issue in the domain of literary translation as well.

The 2015 publication of influential Haitian novelist Kettly Mars's *Saisons sauvages* in English is a troubling instance of this phenomenon. The novel's talented and much-decorated translator Jeanine Herman made (and has since defended) the decision to render "Vodou" as "voodoo" in the English text.[22] Queried about this choice in a published interview, Herman explains that after thinking "long and hard about *voodoo* vs. *vodou*," she and her editor "finally decided *voodoo* seemed more accessible." She continues, "I thought *voodoo priestess* had a nice ring to it, something almost Baudelairean about it." The insouciance of Herman's rationalization suggests, at best, an unawareness of the real stakes of such a choice. At worst, her position echoes "centuries of ahistorical arrogance and racial and cultural supremacy."[23] Granted, as Herman readily acknowledges, she had little to no familiarity with Haiti or its cultural and political realities prior to embarking on the translation of Mars's novel.[24] But this is distressing in and of itself. The absence of cultural sensitivity resulting from the translator's lack of information about the source (con)text is a function, ultimately, of the U.S. publisher's relative unconcern with the fact of Haiti's precarity on the world stage. The careless assertion that the term "voodoo" is, currently, most "accessible" begs two critical questions: 1) what anglophone audience is the novel meant to interpellate? and 2) what pedagogic and ethical responsibility do the translator and publisher bear?

These questions bring me to my second point of entanglement in approaching the translation of Depestre's novel: the matter of audience. Haiti is in many ways as foreign to non-Haitian Afro-diasporic communities in the United States and elsewhere as it is to Europeans and non-Black Americans. Although largely marginalized as second-class citizens within their national contexts, Afro-diasporic consumers of 'First World' media have been necessarily influenced by anti-Haitian stereotypes of Vodou. U.S.-American Blacks, especially, are situated by virtue of their nationality (albeit only ostensibly and precariously) on the privileged side of the developed/underdeveloped, imperialist/colonized divide, and so may not recognize Haitians as political and cultural kin. Afro-diasporic populations in the anglophone Caribbean (Jamaica, Barbados, the Bahamas, etc.), also have tended to see Haitians as unwanted populations. Though geographically proximate and 'racially allied' with Haitians, Afro-anglophone communities throughout the Americas have remained in many ways distanced from the Black Republic.

There was a second audience/readership for whom I intended my translation of *Hadriana*: anglophone and creolophone Haitian communities outside of Haiti, communities that, by reason of global imperialism and its long wake, have been separated from their *francophonie* and subsequently cut off from their rightful cultural patrimony. Teaching Caribbean literature in New York City has led me to encounter many such students, first-generation Haitian Americans who read and write in English, not French. I thus have witnessed firsthand the phenomenon whereby individuals from a transnational community are alienated from certain aspects of their heritage. Insofar as Depestre is an incontrovertible pillar of the Haitian literary canon, his celebrated contribution to world letters ought to be read by those who can and should claim him as their own.

Targeting these two Afro-anglophone readerships as the personal stakes of my translation project posed a particular challenge. Whereas both audiences could access the novel in the English language, their understanding of Haitian culture diverged. I was thus obliged to balance an effort to render comprehensible certain culturally specific realities, on the one hand, with the desire to maintain the very opacity that can signal resistance or critique in 'minority culture' literature toward a dominant culture, on the other. Depestre's inclusion of the "Prolegomena" and appendix in the original French text served to shoulder much of this 'burden.' His creative integration of explicative elements into the very narrative of *Hadriana*, along with his inclusion of the glossary, effectively lessened my responsibility as mediator of both the language of the source text and the cultural specificities it presented. To a certain extent, translating the non-Anglo-Western elements of Depestre's novel was 'simply' a question of adhering to the foreignizing strategies he himself had decided to implement.[25]

Yet, in translating *Hadriana* I nevertheless was obliged to grapple with what translation theorist Maria Tymoczko calls the "dilemma of faithfulness," that is, the question of what to do with "factors that are particularly problematic for the receiving audience." Tymoczko explains that "to be 'faithful' such problematic factors must be transposed despite the difficulties they might cause to the sensibilities or cognitive framework of translator or audience."[26] As celebrated Martinican writer-theorist Édouard Glissant has argued, peoples from "small countries" affirm "the right to opacity"[27]—the right to illegibility or, better, to untranslatability. They engage a praxis of refusal vis-à-vis the condescending and endangering presumptions of transparency that circulate in countries of the Global North regarding peoples of the

Global South. The translator's task is thus particularly complex in this context, insofar as she must decide whether to unmask "aspects of a text that actively resist being translated" (Basnett 341). Faced with the possibility of a given author's deliberate opacity, what responsibility does the translator then have to allow for the possibility of such active resistance? How can the translator fulfill her obligation to render a text legible while respecting the refusals built into the language of a source text from a 'minority' culture? Moreover, to what extent do matters of race and/or/as culture determine the parameters of the translator's accountability to the author she seeks to carry over into another world(view)?

While I take seriously Edwards's contention that "diasporic reciprocity is above all a call to translate," I also recognize that the process of translation can lead as readily to exoticizing and silencing as to unifying and subverting. There are, in other words, real risks attendant in "attempt[ing] to carry blackness beyond the boundaries of nation and language" (Edwards 118). Given these risks, translating Vodou was of particular concern for me in every aspect of translating Depestre's novel. The very choice of the word "Vodou" to render Depestre's "vaudou" marked a definitive stance vis-à-vis the ethics of representing Haiti in foreign spaces—an acknowledgment of what Ramsey posits as the "history of stigmatization attached to the usage of the word 'voodoo' and thus its inappropriateness to name the religion."[28] Beyond that decision, however, the novel posed the challenge of representing Vodou culture in translation. Knowing very well that Depestre's unabashed incorporation of 'local color' in *Hadriana* might allow certain readers to find a home for their prejudice, I had to resist overstepping my authority and succumbing to "the common translatorial temptation to erase much that is culturally specific, to sanitize much that is comparatively odorous" (Basnett and Trivedi 7). Specifically, I had to reckon with the relatively Puritanical culture of the Anglosphere. *Hadriana* contains several highly erotic scenes, among which are descriptions of sexual encounters between Hadriana and various male and female partners in Jacmel, as well as evocations of the explicit sensuality and sexuality of Vodou.

For the most part, I endeavored to follow the source text's lead: I did my best to identify English terms that would render the extravagance of Depestre's ludic register. There was, however, a particular textual moment that proved more complicated to contend with: an early subplot in the narrative that recounts the terrible tale of Balthazar Granchiré, a young man who has been turned into a demonic butterfly-like creature by a vengeful sorcerer. As legend would have it, Granchiré has been cursed with an outsized penis and insatiable sexual desire, and he is responsible for drugging and penetrating members of Jacmel's female population while they sleep. Several theorists argue that Depestre's humorous rendering of what amounts to predation evinces "the deeply rooted sexism that pervades the text."[29] But there is something more to this story—a something more I have unearthed, through close reading and textual and contextual analysis, in the context of my scholarly work.[30] Taking into account the fact that reports of Granchiré's alleged nocturnal assaults involve only Catholic nuns and teenage 'virgins' and married women of the elite class, the story of Balthazar Granchiré reveals itself to be a satirical riff on the Jacmelian community's bourgeois preoccupation with feminine respectability—a preoccupation that sets the stage for Hadriana's zombification.

Whereas presenting these conclusions in the academic context involved careful and detailed intellectual work, connecting with my aspired-to readerships in the context of translation required a more economical interposition. How could I *not* keep in mind what the 'non-professional' anglophone reader might make of this episode through my rendering? This consideration ultimately shaped my decision in translating the monster-butterfly's name. While "Granchiré" does not have any semantic value in French, it does signify in Creole: the word translates literally to "big gash" or "big tear." This is a ribald allusion, of course, to either/both female genitalia or/and the phallic penetration of female genitalia. I first toyed with the idea of translating this character's name as "Balthazar the Ripper." Upon reflection, however, I realized that such a translation would be a misrepresentation, given what I believed to be the passage's satirical nature. The baggage attached to the "Ripper" etiquette risked shifting the English-language reader outside of Depestre's darkly comic intention into an unambiguously violent and macabre context.[31] I decided instead to render the name in English as "Granchire," thereby maintaining the relative opacity of Depestre's evocative moniker for an anglophone reader while at the same time, by removing the Frenchifying diacritical marker, giving back to the name its fullest Creole signification. I thus hoped to interpellate an anglo-creolophone reader in much the same way the original French would have winked at a creolophone reader in the francophone world.

My personal experiences of presenting *Hadriana* have borne out the notion that cultural familiarity and the context of consumption condition audience response to the most provocative elements of Depestre's novel. In the years leading up to and immediately following the English publication of *Hadriana*, I was invited to discuss the novel in three different academic settings: a Francophone Studies graduate seminar at New York University; an undergraduate class on Caribbean literature at St. John's University; and a postcolonial Caribbean Studies graduate seminar at the University of Miami. Fascinating to me in these encounters was the striking correlation between the overall cultural affiliations of the respective groups of students and their reactions to Depestre's rendering of Vodou and the erotic. At NYU, an elite institution located in Manhattan's West Village, the students—the majority of whom were not of Caribbean origin, and all of whom were well versed in postcolonial and feminist theory as articulated within the frame of North Atlantic scholarship—expressed discomfort with the perceived excesses of Depestre's carnivalesque presentation of Vodou and hyper-sexualization of Hadriana. The students at St. John's—none of whom had yet engaged substantively with Caribbean or postcolonial theory, and the vast majority of whom identified as first-generation Caribbean-Americans—read the same descriptions of Vodou, sex, and carnival without objection. Though only one among them was of Haitian origin, several recognized their own Caribbean cultural experiences and traditions in Depestre's portrayals of popular religious expression and in the narrative's anchoring in the so-called "marvelous real." In Miami, distinct hub of multiple Caribbean diasporas, a diverse cohort of graduate students from across the Americas writ large, and variously invested in Caribbean and postcolonial studies, similarly appreciated Depestre's provocations as at once rooted in and subversive of Haitian cultural realities.

The response of these diverse micro-readerships provides (admittedly anecdotal) confirmation of Huggan's very important caution regarding audience reception, notably that readers "by no means form a homogeneous or readily identifiable consumer group. Postcolonial literatures in English," Huggan notes, "are read by many different people in many different places; it would be misleading, not to mention arrogant, to gauge their value only to Western metropolitan response" (Huggan 30). This is, of course, the case for postcolonial literatures in translation as well.

As a professor at an Ivy League institution in the Northeastern United States, editor of a Caribbean Studies journal, and translator of francophone literature and theory, I belong, I recognize, to that "relatively small, Western-style, Western-trained, group of writers and thinkers who mediate the trade in cultural commodities of world capitalism at the periphery."[32] This positioning within the literary institution motivated me to be very lucid regarding my intention and my responsibility in translating *Hadriana*. Beyond the lexical decision-making and attentiveness to the interests and capacities of my personally-desired audiences, my other interventions as translator had to do with the packaging of Depestre's novel for the anglophone world. I had to find a publisher I could trust to do justice to the novel's deep anchoring in Haitian Afro/Vodou culture, without betraying that culture by pandering to the potentially racist presumptions of the non-Haitian reading public.

I spent over two years 'shopping' my translation. I was able to pitch directly to decision-makers, facilitated by introductions from two colleagues—a prominent novelist and an esteemed scholar of Haitian history—who enthusiastically supported the project. Thanks to these relationships, my queries were always acknowledged and thoroughly answered, enabling me to get a clear sense of what Depestre's novel looked like from a market perspective. I began, optimistically, by approaching an imprint of a major international press that recently had published a Haitian novel in translation. The response was disappointing but encouraging: the editors found the translation compelling but thought the generic instability of the novel (its inclusion of the prolegomena, the glossary, and other pedagogical elements; the collage-effect of its inclusion of a newspaper article, an "imaginary interview," and a love letter in the middle of the narrative; and the change in first-person narrator two-thirds of the way through the story) made it more suitable for an independent press. Undaunted, I approached editors at two such presses, both of whom found the book "fascinating" but "too challenging" for a "casual reader." The novel definitely was not African-American fiction, and its presentation of a white heroine on a Black island was thorny. What was the "publishing hook," one mused. It was suggested that I reach out to an academic press. Still undaunted, I did just that. But this option, too, came to naught. Even with my proposed critical introduction attached and strong praise for the quality of the translation, *Hadriana*'s presentation of the exotic and the erotic made the editor nervous about reception among the press' academic readership.

I was, at this point, decidedly daunted. How could it be that this novel—written by an author who was admired by celebrated contemporary Haitian literary figures, and that had won a major prize and been translated into seven languages—was of so little interest to U.S. English-language publishers? Stymied by the question, I nevertheless tried one last approach: I reached out to contemporary Afro-Haitian-American woman writer Edwidge Danticat, who I knew not only appreciated Depestre's novel, but even had been inspired by it to publish her own chronicle of Jacmel. I asked Danticat whether she would consider writing a foreword to the translation. Her response—"Whatever you need, my dear. I really love that book"—set me back on track.

When it comes to so-called marginal literature, the right preface can make all the difference. As Richard Watts has written, a preface can serve both to "move the merchandise" and to signal to the reader "the quality, seriousness, and perhaps even political orientation of the text in question" (Watts 2, 13). Famously respected (and even beloved) by both scholars and 'non-professional' readers, Haitians and non-Haitians, Edwidge Danticat was the ideal 'shepherd' for *Hadriana* in the (Afro-)Anglosphere. Her own work is renowned for its sensitive treatment of gender and transnational blackness and, accordingly, she is perfectly placed to 'vouch' for *Hadriana*'s value in these arenas. The very presence of her name on the book's front cover, along with a blurb from her foreword on the back, would attest to the legitimacy of the novel's intent and accomplishment.

The elegant preface Danticat ultimately provided generously contextualizes, educates, and reassures. It exercises a measure of control, enjoining the reader to look beyond the superficially exotic to think about the deeper meanings inscribed in the narrative. "Just as one might at carnival," Danticat writes, "one must surrender to this story while not being too easily offended or outraged." She also pointedly prepares the reader for Depestre's unstable generic and other choices—"[t]he novel occasionally veers into *lodyans*—a tongue-in-cheek narrative genre meant to provoke laughter," she explains, "though here perhaps it is intended to provoke other carnal reactions as well." Finally, Danticat subtly gestures to the different layers of access different readers might expect to enjoy: "[Depestre] not only describes a lively town, but also evokes class, color, religion, and gender dynamics, cleverly weaving them into his supernatural plot. He name-drops famous Jacmelians whom locals, and even regular visitors, are likely to recognize" (Depestre 14, 15). Highlighting *Hadriana*'s at once universal and insular scope, its invitations and its refusals, the whole of the foreword offers guidance without preachiness, explanation without condescension. It is, in and of itself, a very graceful instance of translation.

Danticat's paratextual imprimatur secured, I went on to pitch the project with renewed confidence. The obvious target this time was Akashic Books, which had published Danticat's groundbreaking edited short -story collections *Haiti Noir* and *Haiti Noir 2: The Classics*. A well-reputed and widely admired small publishing house, Akashic's self-declared ethos—"reverse-gentrification of the literary world"—seemed promising. Moreover, the very first two subject headings of the press' catalog read "Black Interest" and "Caribbean Interest." While the vicissitudes of alphabetization account for the prominent placement of these topics, a closer look through Akashic's list categorically confirms the press' deep commitment to Afro-diasporic literatures: the list features multiple titles related to 'blackness' and race in a U.S.-American frame, including works by Amiri Baraka, Bernice L. McFadden, and Melvin Van Peebles, as well as a wide-ranging and extensive list of important titles by Caribbean writers—including Elisabeth Nuñes, Colin Channer, Kwame Dawes, Katia D. Ulysse, Thomas Glave, Robert Antoni, Marlon James, and Danticat herself. All these factors provided me with crucial 'market' context. The presence of these living authors in Akashic's catalog, several of whom write their island from the vantage point of the continental United States—did the work of vetting the press for me. I could feel certain that *Hadriana* would be handled with care.

Akashic's carefulness in fashioning the postcolonial package of my translation is evidenced in the details of the frame placed around the published manuscript. Danticat's foreword does the work of situating the novel; a short "Translator's Note" articulates my conception of the translation as intervention and speaks directly to my desired readership. Perhaps most important from a commercial perspective, there is the cover art—the paratextual element most viscerally responsible for interpellating potential readers. For *Hadriana*'s cover, Akashic proposed, to my great pleasure and relief, an image both evocative and respectful of Haitian Vodou—of Haitian blackness. The design is at once aesthetically arresting and a perfect staging of the story that follows. It features a stylized ensemble of vèvè, sacred symbols of Haitian Afro-spirituality,[33] which form the pattern of a muted background and are integrated also into the typeface of the book's title. These symbols present an opacity that is, once again, invitation and refusal: they appeal differently to initiated and uninitiated readers alike—not unlike Depestre's novel.

"[W]here does 'realism' stop, and doudouist folklorization begin?" asks literary theorist Thomas Spear in reference to Depestre's writing in general, and to *Hadriana* in particular. Spear is perfectly right to pose this question, and he is also right to take it back. "The question is not necessarily useful," he concedes in the following sentence, "literature, a work of the imagination, does not care about any reality."[34] Responses to *Hadriana dans tous mes rêves* very much echo this ambivalence. Depestre has been celebrated as much for his wanderings back and forth across the globe in bold pursuit of political justice and racial equality, as for his deep commitment to Haitian culture as a source of aesthetic beauty and creative inspiration. At the same time, he has been much criticized for unguardedly presenting aspects of that culture—its Afro-spirituality, its ebullient erotic expressiveness—for consumption by those likely to disdain such cultural traits. To translate Depestre's French into U.S.-American English has meant being caught up in this contradiction. It has meant facing the risks inherent in extracting Haiti's 'blackness' from its original francophone context and carrying it over sensitively—mediated and repackaged—to the English-speaking world.

Barnard College, Columbia University

ENDNOTES

1. Brent Hayes Edwards, *The Practice of Diaspora: Literature, Translation, and the Rise of Black Internationalism* (Cambridge: Harvard U P, 2003), 211.

2. To date, I have published three works of Haitian fiction in translation: Frankétienne's *Ready to Burst* (New York: Archipelago Books, 2014); Marie Vieux-Chauvet's *Dance on the Volcano* (New York: Archipelago Books, 2016); and René Depestre's *Hadriana in All My Dreams* (New York: Akashic Books, 2017).

3. "Translation is, etymologically, a 'carrying across' or 'bringing across': the Latin *translatio* derives from *transferre* (*trans*, 'across' + *ferre*, 'to carry' or 'to bring')." Christopher Kasparek, "The Translator's Endless Toil," *The Polish Review*, 28:2 (1983): 83.

4. John Keene, "Translating Poetry, Translating Blackness," https://z.umn.edu/443a.

5. Stuart Hall, "Cultural Identity and Diaspora," *Colonial Discourse and Post-Colonial Theory: A Reader*, Patrick Williams and Laura Chrisman, eds. (New York: Columbia U P, 1994), 402.

6. Tejaswini Niranjana, *Siting Translation: History, Post-Structuralism, and the Colonial Context* (Berkeley: U of California P, 1992), 1.

7. René Philoctète, "Entretien," *Callaloo*, 15:3 (1992): 626. See also Kaiama L. Glover, "Haitian Literature and the Insult of Dust," *sx salon* 23 (october 2016), https://z.umn.edu/443g.

8. That year, the novel also won the Prix du roman de la société des gens de lettres and the Prix de l'Académie royale de langue et de littérature françaises de Belgique, among other prizes.

9. See Colin [Joan] Dayan in "France Reads Haiti: René Depestre's *Hadriana dans tous mes rêves*," *Yale French Studies* 83 (1993): 154–75 for citations from contemporary French reviews of the novel.

10. Katell Colin-Thébaudeau, for example, accuses Depestre of courting "a Western readership" and casts suspicion on the literary merit of the novel due primarily to the fact of its success among a North Atlantic reading public: "René Depestre

wants to be read in Europe, in North America [...] he does his best to entice this foreign reader to the island of Haiti by reflecting back to him a host of delectable exoticist images" (Colin-Thébaudeau 43-46). Colin-Thébaudeau goes so far as to suggest that all of Depestre's theoretical writings on Haiti's popular culture are designed to mask and legitimize his troubling fiction writings.

11. Graham Huggan, *The Postcolonial Exotic: Marketing at the Margins* (Liverpool: Liverpool U P, 2001), 7.
12. Richard Watts, *Packaging Post/Coloniality: The Manufacture of Literary Identity in the Francophone World* (Lanham: Lexington, 2005), 11.
13. In an early section of the narrative titled "The Zombifier's Secret Code, or, A Zombiferous Pharmacopia," one of Depestre's characters describes the various steps undertaken by practitioners of 'black magic' to turn human beings into the living-dead.
14. It is worth noting that Depestre is trained in the field of anthropology, a domain that both practices and relies on cultural and racial translation.
15. In the hours following Hadriana's death, a debate arises as to whether to mourn her according to the rituals of Catholicism or Vodou. A compromise is reached wherein the local Catholic priests are convinced by local Vodouisants that certain tenets of the Vodou faith must be honored so that the people of Jacmel might accept and heal from the loss of Hadriana. In addition, it becomes clear by the novel's conclusion that Hadriana herself is very much imbued with a psychological strength that comes from her having been cared for by domestics who initiated her to a degree into Haiti's spiritual universe.
16. Charles Forsdick, "Translation in the Caribbean, the Caribbean in Translation," *Small Axe*, 48 (November 2015): 161.
17. Susan Bassnett, "Postcolonialism and/as Translation," in *The Oxford Handbook of Post-colonial Studies*, Graham Huggan, ed. (New York: Oxford U P, 2013), 345.
18. Stuart Hall, "Race, Articulation, and Societies Structured in Dominance," in *Black British Cultural Studies: A Reader*, Houston A. Baker, Jr., Manthia Diawara, and Ruth Lindeborg, eds. (Chicago: U of Chicago P, 1996), 20.
19. Kaiama L. Glover, "'Flesh Like One's Own': Benign Denials of Legitimate Complaint," *Public Culture*, 29:2 (May 2017): 235–60.
20. Kate Ramsey, *The Spirits and the Law: Vodou and Power in Haiti* (Chicago: U of Chicago P, 2011), 1. Ramsey's masterful study offers to date by far the most thorough, nuanced, and exhaustive account of the Haitian spiritual practices that "in official Kreyòl orthography and most scholarly writing" (6) have been encapsulated in the word "Vodou." As Ramsey notes, both "Vodoun" and "Vodun" are also acceptable terms among scholars and practitioners.
21. Colin Dayan, "And then Came Culture," *Cultural Dynamics*, 26:2 (2014): 144.
22. "Haiti in Translation: Savage Seasons by Kettly Mars, An Interview with Jeanine Herman," https://z.umn.edu/443h.

23. Patrick Bellegarde-Smith, "Broken Mirrors: Mythos, Memories, and National History," *Haitian Vodou: Spirit, Myth, and Reality* (Bloomington: Indiana U P, 2006), 21.

24. "I didn't know much about the political situation in Haiti," Herman notes, "I had not heard of the Haitian classics, and I didn't even know that French was not [Mars's] first language. I was not at all familiar with Haitian culture or literature." Herman, "Interview."

25. By "foreignizing strategies," I mean the inclusion of textual and paratextual materials that explicate elements of the source culture, as opposed to domesticating the text so to conform with the target culture.

26. Maria Tymoczko, "Post-colonial Writing and Literary Translation," in *Post-colonial Translation: Theory and Practice*, Susan Bassnett and Harish Trivedi, eds. (New York: Routledge, 1999), 21.

27. "Nous réclamons le droit à l'opacité!", Édouard Glissant, *Le discours antillais* (Paris: Gal limard, 1981), 11.

28. Kate Ramsey, "From 'Voodooism' to 'Vodou': Changing a US Library of Congress Subject Heading," *The Journal of Haitian Studies*, 18:2 (2012): 14.

29. Lizabeth Paravisini-Gébert, "Women Possessed: Eroticism and Exoticism in the Representation of Woman as Zombie," *Sacred Possessions: Vodou, Santería, Obeah and the Caribbean*, Margarite Fernández Olmos and Lizabeth Paravisini-Gébert, eds. (New Brunswick: Rutgers U P, 1997), 50.

30. *In Disorderly Women: On Caribbean Community and the Ethics of Self-Regard* (Durham: Duke U P, 2021).

31. I am referring, of course, to the never-identified nineteenth-century serial killer, Jack the Ripper, who brutally murdered several sex workers in the East End of London. Jack the Ripper's story was highly sensationalized by the media in its time and has since given rise to hundreds of works of both fiction and non-fiction.

32. Kwame Anthony Appiah, *In My Father's House: Africa in the Philosophy of Culture* (Oxford: Oxford U P, 1992), 149.

33. *Vèvè* are powerful religious symbols used during Vodou ceremonies to call the *lwa* (spirits) into attendance. They are traced on the floor of the ritual space using a mixture of cornmeal and wood ash.

34. Thomas Spear, "Carnivalesque Jouissance: Representations of Sexuality in the Francophone West Indian Novel," Richard D. Reitsma, trans. (1998), https://z.umn.edu/443i.

3. THE LION OF THE TRIBE OF JUDAH IS DEAD!

Aaron Robertson

> "Dear friend, of course I remember. Wasn't it just yesterday? Yesterday, but a century ago. In this city, but on a planet that is now far away. How all these things get confused: times, places, the world broken in pieces, not to be glued back together again. Only the memory—that's the only remnant of life." — From *The Emperor: Downfall of an Autocrat* (1978) by Ryszard Kapuściński (tr. William R. Brand, Katarzyna Mroczkowska-Brand)

May 26, 2021 — The one indication that my grandmother ever had a strong opinion on foreign affairs was a curio on her fridge. I can't remember if it was a magnet or a brochure that read *Support Israel* and pictured the gleaming Dome of the Rock, my only reference point to Jerusalem outside of the sermons I'd been hearing and the scriptures I'd been reading since I was young. I had questions and much to learn. Were we not Christians reared in the gospel tradition?

I was in college at the time but had never learned of the Jewish pioneer movement or the Arab League; the Balfour Declaration or the Partition of Palestine; the 1948 Arab-Israeli war or the many that would follow. Zion was just an impressive hill, a city on a mount where our family's god resided. One of the names most familiar to me was Yahweh. It evoked the Old Testament Hebrews, thunder, bloodshed, and eradicated tribes. There was something enigmatic about *Support Israel*, which managed to be an apolitical comment on an issue for which people died and were killed. The intended message had less to do with the Jewish people than with my grandmother's concern for her own kin, descended from a line of African-American pious folk who began dreaming about the end of the world in childhood. Supporting Israel meant hastening the ingathering of exiled Jewish peoples. It was also inviting the apocalypse to come as swiftly as the Lord would have it to sweep up the saved and abandon the damned. Whatever animosity lingered between American Blacks and Jews did not alter the message of Exodus: both groups knew the hard hand of Pharaoh. The forecast of the biblical prophets, which promised the restoration of bountiful land to the Jews, boded well for all beneficiaries of Christ's second coming.

The meaning of "Black Zionism" has never been definitively settled. It is most famously associated with Marcus Garvey's mass movement of the 1910s and '20s, the United Negro Improvement Association (UNIA). Sometimes it stands in for any "back-to-Africa" campaign—Sierra Leone and Liberia were prominent destinations in previous centuries, and one could say the sentiment applies to countries like Ghana and The Gambia today. Various subgroups under the umbrella term Black Hebrew Israelites believe that Black people are the "real" Jews described in the Bible. The bigoted elements in some of these sects are garishly anti-Semitic; on the other hand, African Hebrews in Dimona—a community that began in the 1970s as a project of the African-American spiritual leader Ben Ammi Ben-Israel—have lived in an ambivalent state of integration within Israel for generations.

The comparatively dim public interest from progressives in the Tigray War, a brutal regional conflict in the Horn of Africa that began in the fall of 2020, may have dismayed African-American supporters of a popular, proto-Black Zionist sentiment known as "Ethiopianism" nearly one century ago. For decades after the Italian government felt its first stirrings of *mal d'Africa*, its longing for an African protectorate that culminated in the Italian army's historic defeat by Ethiopians at the Battle of Adwa in 1896, Ethiopia enjoyed a world-wide reputation as a symbol of Pan-African promise. Not since the Haitian Revolution nearly a century prior had Black-led martial success inspired such acclaim. The Ethiopians' resistance against the Italians lent legitimacy to a well-known verse from Psalms 68, referenced in the writings of 19th-century African-American abolitionists like Frances Ellen Watkins Harper, Henry Highland Garnet, Martin Delany, and Frederick Douglass: "Princes shall come out of Egypt; Ethiopia shall soon stretch out her hands to God." Downtrodden peoples everywhere could wrap their arms around *soon*. *Soon* was a date on the calendar. October 23, 1896 for the Ethiopians, when the Treaty of Addis Ababa was signed, seemingly immunizing the nation against colonial rule.

Inoculation lasted until Mussolini yearned for an empire of his own, Italy's "place in the sun." In 1935, a surprise launch by the Italians on Ethiopia from Eritrea, one of Italy's colonial possessions at the time, ignited a years-long pacification effort, which included acts of genocide, that resulted in hundreds of thousands of Ethiopian deaths by the time the Allies dissolved Italian East Africa in 1941. The apocryphal tale of the Second Italo-Ethiopian War was that Black kids from Mississippi to the Gold Coast wept.

The Ethiopians garnered nominal support from African-American clergy and organizations like the NAACP and the Urban League. Historians like Nemata Amelia Ibitayo Blyden, William R. Scott, James Quirin, and Fikru Gebrekidan have shown how, even as many African-Americans longed to help the devastated Ethiopian populace, ideological and material obstacles often stood in the way. Although groups were established throughout the country to raise money for medical supplies and other goods, and a number of African-Americans expressed their desire to fight alongside the Ethiopians, very few resources made it abroad. Citing a federal statute prohibiting U.S. citizens from enlisting in foreign armies, the government pressured the Ethiopian Consul-General to halt recruitment projects. Stateside tensions led more often to clashes between African-Americans and Italian-Americans, notably in Jersey City in 1935.

Besides, Black diasporic resettlement schemes in Ethiopia didn't have a great track record, whether initiated by the African-American millionaire William Henry Ellis or the Barbadian-American rabbi and former UNIA musician Arnold Josiah Ford. As Du Bois himself admitted—once he had matured from his earlier condescension toward African people—not all Ethiopians cared to have American Blacks issue "the last word in civilization and manners." Although the Ethiopian emperor, Haile Selassie, eventually recognized the efforts of "Negro Americans during the crisis [who] did not abandon their embattled brothers, but stood by us," effusive claims to camaraderie often spoke to a vague, deflated yearning. Du Bois felt it ("The only salvation of Ethiopia and the black races is to find new ideals different from the ideals which have dominated white Europe and America since the seventeenth century"). C.L.R. James, the Trinidadian historian who founded the International African Friends of Ethiopia, felt it ("I believed also that I could have been useful in helping to organize anti-Fascist propaganda among the Italian troops"). In one of Langston Hughes's startlingly honest moments, he felt it too: "I was only an American Negro who had lived the surface of Africa and the rhythms of Africa, but I was not Africa. I was Chicago and Kansas City and Broadway and Harlem."

There were civilizational hang-ups, too. Blame what you will—anthropologist Melville Herskovits' theories about "Africanisms" and "survivals" making their way to the New World, Harlem Renaissance-era debates about the "New Negro," propaganda promulgated by Victorian-era imperialists and missionaries, or something else—the African continent has long occupied a position of dubious prominence in the political and cultural imagination of African-Americans, particularly those who, like my family, have no immediate kinship ties. Few African-American writers were more tortured by questions of race loyalty and consciousness-raising than George Schuyler. In 1938, one year after the Italians completed their decimation of Ethiopian forces and slaughtered tens of thousands after an attempt on an Italian viceroy's life—an event known as Yekatit 12—Schuyler began serializing his *Ethiopian Stories* in the *Pittsburgh Courier.*

One of his novellas, *Revolt in Ethiopia: A Tale of Black Insurrection Against Italian Imperialism*, was a fantastical political thriller. The protagonist is a Black man, Dick Welland, who inherits great wealth after an oil tycoon relative dies. With his money, he heads to Europe and, on the *S.S. Metallic*, meets a woman named Ettara Zunda who turns out to be traveling incognito. She is, in fact, the niece of Emperor Selassie, an Ethiopian princess on a mission to locate treasure that would finance a vigorous resistance effort against the Italians. Historian Ivy Wilson notes that the novella "links the Ethiopian opposition against Italian fascism as the twentieth-century analogue of black resistance against the peculiar institution in the nineteenth and thereby creates a racial continuum that is both transhistorical and transnational." Schuyler, though not exactly known for his optimism, gives the reader the kumbaya ending that history denied. Dick and Ettara evade their fascist pursuers, find the hidden jewels, and acquire military equipment from the Germans which they funnel to the Ethiopians. Ethiopia is saved, the Italians are once again defeated, and the literal marriage between Dick and Ettara forges a bond that makes for a beautiful fireside tale.

★ ★ ★

What is the measure of a good sympathizer? The question captivates the good translator and the good civic actor. In some cases, it is the difference between memoria and rimozione, memory and repression or, some translators of the Italian may prefer, removal. As it became clear that Ethiopian Prime Minister Abiy Ahmed was not the man the world believed he was, and as I watched U.S. sympathies being channeled into some vast tragedies but not others, I thought of another Ethiopian princess. A real one. Where would Martha Nasibù have placed her sympathies?

I had decided years ago that my only translation assignments would be at my leisure and center on connections between Italy, the nations in the Horn of Africa that it once colonized, and the individuals who moved between these places in body or in spirit. I only glanced at the sepia-toned cover of *Memories of an Ethiopian Princess* (*Memorie di una principessa etiope*) before I settled on translating it. A young Martha Nasibù, the author, smiles and looks off to the side. A gauzy shamma, an Ethiopian shawl, frames her thinly oiled face. Nasibù (or Nassibou, depending on the context) survived the Second Italo-Ethiopian War, though she was also one of its victims.

She was born in 1931 to Atzede Mariam Babitcheff, the daughter of a Russian noble who fled the bloody October Revolution, and Dejazmach Nasibù Zamanuel, a former mayor of Addis Ababa and one of Emperor Selassie's most-trusted wartime generals. Martha's family were members of the mekwanint, which Major Asseged describes as the "noble-warrior ruling class," and which the emperor increasingly favored over the hereditary nobles known as the mesafint. Before the

Italians invaded, Emperor Selassie had been replacing an old system of localized, feudal lords with a centralized state apparatus that was seen by some as progressive for its time. Millions of poor peasant-tenants throughout Ethiopia were the backbone of a complex land tenure system that gave landlords wide judicial and administrative jurisdiction over their tracts. Asseged, writing of the lead-up to the Ethiopian Revolution in 1974 and the subsequent dissolution of the empire, describes Ethiopian society as one that was "divided into a class of owners and a class of dispossessed."

Martha was living in the south of France when I wrote to her publisher a few years ago asking after the English rights. One of Martha's daughters was handling business for her, though we never connected directly. Martha died at some point in 2020. She would have been around 90 years old. The memoir was her only book; those who know of Martha at all remember her mainly as a skilled visual artist whose paintings of Ethiopian people and rituals appeared in European and Ethiopian museums. I'd studied her book for my graduate dissertation and was charmed by its odd, tragic, fable-like account of the decline of an empire and the eight years Martha, her mother, and her siblings lived as exiles in countries including Italy, Libya, Greece, and Egypt. After fighting against Italian forces and pleading for aid before the UN, Dejazmach Zamanuel died in a sanitorium in Switzerland, his lungs ravaged by illegally deployed mustard gas.

Until her passing, Martha was likely one of, if not the last living witness to an Ethiopian court that flourished before the Fascist invasion. I joke that the book is my little secret, namely because my translation remains unpublished, but as I thought about it more, the secret started to feel like something illicit. In the first half, scenes of lavish banquets, carefully conducted rituals, and aristocratic children at play abound. Descriptions of sumptuous clothing and European-inspired architecture are everywhere. To the extent that there is a plot, it unfolds in the second half after the dejazmach dies and the dislocations of Martha and her refugee family begin.

Probably because I do not ask, I rarely hear translators speak equivocally about their source texts. Certain passages may inspire more than others, and some elements might annoy—plot inconsistencies or stylistic conundrums—but most translators I have met understandably devote their time to work they believe is doing something more generative than not, artistically or socially. That was true for me as I worked through various drafts of *Memories*. I was sensitive to its narrative monotony, but I could overlook that because it was an important work of testimony with flashes of descriptive power written from an exceptionally rare perspective. I still believe this. But for how long could I ignore the Italianist Franco Manai's discomfiting assessment of Nasibù's project as one that overlooked "the true dynamics of social relationships which are otherwise apparent"? Though it was a small publication when it came out in Italy in 2005, the book was critically well-received. The introduction was by Angelo Del Boca, a white man and arguably the most prominent historian of Italy's colonial endeavors. It was Del Boca who encouraged Nasibù to go forward with the book, and for that we thank him, but I spotted a red flag when he concluded:

> It is because of [Atzede Mariam Babitcheff] that after being put through the wringer of exile, her five children showed no signs of resentment, no abhorrence of Italy—particularly Fascist Italy, which stole both Martha's father and brother from her, and took away her freedom for eight long years. The incontrovertible evidence of Martha Nasibù's forbearance lies in her second marriage, to a Neapolitan aristocrat, Marchese Francesco Tortora Brayda di Belvedere.

In this moment, Del Boca struck a tone reminiscent of one of the "authenticators" of an American slave narrative, often a white abolitionist who wrote a short preface to promise a predominantly white readership that the testimony they were about to read was genuine and devoid of offensive content. (Or perhaps I was thinking of Georgina, the housekeeper in *Get Out* who weeps, smiles, and shakes her head: "No, no, no, no, no, no...!")

After I read part of my *Memories* translation at an event, an older Italian woman approached to compliment and assure me that most Italians paid no mind to fascism, race, or racism; so, I was prepared for Del

Boca's introduction. But the longer my translation went untouched in Google Drive, the more carefully I considered the single passage in the book in which Martha directly addresses the situational disparity between her family and most other Ethiopians. Martha and Atzede visit an old hermit monk who once predicted the coming of the white men, the Italian *ferenj*:

> "I am going down to the hot baths now, the ones in the basin where the Gondar River flows. Watch how the puddle water down there in the foliage steams," he said, pointing. "The needy immerse themselves there, as do the derelict and the diseased who come from every part of the country, hoping to convalesce or to alleviate their wounds. Paralytics who arrive on gurneys are also put under, supported by the compassion of those who dedicate their lives to their neighbors so that they may carry out Christ's teachings. I'm going there, among them, to bless them and pray for the remission of their sins, which are the principal cause of the body's ills. The springs you swim in are made beautiful with artificial things, majolica tubs and sinks in which water gushes. Those are for the rich, who pay to find youth in hot water that tickles their skin with bubbles." He was quiet for a moment. My mother and I felt pangs of guilt—clearly, he had blamed us—and I sensed that he read it on our faces. But the old man burst into laughter and shook his head, saying, "Don't be alarmed, children, you aren't at fault."

Not every mouth that opens produces song. It wasn't immediately obvious to me that an act of authorial self-absolution, mediated through a minor character, could be one of *Memories* more unsettling moments. As Manai writes, "Postcolonial discourse often greets whatever a native [author] says as a pronouncement of the voiceless. As such, this pronouncement is regarded positively. Often, however, as in Nassibou's case, what is said comes from those who have always had a voice insofar as they are part of the ruling class." Zora Neale Hurston said it well: *All my skinfolk ain't kinfolk.*

As stunning as *Memories* is as a portrait of a moribund court, it is also an incomplete analysis of power. This is not as much an imputation against the author (her skin color does not make her responsible for defending the underclasses) as it is a warning to the avowed anti-colonial reader. The late Africanist historian Robert L. Hess once reminded us that until 1935, Ethiopia was seen as "in so many ways the least African of the African states," referring to its relative insularity. The parochialism of *Memories* is in some ways a measure of Nasibù's limited gaze. Rarely did she look beyond the walls of her father's palatial estate, or the pacific orchards of her grandfather's plantation, where the family retreated shortly after the invasion. I don't want to come down too harshly on Nasibù or conjure a book that could have been. Like Nasibù reflecting on the serenity of her early childhood, I saw what I wished to see in her writing. The task began as a basically uncritical acceptance of the world Nasibù wanted to preserve, a Zion not meant for all. It was me living "the surface of Africa" as an African-American seeking allyship through translation but not always convinced that I had found it here.

As ideological stratification within the United States sharpens, how we choose to empathize, and with whom, becomes a consequential matter that goes beyond individual allegiances. It feels as if every act is one of care or neglect, down to what we choose to read, and these decisions determine what the beloved community can be. I have nothing against majolica tubs. My worry is that I have lingered in tepid bathwater for too long, watching the suds fizzle away as elsewhere, bombs drop.

4. RIGHT TO ACCESS, RIGHT OF REFUSAL: TRANSLATION OF/AS ABSENCE, SANCTUARY, WEAPON

Khairani Barokka

Translations are as complex as the concept of literatures at large – multiple, layered, shaped regionally and transnationally, never neutral, always deeply nuanced, inflected with cultural biases and the baggage of cultural workers. Ever employed to advance political mindsets, to continue or disrupt regimes of language.

This essay centres disability justice(s) as anti-colonial praxes, fundamental to any conversation on decolonising translation; further, it shows the complexities of 'decolonising' when the right of access and the right of refusal interact with translation, disability justice(s), and indigeneities.

By 'decolonising', I invoke the definition popularised by Eve Tuck and K. Wayne Yang, long held firm by indigenous communities around the world:

> Decolonization brings about the repatriation of Indigenous land and life; it is not a metaphor for other things we want to do to improve our societies and schools. The easy adoption of decolonizing discourse by educational advocacy and scholarship, evidenced by the increasing number of calls to "decolonize our schools," or use "decolonizing methods," or, "decolonize student thinking", turns decolonization into a metaphor. [...] The metaphorization of decolonization makes possible a set of evasions, or "settler moves to innocence", that problematically attempt to reconcile settler guilt and complicity, and rescue settler futurity.

When I write of 'decolonising translation', I specifically refer to translation that can bring about the said repatriation of indigenous lands and lives – not only from settler colonial states such as the US, Canada,

Australia, and New Zealand, but in terms of a repaying of colonial debt and repatriation of objects by European and other colonisers, and in terms of returning indigenous lands that are, for instance, now owned by companies such as Shell in Indonesia (for extractive activities of all kinds including mines, refineries, plantations, and 'carbon offsetting' that allows such companies to increase their pollution emissions) that are thefts of land from indigenous peoples.

With regards to translation, I've been thinking about the right of refusal to be translated, the right to access, and decolonising 'disability justice'. The latter is a term coined by Sins Invalid, a queer crips of colour collective based in North America, and it is a phrase which I seek to emphasise as open to plural, decolonised, localised interpretations. Sins Invalid define 'disability justice' with ten principles, including anti-capitalism – the term is distinct from the framework of 'disability rights', something I understand as a bequeathing of rights onto populations by colonial states. As a disabled writer working on these issues, I also often invoke Jasbir Puar's *The Right to Maim* for a truer concept of access that seeks to stop ongoing colonial maiming and disabling of, and inaccessibility for, Black and brown people globally in places like Palestine and Indonesia.

The right of access to information is part of the set of colonial metaphors and frameworks for translation – the 'universal right to access information being translated' is often used to mean 'the colonial right of people privileged by Empire to access all kinds of information'. In other words, translation as colonial extractivism, a framework we are forced to reckon with, especially as we try to perpetuate translation that is not only decolonial, but anti-colonial.

An example I give with regards to the distinction between decolonial and anti-colonial: repatriation of items in the British Museum belonging to communities in Indonesia is an act of decoloniality. Anti-coloniality, which I believe we should strive for, is the simultaneous awareness that Indonesia is itself a colonial nation-state formation, the occupier of Papuan regions, for instance. 'Asian languages' exist within different localised social hierarchies. Languages used and created in the majority world by people denoted as non-disabled have a colonial relationship to those in the majority world that are not. Majority world (a term myself and others sometimes use instead of 'Global South') authors and translators whose names 'sound Western' are given more opportunities, by virtue of proximity to whiteness, as are those of us who are, for instance, fluent in languages such as English and French as well as other 'Asian languages'.

In the two case studies below, which demonstrate translation as always being bodily, the blanket application of false binaries to encompass one work, such as 'transparency' versus 'opacity', or 'accessible' language versus 'inaccessible' language, is shown to be reductive and broken open. In both Cok Sawitri's performance of bravado and deliberate withholding of translation – the right of refusal to translate as a political and decolonising act – as well as in the conceptual framework for my book, *Indigenous Species*, creative choices reveal what assumptions of translation we can work to dismantle: how the notions of absence, sanctuary, and weapon are employed. In particular, these frameworks reveal how deeply, indelibly translations are tied to perpetuating or unpacking ableist, colonialist notions of the 'good' bodymind.

I. COK AND THE NIGHT AMBUSH

Several years ago, at the opening ceremony of Ubud Writers and Readers Festival, Balinese poet, theatre artist, and activist Cok Sawitri gave a bravura performance – open-air, under the stars, surrounded by traditional local architecture and a plenitude of foreign tourists and writers. Senior performer Cok did not circle that space as much as prowl it, hilariously monologuing in Indonesian and Balinese about tourism's impacts on her home province, local homestay owners putting their bodily detritus in banana pancakes, the 'paradise island' myth beaming in tourists' imaginations. She was ferociously shattering myths of locals as ready to appease, to heal, and to cater to foreigners' whims, of the island, struggling under the weight of overdevelopment and environmental destruction, as existing purely for incomers. Pulsing throughout her piece was the blatant discrepancy between what outsiders expect of Bali, and the performative acts of compliance, as well as acts of resistance, that Balinese people enact.

'The Night Ambush' is not the title of the piece, but my own personal naming of this performance, in my recounting. The genius guile here: Cok performed the piece in two local languages, in front of swathes of foreigners who understood neither. She was teasing them at a high-profile literary event in Southeast Asia, without them being the wiser – to them, she was a woman attired in elaborate Balinese clothing, running around vocalising what was probably a sacred traditional welcome. When all of us—non-Balinese Indonesians, Balinese Indonesians, and foreigners—clapped loudly for her, we were clapping *for entirely different reasons*. Those of us who understood Cok's monologue, untranslated that night, were complicit in her conceit, and it made us proud. Those who did not understand her words were, with their applause, extending the piece's affect, confirming how successful it was, a double-edged sword.

This remains one of my dearest memories of performance of any kind. It was one I will always feel privileged to have been privy to, particularly being Indonesian-fluent but not Balinese-fluent, both outsider and insider. I am Indonesian but not Balinese, though I have Balinese cousins and friends who live on the island, and have often visited. By virtue of Indonesian-fluency, I understood the code-switching and richly layered sociopolitical critique at play, and the stratification of Cok's intended audience. Yes, it was for Indonesians and Indonesian-speakers, but only to a certain extent. Most of all, it was for Balinese people, those local to Ubud in particular. What could easily have been yet another act of cultural production primarily for outsider consumption became one of generative and covert, yet wildly open, refusal. To my knowledge, the script has never been published nor translated into English, lending further power to Cok's cunning move through her work's ephemerality.

Years later, reminiscing, the question arises: what if there had been sign language interpreters at Cok Sawitri's performance? The notion of inclusivity here becomes: inclusivity for whom, and to what ends? Which sign languages would have been used – or would there only have been one? If so, which one: Australian Sign Language (Auslan), reflecting the origin of most festival attendees, thereby including only D/deaf Australians and others who understood this Australian language,

in the grand scheme? BISINDO, the term for Indonesian Sign Language? It might seem most implausible that there would be any interpretation in Kata Kolok, a sign language indigenous to only one village in Bali, which has a large number of D/deaf residents and has proudly developed a language of its own. The choices of sign language, as with any other language, are political.

What if there had been audio description at the performance? Audio description too is never 'objective'; the description itself is a scripted performance, and when conceptualised as its own artwork can ignite exciting possibilities. Would there have been a split between audio descriptions in English, Balinese and Indonesian?

The absence of translation in Cok's performance was a beautiful sanctuary for her defiance and our basking in it, yet this was a partial sanctuary, as every artwork is. The absence of translation for D/deaf Indonesians made it partial sanctuary of a very different kind than the absence of translation in Auslan, though I believe choosing the latter over the former would have gone against Cok's principles.

A disability justice framework for translation requires an understanding of nuance, a comprehension that there are gradations of absence, of sanctuary, and of translation as weapon. Having sign language translation in BISINDO and Kata Kolok, but not in Auslan, for instance, would have been weaponry in keeping with Cok's creation of sanctuary, for respite from having to exist in one's own land as fodder for others' fantasies. Yet would the very announcement of these translations have been a 'tell' that gave away the artist's plan?

Translation that may be a shared sanctuary, a bridging to some, is an absence of this connectivity for others, and not always in ways we've internalised as intuitive. There is nothing that has been translated into every language ever known and used, especially as more and more languages face extinction at an alarming rate. The subject of which languages and poetries are chosen for translation, and how they are translated, is always infused with biases.

Understanding gradations of absence, of sanctuary, and of translation as weapon also requires an innate humility of all that we as individuals do not know, and have yet to learn, in order to translate with requisite awareness: that feminisms are as plural as literatures, and that western or white feminisms are not the same as Indonesian feminisms, with different regional histories and emphases – this matters for an analysis of Cok's performance. For instance, I come from a matrilineal culture, Minangkabau, that predates use of the word 'feminism' by centuries, yet I now proudly call these West Sumatran roots feminist.

Further, ''65–'66' does not mean the same thing to Indonesian feminists as it does to those from elsewhere – these are the years of state-sanctioned mass murder, with victims possibly in the millions, targeting minorities and those accused of being leftists, including many feminist organisers, and was at heart part of imperialist Cold War tactics. Yet I have read text after text after text that presumes to subsume all of the world's women into a version of 'the sixties' that is Eurocentric or US-centric, even as the politics of those retellings are indelibly tied to what Indonesian feminists endured. I'm not sure Cok would entrust a translation of her poetic ambush that night in Bali years ago to someone who did not know these histories, to someone unaware that Bali contains mass graves as well as tourist resorts.

By the same token – just as a word such as 'feminism' is loaded with knowings and unknowings, and the deliberate ways politics and economics shape what we know and are not meant to know – there is an innumerable variety of bodyminds on the planet, contributing to linguistic diversity that remains unacknowledged. Even those of us who identify as disabled (with many, but not all, taking the social model approach whereby the term implies the opposite of 'enabled', not 'unable'), who've worked in disability studies and research, are liable to be completely unaware of various kinds of languages used, whether sign languages, Brailles, the languages of autistic people and communities, and on and on. These languages are also regionally and historically shaped. These languages are also less likely to be treated as worthy of being translated into and from, as literatures and poetries to be archived, disseminated, studied in schools and universities, celebrated in all the ways some languages belonging to more normative bodies are.

The offshoot of these inequities is that the bodies to whom those languages belong continue to be disenfranchised, excluded, and endangered. I am thinking here particularly of artist Mel Baggs's video *In My Language* (available on YouTube), which uses the word 'translation' quite prominently to convey the discrepancy between how people interpret hir communication as an autistic person, and what sie is actually saying:

> We are even viewed as non-communicative if we don't speak the standard language, but other people are not considered non-communicative if they are so oblivious to our own languages as to believe they don't exist. [...] And in a world in which those determine whether you have any rights, there are people being tortured, people dying because they are considered non-persons because their kind of thought is so unusual as to not be considered thought at all.

Ableism, as fellow disabled writer Talila Lewis points out, affects everyone, not just people self-identifying as disabled; it is, Lewis writes:

> A system that places value on people's bodies and minds based on societally constructed ideas of normalcy, intelligence and excellence. These constructed ideas of normalcy, intelligence and excellence are deeply rooted in anti-Blackness, eugenics and capitalism.
>
> This form of systemic oppression leads to individuals and society determining who is valuable and worthy based on people's appearance and/or their ability to satisfactorily produce, excel and 'behave'.
>
> You do not have to be disabled to experience ableism.

I would add that ableism is also rooted in colonialities, anti-indigeneities, anti-pluriversalities.

Biases regarding the 'good' bodymind shape language, and language – as we know – shapes the felt world, and moulds what universe our selves as bodyminds live through. These biases have, in Indonesia, been shaped for hundreds of years by colonial regimes including the Dutch and English. In his book, *Disability in Java: Contesting Conceptions of Disability in Javanese Society after the Suharto Regime* (2013), Slamet Thohari explains how colonial and missionary medicine propagated on Indonesia's most populous island the medical model of disability, in which all non-normative bodies are seen as impaired and in need of cure, regardless of whether or not the people involved perceive themselves as such – despite Javanese culture having disabled gods, and a previous understanding of disabled people as closer to the deities.

In other words, the likelihood that any poetic performance in Indonesia will be translated into BISINDO or another sign language, be audio-described, or be a 'relaxed' performance inclusive of disabled bodyminds, has been decimated by deliberate choices to regard certain bodies as less-than- or non-human. Thus we lose chances to disseminate poetry. Thus we lose chances to honour poets in non-'abled' languages, and to nurture more poets in those languages. Thus we lose chances for people to learn about their poetic heritages of languages outside those perceived as normative.

II. *INDIGENOUS SPECIES*

Considering translation as a cleaving, a refracting, I think of how the word 'refracting' calls to mind for me (coded as a seeing person despite severe short-sightedness, only because glasses and contact lenses are not as stigmatised as other assistive devices) a ray of light's direction being manipulated, and how this word, as a visual image, is tied to its ocularcentricity. When I first began to delve into the world of arts research from disability justice frameworks, in 2011, I became aware of how cultural consumption is skewed towards those of us both hearing and seeing. As though blind and sight-impaired artists don't also create and come from cultures of their own, as though D/deaf cultures aren't linguistically rich.

Ocularcentricity is societally shaped, as are audiocentricity and verticalcentricity (full disclosure: I write these words in a horizontal position, assumed most hours of most days so I can be vertical more often when I choose to be).

Part of my project with *Indigenous Species*, informed by the work blind and sight-impaired artist-activists have long been doing, is a translation of absence: the word Braille in 'flat Braille' is on every left-hand page, to emphasise to sighted readers that we are, in fact, sighted. Originally conceived as a sight-impaired accessible art book, which grew out of a poem first written and performed for the Emerging Writers Festival in Melbourne, Australia in 2013, I stipulated to the publisher that there would be a 'sighted version' that proclaimed itself as such. I tried to create enough contrast on the illustrated pages, so that as many colour-blind readers as possible would be able to see the artwork. In addition, two kinds of accessible e-books were created for purchase.

The hope is that in addition to ensuring more accessibility for non-seeing demographics, an awareness is created in multiple ways for sighted readers: of the absence of access in publishing, made more prominent when one understands a book as object, but also the absence of access to blind and sight-impaired cultures for us sighted people. 'Plain sight' is never just that. Sightedness and gearing arts resources towards sightedness – and hearingness, neurotypicalness, etc. – are political, as being a cis-gender woman is political, as living and breathing in the United Kingdom is political, as visa statuses are political, as the sources of our breakfasts are political, as our choice of poetry consumption and production and engagement beyond and within capitalist models is political.

It is difficult to categorise such translation of absence as 'opaque' or 'transparent', considering both terms are so predominantly interpreted through the dominant frameworks of seeing cultures and thus limited, but also because one could ask what is being made transparent, and how. If I say I am making absence of language to blind readers on a flat page 'transparent' for sighted readers, was it not the case that those of us who are sighted already knew that flat pages of a paperback book – without audiobooks, accessible e-book versions and Braille – are inaccessible to blind and sight-impaired readers? What socialisation has made this exclusion seem natural?

As with every translation or artistic project, *Indigenous Species* as intended weapon, absence, and sanctuary has limits. Not all blind and sight-impaired people use or read Braille, for one. However, it feels like a small gesture in response to sighted privilege, as a sighted creator who has learned from the work of many blind and sight-impaired creators, apart from the story itself as gesture: an abducted girl in a river boat tries to escape, conveying her thought process with power, fiercely aware of the environmental destruction around her and its social consequences. It feels like only one of many, many possibilities to respond to the limiting of respect and care for bodyminds deemed to be aberrant, unimportant, used as imagery in non-disabled writers' poetry yet still excluded as poets and poetry lovers.

> Privacy is impossible
> If one's community
> Is not bound by love
> - Shane McCrae, *In the Language of My Captor*

The two examples above both involve the right of refusal: Cok's to translate, and mine, as a person coded 'sighted', to maintain an unfair publishing hierarchy and non-acknowledgment of the criminal lack of access for blind readers.

How do these instances of right of refusal interact with the right to access? Shouldn't every D/deaf person have the right to access every part of a performance such as Cok's? Again, we need to think of 'right' in the context of 'disability justice' rather than 'disability rights'. I believe colonial pasts and presents always need to be taken into account with regards to the dynamics of refusal, who is refusing to translate or be translated, and how they/we are racialised or otherwise configured within colonial power dynamics.

Access rights, particularly in terms of disability justice, need to be understood multidimensionally, in local contexts, and in terms of their interaction with the right of refusal to translate, to be translated, or to otherwise be involved in a translation activity.

As someone whose language heritages include Baso Minang, Boso Jowo, and Baso Lintau (a dialect of Baso Minang, and a language I perceive as under threat), I've observed a tendency among some white translators to express sentiments along the lines of 'there is nothing that we can't translate'. But there are things that they *should not* translate, and that, as indigenous peoples, we do not want them to even have access to, in whatever form.

Indigenous peoples are being displaced, kidnapped, beaten, and killed at a still-relentless pace, and despite being the best caretakers of land for environmental and climate justice, our land practices are criminalised and banned, and our land is stolen from us (often in Indonesia under the guise of so-called 'carbon offsets').

There are innumerable local knowledge systems – the names of fruits, the medicinal uses of plants, aspects of land-based indigenous spiritualities, maps of indigenous areas – that need to be actively protected from outsider knowledge, as they and we are in imminent danger. Corporations' and nation-state formations' knowledge of these leads to appropriation, to theft, to capture. In an age of digital surveillance, where our digital devices spy on us for any number of companies we cannot even name offhand, it is increasingly difficult to prevent language from abetting capture. And once language meant to be protected by indigenous communities is captured by a mega-corporation, it is subject to the inherent biases and unwanted 'inclusions' of language in those racist and sexist algorithms, as Safiya Noble writes in *Algorithms of Oppression*. It is always fundamentally necessary to ask, with regards to 'inclusion', what we are being included in, and why.

There is no 'decolonising translation' without an understanding of these ethics – that all of us, including minority ethnic translators in majority white countries – need to understand that the wonders of translation do not permit any of us to translate without ethical permission. That decolonising translation only for non-disabled people is a fallacy. That disabled people's right to access needs to be contextualised locally and in terms of power dynamics.

Sharing screenshots of poems on social media without captions – either in the body of the text or through Twitter's alt text – excludes blind and sight-impaired readers from poetry even as it includes seeing people, while also including these posts in Twitter's trove of images owned by the company. We must reckon with all the complexities and realities of how language and translation work, of the multiple forces our language work is subject to. I continue to caption my images on Twitter – but I have become increasingly wary of writing or photographing things for social media, or even at all (as our phones also contain algorithms of image-making and capture, which Hito Steyerl writes of brilliantly in *Duty Free Art*) from my home communities, without as clear an understanding as possible of the potential risks as well as rewards.

Many translators are responsible for the induction of what we translate into 'globalised' economies, but ethical publishing practices that centre stolen-from communities have also been burgeoning – these facts co-exist. If one understands all translations as forming future archives, what are the access rights as well as rights of refusal that come with the creation and maintenance of these archives? Again and again, I refer not only to the right of access (particularly with regards to D/deaf and/or disabled people) and the right of refusal, but to what Yoshi Fajar Kresno Murti, writing in the book *Arsipelago* about archives, refers to as the 'politic of claim' and the 'politic of access'—the justice of the thing.

I think of Cok's calling out of the forces pushing us to perform for a western gaze, of all the ways culture pushes us to perform for a non-D/deaf and/or non-disabled gaze, how these norms of bodily functioning have contributed to current policies in Indonesia, in the UK, and elsewhere: elevation of certain bodies and desires and ways of connecting with literature over others – an elevation of non-disabled translation and languages, and an elevation of colonial frameworks for translation. And in response, as resistance, I think of how translation can always be, in myriad ways, absence, sanctuary, and weapon.

5. THE MYTHICAL ENGLISH READER

Anton Hur

AWKWARD

When I started my career as a professional literary translator, I began coming up against a mysterious "English reader" whom academics and editors kept referring to when they looked over my work, leaving comments like, "the English reader will find this line awkward" or "I understand, but we need to make things more accessible to the English reader" and so on. This was very puzzling; I am an English reader, I've been reading English the whole of my reading life. I have a master's degree in Victorian poetry from a prestigious university and worked professionally for years in literary translation, which means, frankly, I tend to be more normative in my English usage, if anything. Look at this paragraph, for example; I sound practically archaic. But I kept coming up against this hypothetical English reader, and not just in terms of language. When acquiring editors invoked the English reader, they would say things like, "English readers won't go for that sort of thing" or "English readers don't like short story collections."

But who was this English reader, and why did he hold so much sway over my practice? He (he seems to be a he) is actually a minority in the reading world, but everyone in publishing defers to him. Women read more than men, and translated fiction outsells English fiction in the UK, but the Mythical English Reader won't read women writers or non-European translations (which begs the question: Then why should I care about him?!). He is incredibly finicky, in a way that suggests people have been indulging him all his life instead of challenging him or encouraging him to try new and different things. What he likes seems to be other white men and whatever other white men produce; if he reads translated literature, he might read an obscure dead white male from Germany or Italy, or even some author from a non-European country if at least the translator is white. He likes very few things and hates an awful lot of others. Over the years, I would constantly be nudged or told outright to write like "the English reader," to think like "the English reader," to like the things he likes and disdain the things he disdains, to make the world comfortable for him, my sentences and content easier for him. And soon, this constant presence of outside voices seeped into my inside voice until I found myself automatically trying to fit into the Mythical English Reader's ideas of what my work should look like.

It was a long time before I realized that the problem wasn't my flawless English or the amazing books I tended to pick to translate; saying, "the English reader won't like this," really just meant, "You're not white." Proper English wasn't proper because it followed a set of rules per se, proper English was proper because that was the way white people spoke, and whatever I said was incorrect by default until it was approved by a white person. While this revelation came as something of a shock, perhaps it isn't so surprising to you. If you're a person of color reading this essay in English right now, chances are you grew up under the pervasive and ubiquitous gaze of the Mythical English Reader and understand it very well. I didn't grow up like that, or at least, not to any meaningful extent. I grew up mostly in Korea, have lived my entire adult life so far in Korea, and even when I wasn't living in Korea, I was mostly living in Asia. Throughout my life I couldn't care less what white people thought because white people had nothing to do with the grades I got in school, what my clients paid me, the men I dated, or what I thought of myself. Then I fell into this "literary translator" job and suddenly I had to figure out exactly what white people thought—and fast.

They are truly a different people from us Koreans. First of all, as far as I can tell, "white people" seem to be a colonial invention, an identity that almost only appears when they go up against brown-skinned people in their conquests and exploitation. In America, while there are still people there who talk about being Italian or Irish etc., white people are for the most part a very distinctive and cohesive monolith who are mostly defined by the fact that they are Not Brown. It was historically important that they were white because being not-white meant being a target of Indigenous genocide, a slave in the chattel slavery system, or a second-class brown person who was treated differently from a white person who does the same job and pays the same taxes and dues. I say "historical," but all the above systems continue to be perpetuated in America in some form today (for example, just look at who does most of the forced labor in the US prison-industrial complex). Whiteness craves power and money and is unwilling to concede that power and money to non-whites. Sometimes, it will throw a bone to a few brown people when it looks like they're going to stage a revolution—aficionados refer to this as "tokenism"—but for the most part, whiteness will bend over backwards trying to keep people of color in line.

Given that such white supremacy still exists in the Anglosphere, of course it would exist in the world of letters as well. The Mythical English Reader is, therefore, not a form of benign snobbery (if snobbery can ever be benign) but serves as a superego of whiteness, policing all literature so that it continues to affirm the superiority and cultural capital of whiteness, because in the end, cultural capital leads to actual capital, and the goal is to keep the money within the family. An Asian American writing instructor once warned me that the Anglophonic literary world used phrases like "the beauty of the language" as a reactionary code for excluding writers of color from the center of the establishment. I wondered what he was talking about at the time, but understood well enough as I entered the industry and kept on encountering weird situations where "beautiful language" honors were conferred on some truly mediocre white writing that followed the style of the status quo—which is a kind of flat and overly "clear" pseudo-Hemingway pastiche of workshop-ready minimalism—while anything else was branded as "bad writing" or "awkward." Note the mention of Hemingway here (talk about a white person going up against brown-skinned people in his conquests and exploitations). Hemingway, because of his privileged-expat life among brown people, was the whitest of all white authors, the god of all Mythical English Readers, and this is why his DNA runs so deep in American letters today.

In the end, "awkward," for me, always invites the question: awkward to whom? (White people.) And what makes it awkward? (A white person didn't write it.)

THE LITERAL ENGLISH READER

I was once asked to submit to a publisher who is infamous in Koreanist circles for pairing Korean translators with white monolingual writers, as "co-translation" teams. These are setups where the Korean translator gets stuck with doing a crib translation and the white monolingual does some editing and gets credit for imbuing "artistry" (whiteness) on the work of the Korean translator, who is relegated to being a mere technician. I had just come off a similar "co-translation" where an editor was given co-translator credit despite only having been an editor of the work. It was a completely insulting process from beginning to end (interestingly, the edits flattened the prose dramatically). I also had to practically bludgeon this editor repeatedly about getting the paperwork for my payment, which just goes to show how little they cared about my work, my time, and my rights as a translator. In cases like this, the Mythical English Reader becomes a literal English reader, a living, breathing reader who has the power to change the very words of your translation merely because they are white and you are not. They are the white gaze manifested into flesh. And in this case, they take your credit and your very real money and advance their own interests by exploiting your labor.

Or ruining it. A literary translation school in Korea, without bothering to inform me, once replaced me with a white instructor who immediately alienated my former students by openly disparaging Korean women writers in his first session, and proceeded to destroy the workshop I had painstakingly helped to build up over the years. The fiasco left aspiring translators in Korea, most of them people of color, with one less route into the profession, further enabling white people's social and actual capital to be kept within their possession.

Submitting my sample, I told the publisher that I was aware of his publications that engaged in this heinous practice, and that I was categorically unwilling to engage in it. He rejected the manuscript.

BREAK THE CYCLE

In recent years, I have come to the realization that if we want to change the way our translations are published, the way to do it is not only through individual action but through changing the entire landscape of publishing. The best way to help yourself is to change the system for everyone, instead of aiming to become another token for the perpetuation of whiteness. We all have limited time and energy, but there are still many ways to identify the cracks in the system that we can shove a wedge into or the points of leverage we can place a fulcrum upon, and it's going to take all of these little efforts and opportunities combined into a movement to make changes that will truly benefit individuals. Examples of this include Indonesian author Khairani Barokka's refusal to italicize non-English words in her writing, translator Rosalind Harvey offering free mentoring slots specifically for translators of color, and joining a translator collective or creating one yourself (you only really need three people to make a collective). I'm currently in three, and each makes a big difference to how I think about my practice. For example, the ALTA BIPOC Caucus, founded by some talented translators whom I deeply admire, provides a treasure trove of information and connections, not to mention an easy way to give back to the BIPOC translator community in various ways. Collectives make sense for translators; our work is inherently collaborative (we deal with virtually every level of publishing, from rightsholders to editorial to publicity to readers), and the publishing world is so opaque that you need all the help you can get to pass the gatekeepers.

Point being, we need a movement to make real changes in the landscape, and movements mean collective action, the sum of all of our individual efforts coalescing into a single, anticolonial direction.

THE TRUE ENGLISH READER

When I'm translating, I always imagine the author across the table from me, telling me the story in Korean. I never feel alone when I translate, and by the end of the book I feel as if the author and I have been sitting and working together for a long time.It is always a shock to meet the author in person because I feel extremely close to them but they haven't spent nearly as much time with me. It's really the author whom I'm thinking of when I translate, and it's really me for whom I'm translating—I am the true English reader.

So, the next time someone tries to gaslight you by asserting the authority of a mythical being over your own reading, call it out. No, you may not use that excuse, you need to come up with a real reason. No, either take ownership of your own prejudices or stay silent. This is your time now. You have entered the landscape. You're the realest thing in it.

6. PRESERVING THE TENDER THINGS

Ayesha Manazir Siddiqi

'I will have my serpent's tongue – my woman's voice, my sexual voice, my poet's voice.' – Gloria Anzaldúa

Translation is often seen as a kind of bridge-building, a way to make difference understood, thereby creating a path to a more tolerant, globalised world. Through this personalised and semi-fictionalised 'case study', I challenge that conception, examining the idea of the translator as intermediary between the West and her local culture, and how this role of intermediary can in fact be very much a part of the colonial project. This essay is also a prayer for the tender things, those that become lost, damaged, or forgotten when a dominant language overtakes one less powerful.

أشهد أن لا إله إلا ٱلله

The words of the azaan were whispered into my right ear immediately after I was born. They were recited in the original Arabic even though we do not speak the language. It is preferable, they say, to recite verses from the Quran without translation. Maybe because there is less opportunity for distortion when the words are poured from the original cup.

The daily prayers are also, of course, recited in Arabic by those who practice. And at the same time, there has been a movement in Pakistan against the Arabicization of Urdu: things like the replacement of Ramzan with Ramadan and Khuda-hafiz with Allah-hafiz. These translations are resisted in the name of protecting one language from the dominance of another. Although the two cases may seem contradictory, in both, there is a resistance towards translation and a wish to preserve.

Even though we lived in Karachi, Urdu was not intact on our tongues the way it was on our parents', whose Urdu was also weaker than that of their elders. In our household, the language continues to weaken, to practically disappear. I live in London now, but my three-year-old niece is growing up in Karachi. She's incredibly chatty in English, but doesn't speak a word of Urdu. I try to teach her: mera naam Anya hai. She responds in gibberish: baba boo blala la, and makes a funny face while doing it. There is a mockery in her imitation that surprises my sister and I. Maybe the child is already picking up on the fact that it is the servants that speak in Urdu. English is the language of the elites in Pakistan, and maybe the child can already sense the quiet respect that comes with this tongue. The colonisation begins before the words have even arrived.

All her schooling is, of course, in English. In this beautiful city where even a jumper (we call them sweaters, but my tongue has been policed since its arrival in the UK into making the necessary shift) is rarely necessary, she comes home from school one sunny December afternoon singing Jingle Bells and saying she is excited for the snow.

The shift from regional languages to English in colonised countries is not incidental but, in fact, strategic. In the subcontinent, one of its seeds was firmly planted by a man called Thomas Babington Macaulay, a civil servant responsible in the 1800s for the spreading of Western education in India, who infamously said in his 1835 treatise 'Minute on Indian Education':

We must at present do our best to form a class who may be interpreters between us and the millions whom we govern, a class of persons Indian in blood and colour, but English in tastes, in opinions, in morals and in intellect.

Macaulay established the teachings of English in all schools, and the training of English-speaking Indians to be teachers. He also supported establishing English as the nation's official language. This linguistic rupture meant a rupture, also, in traditional Indian vocational, educational, and scientific processes. And this was necessary because, as Ngũgĩ Wa Thiong'o reminds us, 'Economic and political control can never be complete without mental control'. This mental control, he says, involves two aspects: 'the destruction or the deliberate undervaluing of a people's culture' along with 'the

Although my niece was born into a largely English-speaking household, I feel like I witnessed the transition in real time, watching one language dwindle in favour of another. This was partly because of socio-political factors – the country was changing after Zia-ul-Haq's regime – and partly familial. When I was ten or so, my father started building up a business in Karachi, a process that involved socialising with an English speaking elite class, that was also, no surprises, devoutly secular. 'At some point,' my mother says of the growing secularism of the elite with her characteristic insight, 'they decided *they* were God.' And I saw the consequent changes. I saw, amongst other things, God gradually stream out the window. I saw, amongst other things, alcohol quietly trickle in. I am basing this on the vague recollections of a child, but my impression is that many tender things are sacrificed for entrance into the world of the so-called 'progressive elite'. Changing a language is so much

conscious elevation of the language of the coloniser'. 'The physical violence of the battlefield,' he says, 'was followed by the psychological violence of the classroom'. In other words, first the cannons, and then the canon.

Fanon says of the elite in the formerly colonised country:

The national bourgeoisie steps into the shoes of the former European settlement: doctors, barristers, traders, commercial travellers, general agents and transport agents … From now on it will insist that all the big foreign companies should pass through its hands, whether these companies wish to keep on their connection with the country, or to open it up. The national middle class discovers its historic mission: that of intermediary.

There's that word again – intermediary. Fanon deplores the formerly colonised country's neglect of its own resources in favour of becoming what he calls 'the Western bourgeoisie's business agent', also writing, 'The national bourgeoisie of under-developed countries is not engaged in production, nor in invention, nor building, nor labour; it is completely canalised

more than just that – languages come with ideologies attached.

Of course, much was also gained. Privilege involves an ease, an access, a carelessness and comfort that is easy for its holders to take for granted. The gifts and opportunities that *everyone* should have access to came, and this kind of privilege can, no doubt, protect other kinds of tender things.

There were other languages in the household too. My mother taught us 'fay-boli' (ف – بولی), a secret language she used with her cousins as a child. Us siblings used it to communicate secretly in front of family and friends. After my move to London, Urdu became a kind of ف – boli at times, when I want to share something private with desi friends and family in white spaces. Such secret tongues can be useful for protection, privacy, and revolt: I spoke in Urdu, for example, with my sister on the tube to joke about the people around us, and with a colleague to talk about unfair work practices. Once, I used it with a friend in a café when she wanted to share something intimate about her dating life but we soon found it impossible to talk about sex in Urdu, having only used the language to converse with elders, with whom we'd never discussed that

into activities of the intermediary type. Its innermost vocation seems to be to keep in the running and to be part of the racket'.

kind of thing. And so we found that we just didn't have the words.

My school only offered English Literature up to the age of twelve or thirteen. After that, I had to choose between business and science. In retrospect, I think this absence of English Lit may have been a blessing. Maybe I was spared a dangerous indoctrination. Many who have been educated in colonised countries have testified to the absurd disjunction between the people and settings of the books we are taught with the world around us, and the effects of this on the psyche. The novels of Dickens and Hardy, for example, ubiquitous in Pakistani schools, can remove us from our own landscape in favour of an imaginary 'superior' setting, leaving us ungrounded and detached from our lived experience. Books, by their nature, are reflections, and when these reflections do not match with our surroundings, we make internal shifts to accommodate the distortion. The problem is not just the books, but that it was *only* these books, leading us to believe other books, and therefore other stories, did not exist.

Wa Thiong'o, writing of his own schooling in Kenya, says, 'English was the official vehicle and the magical formula to colonial elitedom'. My school offered compatibility with the British educational system, thereby granting us the possibility, which I later took up, of going abroad for university.

One of the books we studied was *King Solomon's Mines*. The book, dedicated to 'all the big and little boys who read it', is about a white adventurer from South Africa, who, learning about the 'history of the dark land' that is modern-day Zimbabwe, goes there in search of King Solomon's diamond mines, which lie on 'the north side of the nipple' of a pair of mountains nick-named 'Sheba's breasts'. Ultimately, spoiler alert, the men get the diamonds by tricking the 'superstitious old Kafirs' with their advanced ways i.e. showing them a pair of dentures and a gun in order to mystify them. The novel is basically an adventure story, where both the African continent and the female subject serve as canvases on which to project the writer's demons and ogres, witches and barbarians, along with its deepest desires, its lusts and passions. It is a paint-by-numbers *Heart of Darkness*, a book that may well have reinforced the prevailing anti-blackness of our culture while allowing us to align ourselves more firmly with whiteness.

Of course, the embodied and overt anti-blackness in South Asia doesn't just come from old European novels like *King Solomon's Mines*. South Asians embody a violent and pervasive anti-blackness, consistently exploiting the position of 'intermediary' via our proximity to whiteness. Our media also encourages and perpetuates anti-blackness at every turn.

As for Urdu, we studied it as a second language. But one of the joys of that experience, and this only happened because the school I was in up to the age of sixteen was not an elite school,

Urdu too is a dominant language in its own context, crushing other regional tongues like Punjabi, Sindhi, Balochi etc. These supremacies within supremacies can be seen more clearly when we face away from whiteness.

was an Urdu calligraphy class. I still see the results of this in my Urdu handwriting.	
What are these columns, by the way, meant to divide? Is it …	
Personal	Impersonal
Biography	Academic
Body	Mind?
How arbitrary all these borders are. They dissolve	the moment you come in closer for a better look.
I flew over one when I moved countries. A big border. One that turned out to be pretty definitive. The flight was long.	Some borders solidify after you cross them. I was not expecting this to be one of those. I was supposed to go back home straight after my undergrad.
I flew over the border at eighteen, when I moved to England for university. I'd come with a kind of training, as I've outlined, that meant I could fit in, and even succeed. Of course, it wasn't entirely easy. The cold was shocking, the food terrible, the transport system confusing and the lifestyle entirely different. It also took a long time for my body to settle. My	A friend told me my bodily unease was occurring because, although I had taken a plane, the soul travels by foot. 'Your soul,' she told me, when I'd been in England for about two months, 'it's probably only in Afghanistan at the moment, or maybe Iran, maybe Turkey, still making its way over to you.'

skin turned flaky, my bladder confused, my belly grumbly, my thoughts jumbled.

Most of the friends I made in England were British Asian. The way that these friends held their 'other' language was interesting to me. They spoke it in a way that I had not seen before, as if it inhabited an entirely different part of themselves than the English-speaking part. Sometimes, it felt performative and at other times, like a genuine resistance, a wish to recover something lost. (My gaze here is simplistic, but I leave this here to show the correction that parallels, as well as to allow for the unformed. The polished essay with all its flaws edited out had frozen my writing for so long that I wonder if an exposure of the process can be helpful.)

A word floats around me in those early years: 'Freshie'. Freshie – fresh off the boat, is a derogatory term that British Asians (and I think other diasporics) use for people who have just come from back home, to signify, mainly, a kind of ignorance or naivety, or customs and accents that they see as backward. The term, with regards to me, was often (not always, but often) in the context of how not like 'a freshie' I was, as if this were a

Kavita, the editor of this anthology, writes in a note to this second paragraph that sometimes this process I describe of British Asian people's relationship with their tongue is neither a self-conscious taking on, nor resistance, but 'just continuity'. She mentions those immigrant households where the language has not been lost and says, 'English is probably more pervasive and normalised in certain contexts in Pakistan than some UK communities'.

It is a crucial bit of nuance, and there is a further implication here, possibly, or a question at least, of whether, in fact, certain native elites inhabit a positionality closer to whiteness than certain members of diasporic communities.

M. Moiz, in her podcast #stonedalive, also reminds me that these distinctions I'm trying to make are not so clear-cut when she speaks, more than once, about 'Defence kay rehnay walay' and their 'diasporic gaze' (I was very much a 'Defence ki rahnay wali'). This relationship between the elites back home and their working class diasporic counterparts is an essay in itself.

compliment. Other times, it was used with gentle mockery, when my language, actions, or turns-of-phrase were 'not-quite-right'. The equivalent, the term Pakistanis use to mock their British counterparts, is BBCD, British Born Confused Desi, and the stereotype veers between the 'coconut', cut off from desi culture, and those holding on to a culture that has frozen in time instead of the 'real' thing, that has continued to flow and transform while they have been outside of it.

In England, I picked up on the cues around me and adapted accordingly. Code-switching is also a kind of translation, and my vernacular, clothing, and behaviour gradually changed. The process was largely unconscious, but the intent, of course, was to be accepted and to be understood more coherently. A primal need for community fuels the enterprise, and the idea of all that has been lost only filters in much later. Translation, you see, does not serve to preserve. It serves to make legible.

After my first year at university, I was back in Pakistan for the holidays, watching *Mrs Doubtfire* on TV with my siblings in my

There are elements of a classist, colonial gaze in both terms: freshie and BBCD. It is usually the urban, English-speaking Pakistani who uses the term BBCD for their British counterparts who migrated mainly from rural areas, and 'freshie' too, is a term more frequently used for the economic migrant, not those urban English-speaking Pakistanis who are moving not out of obligation or necessity, but instead perhaps for what George Lamming calls 'the pleasures of exile'.

My friend, when he proofread this, joked (well, the academic version of 'joked'), 'I like that term, 'code-switching'. I prefer it to assimilation. It implies more agency.' His comment made me think about how, at some point in your code-switching, you can find that the switch has suddenly … jammed. And you think you're an expert, switching ways of being according to who you're speaking with, but then you find that some irreversible transformations have taken place in the process. And since they've happened without your noticing, the necessary funerals were not conducted in time.

This is the first time I have acknowledged the fact that we kept watching *Mrs Doubtfire* after hearing the news. I think

parents' room when my father called. He said some planes had hit the World Trade Centre, an important building in New York and told us to switch on the news. I relayed what he'd said to my siblings, but I think Robin Williams had just stuck his face in the cake to create an impromptu face mask and we decided that we should keep watching the film. The truth is, I didn't think, at the time that this incident was any bigger an event than the countless bomb blasts that punctuated my childhood in Karachi. I did not fully realise then that an act of violence translates to something very different depending on the power of the person it is imposed upon. No, this was (allegedly) a backwards attack – from East to West – it wasn't allowed in that direction. There would be severe retaliation.

When I went back to England after those holidays, it was as if *everybody's* gaze had shifted. Suddenly, I was *Muslim*, and everyone wanted to know what that meant. They wanted me to clear up their prejudices and misconceptions, to elucidate, to explain. I was absolutely unqualified, but I willingly obliged. Maybe it gave me a sense of importance. Or maybe I wanted to defend my people. Or maybe I just didn't know how to say the event became so all-important that admitting that I had accorded it little importance at first felt like sacrilege. Like blasphemy.

In *The Muslims are Coming*, Arun Kundnani cites a joke told by the Arab American comedian Dean Obeidallah:

It's so weird. Before 9/11, I am just a white guy, living a typical white guy's life. All my friends had names like Monica, Chandler, Joey, and Ross … I go to bed September tenth white, wake up September eleventh, I am an Arab.

I find the joke incisive because it suggests that this sharp pivot of the gaze is disorienting not just because of the prejudices it reveals through the 'terrorism' filter that Muslims are viewed through after 9/11, but also because of how invisible the person was the day before. Obeidallah, was, of course, never a white man out of *Friends*. He had simply been swallowed up by the entirely self-involved white gaze, first as a non-entity, and now as a problem.

no, and assumed, since they were asking, that it was my duty to translate.

Eventually, I started to build up translation as a vocation. I have held on to my Urdu with diligence through the years, reading novels with a teacher, poetry with my elders, asking to be taught, basically from whoever would teach me.

My translation work began with translating texts written by family members. A short story written by a great-uncle, then some essays published by my grandmother's father, and then a memoir by a great-aunt.

Later, I applied for a job translating a play into Urdu. The story was set in Birmingham and was about Islamophobia in the UK. It sounded like a great gig at first, but as I embarked on the translation, I grew increasingly uncomfortable with the project. Although it was a well-intentioned piece, it seemed to me that the whiteness of the writers had very much seeped

My great grandfather is hailed in family lore as an intellectual and a freedom fighter. When my grandmother, his daughter, was a child, he left the family for *seven years*, apparently for the sake of his activism. This leave-taking is romanticised and mythologised in our family, but as I read his work and unravelled his views, I started to ask questions, adding layers to a passed-down narrative. I saw that words previously taken as gospel were actually mere opinion, and that men considered legends can be brought back to the ground, allowing, potentially, for not just a celebration of their pursuits but also an assessment of damage done. This is an ongoing and difficult project.

I wrote in my critique:

I found myself playing a strange role in this work, somewhere between translator and consultant, when I pointed out the obvious inconsistencies. The writers seemed attentive to my feedback, eager that I point out anything that may be offensive or inappropriate. However, this is not

into the work, as is inevitable. I worried that, with my translation, I was giving the play a stamp of authenticity and I decided, with some terror, to write a critique of the very text I was translating. I published the critique and it was well received but I was anxious about having upset the writers and felt a desire to disappear. I don't know if all writers feel this way when they write critiques, but it has happened so often that I start to think maybe terror is a prerequisite to writing something new.

It is a complicated equation though, the translator's relationship with their text. Ideally, you want to translate something that resonates, but such things are difficult to find. The next project I embarked on, for instance, was a treatise, written in Urdu, on the condition of Sindhi women in Pakistan by a Karachi-based writer whom I admire. Since I had only read extracts and the actual book was out of print, I had someone pick up a copy from the writer's house herself, photocopy it, and post it to me. But, after all this excitement and effort, I abandoned the project. I worried, for one thing, that the way in which the women's oppression was framed only served to reinforce a racist narrative. This book, I decided, didn't need to

the solution; this is just a smoothing over of surface imperfections to create an image of political correctness. In fact, in this smoothing-over of obvious blunders, I became complicit, making the piece seem more acceptable, leaving room for more subtle, insidious misrepresentations to flourish. I found myself imagining what this play would have looked like if it had been made by a Pakistani Muslim from Birmingham for other Pakistani Muslims from Birmingham; the radical potential of that kind of play. What, in fact, would this play have looked like if it had been written by an Urdu speaker, and I had been approached to translate it into English? When will room be made in the industry for that play?

As a consequence of writing this critique, I was approached by a podcast dedicated to telling this very same story with the depth I had been longing for. It doesn't always happen this way, of course, but the opportunity was validating, a breadcrumb in my journey towards listening to my tummy when it squirms.

be in English. Or at least, I was not the one who wanted to hold that responsibility.

Some people say translation is | a bit like a conversation
A mirroring | gnirorrim A
A dia | logue
But who is in charge here? | Who's doing the translation, and for whom?

We cannot ignore the fact that although translation can operate in different directions, it tends to move towards the historically dominant, imperialistic languages: English, French, Italian, German.

And I don't mean just written translation; when a group of people gather from different parts of the world, they will invariably communicate in English. These dominant tongues hold dominant modes of discourse that can overtake, co-opt, suppress, appropriate, that can, in essence, re-affirm prevalent hierarchies. In light of this, the idea of 'decolonising translation' seems, potentially, an oxymoron. What will we talk about next? Decolonising Colonialism?

Then, Deadly Pandemic began. We do not yet have the words to articulate what this time has done to us, is doing to us.

During the first lockdown, I adopted a cat. A beautiful striped billee who I call Billee, meaning *cat* in Urdu. Someone I know, when he hears Billee's name, jokes, 'Your cat is an English cat, you need to give him an English name otherwise he'll have an identity crisis.' This person, who has been hell-bent on assimilation all his life, recognizes in this joke a disruption, an impossibility; in his joke, he acknowledges the limits of Englishness, which, in his usual rhetoric, he denies with fierce determination.

Billee, as the photo evidences, speaks several tongues. He found this particular book misleading as, he claims, the writer's name gives one the expectations of wolves in the text, a promise left unfulfilled.

Instinctively, I speak to Billee only in Urdu. I use sweet and tender terms of endearment for him that I can't recall where I know from. Sometimes I reason they must have been stored within me from my babyhood. Other times, I think they're coming from ancestral memory, from a primal part of me that just knows those are the words to use for tender things. I have never used these sweet words for another human, and don't tell anyone what they are, and I only use them when Billee and I are alone. A friend, brown, diasporic, shares with me that she has special names for her cat, and from the way she says it I can tell hers are secret too, and I wonder if the same thing is going on with her. But I don't ask – these are regions that have stayed protected, miraculously, and it's best not to probe.

Donna Haraway says of her pet dog, Cayenne: 'We have had forbidden conversation; we had had oral intercourse; we are bound in telling story upon story with nothing but the facts. We are training each other in acts of communication we barely understand. We are, constitutively, companion species'.

The pandemic, which I thought would last three weeks, then three months, did not end. One day, a friend invited me to his podcast, where he spoke to writers of colour about their spiritual beliefs. I mentioned during the conversation that my family had an ancestral pact that impacted our communication with the non-human – with jinns and animals, for example. Before I knew it, I found myself translating the concept to my friend, who is spiritual but of a different religious background, in order to make the idea accessible to him. Later on, I was told

I gave this essay to an ex-boyfriend to proofread, and he highlighted the bit about not using Billee's sweet pet names for any human and asked, 'Could this be shame?' I felt a pang when I read his comment, for all the loving things I felt for him but did not say. And I seriously considered the matter. These names I call Billee. They are so intimate. So desi. Maybe a part of me sees them as backward. As cheesy. Paindu. In 'How to Tame a Wild Tongue', Gloria Anzaldúa writes, 'Shame. Low estimation of self. In childhood we are told that our language is wrong. Repeated attacks on our native tongue diminish our sense of self. The attacks continue throughout our lives'.

An example of this communication with the unseen, offered with prayers, care, and gratitude, only half-told:

If a member of our family finds a snake on their property, they are able to tell it to leave by informing it of an ancestral pact. But it's not that easy. We discuss the very important matter of *tone* on a family WhatsApp group – the information has to be imparted in a certain voice, one that is simultaneously authoritative and submissive. And really, the only way to get the tone

by a family member I should have acted with more care. 'Others won't understand,' she said, 'don't joke about these things.' And I hadn't been joking, but I wondered afterwards whether I had trivialised and disrespected. This sacred information, so tentative, is to be handled with care. Family members were trusting me with this knowledge, quietly and carefully trading information, making attempts to maintain and strengthen ancestral ties through these preserved ways. I wondered whether, with my careless sharing, I had offended the ancestors. But I'll stop there, as some of what I am saying lies between the literal and metaphorical or, actually, on a different plane altogether. It is something translation cannot capture, and will therefore distort.

Now I work mainly as a writer, an occasional translator, and an editor, and I find that the line between translator and contributor is not always clear. Sometimes I only realise in the doing, which of those roles I am performing.

I got a gig, for example, from a TV show looking for a 'sensitivity reader'. And my god, the show was bad. And here I was again. Being asked to make the unacceptable acceptable, to take a thing filled with stereotypes and cleanse it. I told them

right is to summon a certain kind of feeling. This feeling, I suspect, is what is actually being transmitted. Communicating with the other-than-human is no different from speaking with the human: a certain grace is required, a care, a tact, a confidence, a humility, an honesty, a reserve. The transmission is of the energy behind the words, and it is a matter of practice. Our secret language with the other-than-human, however, is quickly being forgotten, overtaken by the dominant tongues of our white supremacist capitalist patriarchal world, which has thought up ways they find more convenient to get rid of unwanted beings from their properties.

I also revisited Urdu/Arabic calligraphy, taking a class at SOAS. My favourite type of calligraphic art is the figurative, where the script also forms the object it represents. Like this one, by Asghar Malik:

how I felt and walked away. I try to learn to recognise these stirrings of disgust and guilt and respond to them, to distinguish whether I'm being asked to be a political correctness filter or a legitimate contributor. And I don't know enough about the role yet but the sensitivity reader, I sometimes suspect, is a hack.

Also, during deadly pandemic, I wrote a novel. It is to be published shortly. The protagonist is, as it happens, a translator, and the novel grapples with what it really means when you take on another's tongue – all that is lost and gained in the process.

In the novel, I am sure I am unsuccessful but nonetheless, I try to find a means to refuse cultural translation, to not translate cultural specificity for a white audience, as this is not my target audience. In fact, sometimes, in order to maintain cultural specificity, I'll do a different kind of translation. For example, when the protagonist, who is from Karachi, eats dahi barey in Delhi, she mentions that in Delhi, they call dahi barey dahi vada. That act of translation felt to me like a translation *within*, favouring the less dominant place and not allowing even for the swallowing up of South Asianness by India. I am influenced, ironically, by the translated literature of Ferrante and Knausgaard, who write in a way that feels to me firmly located, unconcerned with the English language. Although it is not necessarily for me, and I know little about either place, I find it fascinating when Knausgaard, writing in Norwegian, ponders on the small differences between Sweden and Norway in his six-volumed *Struggle*.

Then, in the late stages of my writing this piece, my father was diagnosed with cancer. (It was shit, and he's better now alhamdulillah, but emotions so unexpected and intense emerged that I can only hint at them in brackets for now. I think they will come to my tongue one day. Adrienne Rich writes in 'Planetarium', 'I am an instrument in the shape / of a woman trying to translate pulsations / into images for the relief of the body / and the reconstruction of the mind'.)

In the early stages, we struggled with food prep, and came across dozens of books about cancer and diets, but they were all Western food based. We were unable to find a single book about cancer and South Asian diets. I don't know if we just didn't look in the right places, or if this is connected to the whiteness of the publishing industry, or to South Asian silence and shame around disease. Maybe a combination of those things. We figured it out anyway. Khichri is a good place to start.

My father, who has always been obsessed with the stars and planets, has become even more so. And so on his last birthday, we got him a telescope, and someone came over to set it up and showed him Saturn and its moons, and this seemed an important part of the journey, somehow. Abbu isn't a big talker, but we try hard to listen and to follow his lead, learning the language he would like to communicate in while he journeys this utterly foreign landscape. We train each other, as Haraway says, 'in acts of communication we barely understand'.

We are inevitably using Western language and frameworks to understand what is happening with the cancer, and this is difficult. The language of medicine is intensely alienating.

Ngũgĩ wa Thiong'o articulates one of the problems with scientific and technical terms being communicated in English, when he says that, as a result, 'technology always appears as slightly external, *their* product and not *ours*'.

In speaking of his internal colonisation, my father longs for metaphor. One day, when I tell him I will write about all this, he says, 'you can call it *The Strange Case of the Organ Eater.*'

I want to end with a secret, if that's ok. Come closer, and please, promise this remains between you and me, ok? Ok. Well, this essay is also like a snake. It's shed its skin many times before reaching you. You can't even imagine what some of the discarded skins looked like. For example, maybe there was a thread about translation and eroticism. About how, in the intimacy of the bedroom, lines can be crossed, permissions assumed before they are given. Maybe, in that layer, I spoke of a white man I knew called David, who enthused that if we were to marry and he converted, he could change his name to Daud, like the famous gangster, he said, Daud Ibrahim. Or maybe that story is made up. Who knows. Who knows, for that matter, where the snake begins. Maybe its core is nothing more than a breath of air, a wisp of light. Which is covered, then, by a layer of dung. Or is it the other way around, light over dung? We don't know. We pray that it is light but we continue either way. And we don't know, for that matter, where the snake ends. All we can do, really, is pause at this arbitrary finish to say that there is something untranslatable at the heart of us. Something secret and sacred and serpentine, and it is the reason we go on. May it spread in the way that *it* sees fit while we sit around it, silent, praying for its protection. Ameen.

REFERENCES

All that is good comes from God and all my limitations stem from my own ego.

No text is made in isolation – they are entirely collaborative, formed of conversation, of assistance, of largely invisible labour. Writers draw upon the help and kindness, the activism and healing, even the stories and lives, of so many around them but by the time the piece is done, convince themselves it was a

REFERENCES

Anzaldúa, Gloria "How to Tame a Wild Tongue", in *Borderlands: The New Mestiza - La Frontera*. San Francisco: Aunt Lute Book Company.

Fanon, Frantz *The Wretched of the Earth*. Translated by Constance Farrington. Penguin Modern Classics. London, England: Penguin Classics.

product of their talent alone. We pay homage to the books in our references, but we omit the ones who are even more at the heart of it, and the truth is those struggling to survive are often the same who are nourishing the world.

In my translation work, I turn again and again to my mother Seema Manazir, as well as my Urdu teacher, Zulfiqar Ali Sajjad, for their assistance. Also to my grandmother, Nabeela Manazir/Bari.

One of the editors of this anthology, Kavita Bhanot, suggested the division into two columns in order to address a disjunction in an earlier version. She also probed, with characteristic skill, care, and depth, the arguments put forward. My kind friend Crispin Semmens helped me with the layout of this piece. The brilliant Jasber Singh gave me invaluable feedback. And without the love and support of my two younger siblings, Sara and Bilal, who are doing so much beautiful care work during this time of challenge to the family, I would not have had the resources to write this.

Haraway, Donna Jeanne 'The companion species manifesto : dogs, people, and significant otherness'. Chicago, Ill. : Bristol : Prickly Paradigm ; University Presses Marketing.

Kundnani, Arun *The Muslims are Coming! Islamophobia, Extremism and the Domestic War on Terror*. London: Verso.

Lamming, George *The Pleasures of Exile*, Ann Arbor Paperbacks, the University of Michigan Press.

Thiong'o, Ngũgĩ wa *Decolonising the Mind : the Politics of Language in African Literature*. London : Portsmouth, N.H. :J. Currey ; Heinemann.

M. Moiz's podcast, #stonedalive is on Instagram @unrelentlesslyyours

The snake calligraphy is by Asghar Malik, masgharmalik74@gmail.com

The phrase 'hetero-normative, white supremacist, capitalist patriarchy', stems, of course, from bell hooks.

7. THE COMBINED KINGDOM: `DECOLONISING' WELSH TRANSLATION

Eluned Gramich

'Ga i rif yng Nghaerdydd, os gwelwch…'
'*Speak up!*'
'GA I RIF YNG NGHAER—''
'*Speak up – you'll have to speak up.*'
Siarad lan, wrth gwrs, yw'r siars
i siarad Saesneg.
--- 'Cân y di-lais i British Telecom,' Menna Elfyn

'Ga i rif yng Nghaerdydd, os gwelwch…'
'*Speak up!*'
'GA I RIF YNG NGHAER—''
'*Speak up – you'll have to speak up.*'
Speak up is, of course,
the command to speak English.
--- 'Song of the voiceless to British Telecom,' [Translation by R.S.Thomas]

This is an essay about Welsh translation, and the ways we can – and cannot – talk about the Welsh language in colonial terms. But it is also an essay about how I became Welsh again; how I reclaimed my name and learnt to read the world around me in a radical way, a Welsh way.

INDIGENOUS

In 2018, English-language novelist Alys Conran and Welsh-language writer-translator Sian Northey took part in a London Book Fair panel entitled 'Indigenous Languages of the United Kingdom'. They were there to discuss Conran's debut novel, *Pigeon*, which had been shortlisted for the Dylan Thomas Prize in 2017. For the first time, an English-language novel had been published at the same time as its Welsh translation. I was excited to see Sian and Alys on this stage in front of an international audience who may not have been familiar with Welsh-English translation, with its particular tensions and complexities; who may not have known about the Welsh language at all.

Afterwards, a friend said that Alys and Sian had, perhaps, taken too much for granted. They had assumed their audience 'knew about Welsh'. They'd talked in detail about the processes of transforming *Pigeon*'s hybrid Welsh-English prose and Caernarfonshire dialect into a text that works in Welsh as well as English. My friend was right: many people in the London Book Fair audience didn't 'know about Welsh'. They didn't know about the hundreds of thousands of people who speak Welsh in their everyday life. They didn't know about the communities where English remains a second language, and where people stutter and apologise when switching to English because they forget the correct words, because their grammar is skewed by Welsh phrase-making, saying 'crossing fingers' instead of 'fingers crossed', or 'don't call Will on your father' instead of 'don't call your father Will'. Perhaps some audience members only had the false Welsh stereotypes to hand: a language with no vowels, a dying language, peppered with English words; a weapon used by Welsh people to make English holidaymakers feel unwelcome in pubs.... This lack of foundational knowledge about the Welsh language in a London-based audience is strange when you consider that Wales is only two hours away by train.

The word 'indigenous' in the panel title, too, reveals much about the ambivalent status of Welsh in the UK. The word seems to align Welsh with First Nation languages: endangered languages of communities that have suffered the most from historical and ongoing colonial violence. I don't think that Aboriginal languages or the languages of indigenous peoples in the United States and Canada, for example, can be comfortably compared with Welsh, a language community that has managed to escape from the devastation of imperial greed and linguicide. Since the successful Welsh-language protests in the 1970s and 80s, and Devolution in 1997, Welsh has become one of the languages of government. Fluent bilingualism is now a badge of social status, an aid to political advancement. Not only that, but Welsh is as contemporary and mutable as English – up to date with the new languages produced by the rise of social media ('Trydar' for 'Twitter'), and the Covid-19 pandemic ('hunan-ynysu' for 'social-distancing', 'cyfnod clo' for 'lockdown').

Then again, the label 'indigenous' is not entirely wrong. As a 'junior partner of the expanding British state', according to the historian Chris Williams, Wales was an enthusiastic participant in British colonialism. Yet at the same time, since the 12th century, Wales has struggled with periods of linguistic and social oppression and, today, (to borrow Neil Evans' words) Wales is a kind of 'dependent periphery' that has suffered from a colonial-like or colonial-reminiscent relationship with its financially, culturally, and linguistically powerful neighbour. Welsh people are always having to switch – to 'speak up' – from the language of their family and community to the dominant language: English.

AWAKENING

> *To those of us who speak the Welsh language, that is Cymraeg, there is no such entity as Wales. This land in which we live is Cymru.*
>
> – *Cymru or Wales?*, R. S. Thomas

Knowledge of Welsh history, literature, and language is hard won, even for those who live in Wales. It's an old complaint in Wales that Welsh history is poorly taught in schools (if at all) and Welsh literature, too, is often brushed aside to make way for the English Canon. I'm still learning, slowly, over the years, facts about my own culture that seem almost like secrets.

My ignorance became clear to me in my last year at university. I'd chosen a module in Medieval Welsh, a choice that my course-mates thought distinctly eccentric. (I was the only student in the entire year group who opted for this module.) As part of this, I went on an organised trip with the Celtic department around the ancient sites of the Welsh-English borderland. Marks carved in stone, battered monoliths, cold chapels. There were so few of us that the whole department fit into a 12-seater minibus, and in this bus was a PhD history student I had a crush on. He seemed to know everything, and he spoke a perfect, formal, passionate kind of Welsh while imparting this knowledge to anyone listening.

It was a bright, warm day. There was a tiny pub set in the ruins of an abbey and the men – they were mostly men, the postgraduates in the Celtic department – ordered pints and sat in the tall grass of the abbey grounds and carried on their conversation about Welsh history while I, embarrassed and ignorant, remained silent.

The history PhD said: 'Why are we always taught about 1066? That date means nothing to us in Wales. Better to learn about 1282, when Llywelyn ein Llyw Olaf was killed. That's a date that really matters. Or 1537 and 1542,' he went on, 'The Acts of Union! When Wales became England and we were all forced to speak the language of the oppressor.'

I sipped my beer, nodding enthusiastically whenever he caught my eye. Yes, he was right. He was so handsome, he had to be. The dates were familiar to me – we had learnt about these 'Acts of Union' at school, as a footnote to Henry VIII's many accomplishments, his consolidation of Tudor power. If you'd asked me earlier, I would have said, well, weren't the Acts a good thing?

My glass was warm in my hands; we had seen such old, beautiful things, created more than a thousand years ago, but there were no tourists in these small places. I smiled and nodded, but inside I was filled with shame, because in all my twenty-one years it hadn't once occurred to me that the history I had been taught was *English* and not 'British'.

It was a moment of awakening; it placed a question mark on the narrative I had received at school – not just historical, but cultural too. It was almost as though, having been educated in an English secondary school and an English university, I had forgotten my Welshness. Like the audience at the London Book Fair, I didn't 'know about Welsh' and had to learn anew – an ongoing feat of autodidacticism because, as a minority language, information about Welsh history and culture is not as readily available in the national media as English history and culture.

But there is another reason why this day of the ruined abbey has stayed with me over the years. The professor who drove the minibus from one ancient sacred site to the other called me by my nickname – Ned – the name I had been given at my English secondary school and which, for some reason that I'd rather not reflect on, I had decided to take with me to university. The first time he addressed me as 'Ned' in front of the Celtic postgraduates, I could see the shock on their faces. And more than that, a kind of shared shame that one of us should choose to anglicise their name to the point of ridicule.

I walked back to my room late at night, tired and slightly drunk, hating myself for having given up so easily and so quickly; for not having detected the power dynamics at play. I understood now that the embarrassment I'd felt because of my name was not because Welsh was unpronounceable, but because monolingual English speakers found it unpronounceable. The frustration over my Welsh name did not come from me – although it had felt that way all my life – the frustration belonged to the English monoglots faced with linguistic difference: having to navigate a name that seemed foreign but was, in fact, the opposite.

Llywelyn ein Llyw Olaf, by the way, died in battle in 1282. His baby daughter, Gwenllian, was kidnapped by the English and taken to a nunnery in Lincolnshire where she grew up having never heard her native tongue. She signed her name *Wentlian*.

A NOTE ABOUT NAMES

> '*Wales is a translation; it is part of the process whereby English legislators played havoc with Scottish, Irish and Welsh place-names and patronymics [...]. The changing of mynydd and nant into mountain and stream leaves me an exile in my own country.*'
>
> – R. S. Thomas

I have apologised for my name countless times; I have made fun of my own language. *El-uh-ned*. No, not quite. *El-oo-ned*. Almost! Yes, it *is* difficult, isn't it? When I was younger, I laughed when people said that spoken Welsh was like a coughing fit, and that if I spoke Welsh to them, they'd end up covered in spit. It seems to me, now, that this is common with Welsh people, especially when young and building a picture of the world – *you begin to believe the jokes.* It's easy to think that Welsh is redundant and ugly when articulate and educated journalists in highbrow newspapers say it is. How can they be wrong? They write for *The Times*.

The obligatory anglicisation of the legal and political system in Wales, starting with the Acts of Union, meant that the Welsh patronymic system of naming was replaced by English surnames. So 'Gwenllian ferch Llywelyn' (Gwenllian daughter of Llywelyn) or 'Dafydd ap Gwilym' (Dafydd son of Gwilym) would change to 'Gwenllian Lewis' and 'Dafydd Williams'. It is clear from the names in my mother's generation how strong anglicisation was in the 50s and 60s. Their names are overwhelmingly English in the rural west Wales community where the first language, the language of home, was Welsh, but the language of progress and aspiration was English.

Names carry the bulk of the linguistic strain in Wales. Road signs, place, and house names: these topographic translations, from Welsh to English and back to Welsh again, are metonyms of a wider struggle against cultural domination. Naming the land and owning the land blur together, as in the recent debate surrounding Yr Wyddfa, also known as Snowdon. The motion, put forward by Gwynedd County Councillor John Pughe Roberts, to use only the Welsh name of the mountain was voted down, but not before Welsh was once again ridiculed on *Have I Got News for You*. Or another example (I have many) of the housing crisis in Welsh-speaking areas, is that the traditional Welsh names are disappearing, overwritten by names chosen by English newcomers. Llyn Bochlwyd has become known as 'Lake Australia', Traeth Dynion as 'The Creek' – casual translation by English visitors and locals has to be actively resisted by de-translating, an affirmation of the old names. The truth is that English locals, visitors, and English-language media have the power to wipe out the Welsh names just because it is easier for them to say and write; in other words, the Welsh map is slowly being erased, almost by accident. It reminds me of the Irish schoolteacher, Hugh, in Brian Friel's 1981 play, *Translations,* who warned: 'Remember that words are signals, counters. They are not immortal. And it can happen – to use an image you'll understand – it can happen that a civilisation can be imprisoned in a linguistic contour which no longer matches the landscape of fact.'

WELSH WRITERS IN BRIEF CONVERSATION

So far I've been writing about names and naming. Why not about literature? My answer is that decolonial work (if I may describe it as such) is overwhelmingly located in bureaucratic and cartographical spaces in Wales. Road signs spark protests; house names petitions. Literature seems to slip by unnoticed. And yet many seminal works of Welsh literature comment on, and critique, the anglicisation of Welsh names. So the act of translating this literature into English is a strangely politically contradictory process in that it is, by its very nature, 'anglicising' Welsh writing by transposing it from Welsh into English. Yet, at the same time, it is giving voice to the Welsh protest against anglicisation, encouraging non-Welsh readers to empathise with Welsh-speaking characters whose language is under threat. Kate Roberts' classic 1936 novel *Traed Mewn Cyffion* (Feet in Chains) is a good example: a generational novel set in North Wales in the late 19th/ early 20th century. In my mother's 2012 translation, Welsh place names are left untouched in the text, and explained through a lengthy glossary at the back. 'Place names always mean something in Welsh', she writes, as a reminder that Moel Arian, Yr Eifl, Y Fawnog, can't be ignored or dismissed; they are a part of the story. In the novel, too, one character's name is anglicised by her English husband from 'Sioned' to 'Janet', and children have to be taught correct Welsh words at the local Eisteddfod – 'defnyddio' instead of the Wenglish 'iwsio'. A testament to English's inescapable influence, even at the turn of the century at the heart of Gwynedd's slate-quarrying industry.

'Translation' by Gillian Clarke

after translating from Welsh, particularly a novel by Kate Roberts

Your hand on her hand – you've never been
this close to a woman since your mother's beauty
at the school gate took your breath away,

[…] But you're lost for words,
can't think of the English for *eirin*—it's on the tip of your—
but the cat ate your tongue, licking peach juice
from your palm with its rough *langue de chat*
tafod cath, the rasp of loss.

Few works are published from languages other than English into Welsh (why bother, if everyone can read the English translation?), and the few works of Welsh language literature that are translated into English, or indeed other languages, struggle to find large readerships outside of Wales, even classics like Angharad Price's novel *The Life of Rebecca Jones* and the abovementioned Kate Roberts' *Feet in Chains*, which deserve to be read all over the world.

There are exceptions: acts of resistance, like 'Y brotest ddiderfyn', Elin Haf Gruffydd Jones' translation of the Catalan writer Albert Forns' short story in the Welsh literary magazine, *O'r Pedwar Gwynt*. Here, by means of translation, a Welsh writer declares her support for the Catalan independence movement. But the translation goes beyond that: Jones actively repurposes a short story about a never-ending linguistic, political, and cultural protest in a small European stateless nation, struggling to maintain its identity against a more dominant neighbour, so that it speaks directly to Welsh-speaking Wales. It is one of very few examples of literary translations from a European language into Welsh with no English bridge, a move from one minority language to another that feels almost tender, like an embrace.

Sian Northey's second translation, a memoir entitled *Y Daith Ydi Adre / The Journey is Home* by John Sam Jones, a writer from west Wales, describes a difficult coming-of-age as a gay man in the 1970s. Like *Pigeon*, the two versions were published simultaneously. In an interview for Nation Cymru, Northey is asked whether it's worth supplying a Welsh translation at all, when a Welsh-speaking reader can simply pick up the original? She replies:

> I don't doubt that there will be some people who would not have chosen to read the English version – because they prefer to read Welsh … because publicity for Welsh-language books reaches them … because they wish to support Welsh-language publishing – a whole host of varied reasons. Publishing both versions at the same time will increase the number of people who will read the Welsh language version because they have the choice of either; a later publication date for the translation may have led to fewer sales in Welsh because people who know you would probably have read the English version and then not bothered to read the translation when it appeared. However, one thing that surprised me with Alys Conran's *Pigeon* was that a small group of people did read both – I didn't expect anyone to do that!

Reading this interview with my mam in the kitchen, she tells me that many Welsh-speakers do not read English books. As soon as Mam says this, as strange as it sounds, I know it's true, because I've met such people many times in my life. Great readers of Welsh literature who buy the entire Gwales catalogue every year from the local Welsh bookshop, but who would not pick up an English book.

'It's political,' Mam says. My mam, the real translator, who wishes more than anything that she could translate her favourite South American poets into Welsh and see them published.

'Yes. Sounds it.'

Mam is making coffee, standing in the corner, half-turned to the machine.

'I read an interview with Manon Steffan Ros the other day,' I say.

She smiles then. 'Oh?'

We're both admirers of Manon Steffan Ros, the author of *Blasu* and *Llyfr Glas Nebo*. 'It was about how she translated her novels. You know, she changed things in *Llyfr Glas Nebo* – changed the names from Welsh to English, made up a whole backstory as to why the main character would be writing his diary in English and not his native language.'

'Right,' Mam says. 'Makes sense.'

'And it made me think. The status of Welsh as a minority language is almost always part of the story, isn't it? I mean, for any Welsh author, when their characters speak to each other, or travel… There's always England and Englishness in the background. So to translate it to English, you have to change the story.'

My mother takes out the mugs, looks out of the window; she's retired now and likes to keep a close eye on the visiting birds. 'It must be troublesome to edit,' she replies. 'But good writers can do it. Manon Steffan Ros probably just wrote another bestseller, knowing her.'

'The English translation isn't out yet,' I say, checking my phone. 'There's this other bit in the interview that you'll like. Wait, I'll find it now. Listen. *Writing through the medium of Welsh shouldn't feel like some kind of political declaration; it's just me writing a story. And, in exactly the same way, me deciding to write a novel through the medium of English shouldn't feel political either.*'

'Hm.' Mam pours the coffee. 'Unfortunately, it's not up to her, though, is it?'

'And this is good too.'

'There's more? I thought we were going to have a bit of cake.'

'Wait a sec. This is Manon Steffan Ros again: *I just think the Welsh language is used as a political football and that's not fair. Language is a means of communication and all languages are beautiful. In the same way, I think we tend to politicise the English language. I remember being on a on a panel once with different Welsh language writers, and I had just translated* Blasu *into* The Seasoning, *and one of the other writers, who is a poet, said something along the lines of "Oh, well, you know, Manon obviously feels the need to be acknowledged by the British literary establishment".*'

Mam laughs. 'That's horrible.'

'I heard that the famous Mihangel Morgan refused to be translated into English.'

Mam shrugs. 'That's what they say. He changed his mind eventually, once he found a translator he liked.'

THE COMBINED KINGDOM

> '*Yn yr un byd wedi ei ffalseiddio, eithr heb yn wybod iddo y mae'r Cymro 'Prydeinig' yn byw.*'
> – J. R. Jones, *Prydeindod* (1966)
> (Without knowing it, the 'British' Welsh live in a falsified world.)

Who are these people who have been speaking throughout this essay? Who is J. R. Jones? Who is R. S. Thomas? Or Menna Elfyn? Famous in Wales, but not quite as famous, perhaps, across the border. There is a 'glass wall' between us and England. There should be no border between the so-called 'united' nations, but there are all manner of unseen borders.

Some Welsh-language publications use 'Y Deyrnas Gyfunol' instead of 'Y Deyrnas Unedig' – the 'combined' kingdoms rather than the 'united' ones, dismissing the literal translation from official English nomenclature in favour of a new terminology that more closely reflects the politics of Welsh-speaking Wales. The idea of Wales as England's colony is a common thread in the Welsh-language protests of the 1960s and 1970s, underscored by the investiture of the 'Prince of Wales' in Caernarfon in 1969. Many Welsh people saw the investiture as a colonial act, a confirmation of English power in Wales that reaches back in history to the conquering Edward I. For the philosopher J. R. Jones, 'Britishness' does not exist. It is an ideology designed to conceal the true power relations between the four nations – an argument that became fundamental to the Welsh independence movement. The stance can best be summarised by former Plaid Cymru leader Gwynfor Evans in *Diwedd Prydeindod* (The End of Britishness):

> Beth yw Prydeindod? Y peth cyntaf i'w sylweddoli yw mai gair arall ydyw am Seisnigrwydd; gair gwleidyddol, a gododd o fodolaeth gwladwriaeth Brydeinig, sy'n ymestyn Seisnigrwydd dros fywyd y Cymry, y Sgotiaid, a'r Gwyddelod. Os gofynnir beth yw'r gwahaniaeth rhwng diwylliant Seisnig a diwylliant Prydeinig sylweddolir nad oes ddim gwahaniaeth. Yr un ydynt. Yr iaith Brydeinig yw'r iaith Saesneg. Addysg Brydeinig yw addysg Saesneg. Teledu Prydeinig yw teledu Saesneg. Y wasg Brydeinig yw'r wasg Saesneg. Y Goron

Brydeinig yw'r Goron Seisnig, a brenhines Prydain yw brenhines Lloegr. [...] Yr iaith Saesneg yw'r unig iaith a ganiateir yn honno [...]. Seisnigrwydd ydyw Prydeindod.

[What is Britishness? The first thing to realize is that it is another word for Englishness; it is a political word which arose from the existence of the British state and which extends Englishness over the lives of the Welsh, the Scots and the Irish. If one asks what the difference is between English culture and British culture one realizes that there is no difference. They are the same. The British language is the English language. British education is English education. British television is English television. The British Press is the English Press. The British Crown is the English Crown, and the Queen of Britain is the Queen of England. [...] The English language is the only language that is permitted there [...]. Britishness is Englishness.]

When I was eighteen – this was a few years before my slow awakening – I worked one summer at the National Eisteddfod. The Eisteddfod is a Welsh festival of culture, a fixture on the calendar. One woman I know described it as the place where she could 'feel normal', navigating the two weeks solely in her mother-tongue, and where the presence of Englishness is barely felt. During my summer job, I worked with a boy the same age as me who carried this to the extreme, refusing to speak a word of English to anyone, even to foreign visitors. I was shocked by his refusal to speak English; I did not know that it was possible, had not realised that there were Welsh people (mostly young men) who would go to such lengths to 'resist' English-language encroachment. Later, I learnt of others who refused to acknowledge their own surnames (the surname being an English imposition), insisting on the Welsh 'ap' or their two first names. Others still, like Menna Elfyn in her poem, '*Cân y di-lais i British Telecom*', who spend hours on the phone to utility boards in the hope of reaching a Welsh speaker, or those who went to prison for unpaid tax, as they refused to fill out English tax forms...

What I mean to say by all this history is that Welsh is overwhelmingly politicized. You can, like Manon Steffan Ros, fervently desire to be free of the politics – to just tell your story like you would in any other language – but it's impossible. Welsh almost died out in the 1960s.

It needed Saunders Lewis and his famous radio broadcast, 'Tynged yr Iaith', the Fate of our Language, to spark a protest movement that would eventually save Welsh and succeed in placing it at the heart of Welsh governance. Despite this, there remains a constant struggle to maintain bilingualism in Wales: to translate services, institutions, and media into Welsh. Even supermarket signage and self-service checkouts are politicised so that 'good' shops, like Tesco, make an effort to offer translation whereas 'bad' shops like Morrisons refuse, as it would 'confuse the customers'. Decolonial work in Wales happens with a sign that says 'TOILEDAU / TOILETS' and a robot that says 'DIOLCH AM SIOPA YN TESCO'. As a young girl, my mother taught me to always use the Welsh service whenever I could, 'for the numbers'. Instilled in me from a very young age was the knowledge that I must prove my language is alive every day, by pressing the 'Cymraeg' button on a cash machine, or on a parking meter. If I don't, I put our language at risk.

THE EMPIRE-BUILDERS

> *I am not exonerating Welshmen from having participated in British imperialism. It is merely that when they did so they did so as Britishers, not as Welshmen. The Welsh language was not part of that imperialism.'*
>
> – Ned Thomas, *The Welsh Extremist*

In the wake of Guto Bebb's July 2018 resignation as Conservative Defence Minister, hundreds of posts appeared on Twitter making fun of his name. Inevitably, hundreds more defended his traditional, unremarkable Welsh name, taking monolingual English speakers to task about their prejudices.

A researcher into British Imperial history, perhaps naively, joined in the mockery. Inevitably, there were many people more than ready to point out the hypocrisy of a postcolonial researcher insulting a minority language. Her response? Not an apology, but a sharp, one-line reply, swiftly deleted, to remind them that the Welsh were passionate colonialists, as imperially minded as any Victorian English gentleman.

She was wrong to mock a 'foreign' name, but right to point out that Welsh-speaking Wales is too quick to forget its own involvement in the imperial project. You only need to see the imposing Victorian gothic castle at the centre of Cardiff to have a sense of the wealth created by coal-mining in South Wales – coal that was shipped around the world, fuelling Britain's empire-building. It wasn't simply financial or industrial transactions that connected Wales to the Empire, but ideology too. Welsh missionaries travelled across the British Empire to convert and 'civilise' others. As Charlotte Williams writes in her memoir, *Sugar and Slate*, the African Institute in Colwyn Bay was built to receive and 'train' African missionaries from the Congo, reflecting a Wales that was supportive of imperial aims to dominate the world, not just in terms of its economy, but in social and cultural terms as well.

At a literary festival in Hyderabad, I met an indigenous writer from Australia. During the festival, she was asked multiple times whether she could speak an indigenous language. She replied that she could not. She was also asked why she was white. At first, she was understanding – this was a different country; her role was as a kind of literary ambassador and so she needed to explain the history of Australia's indigenous communities, even if this caused her distress. At the end of the day, however, she was tired of it all. It seemed she needed to explain why these questions were painful; she spoke very quickly, it was late, we were both exhausted, but she talked for a long time as though she had to let out the hurts of the day before she could sleep. 'They took our language away,' she said. 'They even took away my skin.'

She spoke of loss on a scale I could not comprehend, loss upon loss. I could only, in that brief conversation, begin to sense the edges of that grief.

And what has Wales lost? Not as much. We still have our language – or at least, a minority of us do. And, as white Europeans, we were never subject to the systems of racial subjugation inflicted on colonial nations. Historically, Wales participated in a 19th century movement that believed in white supremacy and white rule. Perhaps the academic Simon Brooks is right when he says that Welsh-speakers are partly to blame for the decline of the language, because we so eagerly swallowed

British imperialist ideology; because we were so eager to be British rather than Welsh.

NOTES FROM THE PERIPHERY

> *It is not only the English who were empire-builders [...]. Human beings the world over do not like to be in the minority. How much easier life is in Wales for those who adopt English speech.*
>
> – R. S. Thomas

Years ago, Mam brought one of her then-boyfriends home to meet her parents on the farm near Rhydlewis. He asked to use the landline, and during his conversation, he said very loudly: 'Where am I? I don't know! I'm in the middle of nowhere.' Everyone in the house went silent. My mam's parents were furious, although they said nothing. *The middle of nowhere?* Rhydlewis is the middle of the world.

Mam often says: 'It depends where your centre is.'

Living in Aberystwyth, English friends would complain about how long it took to visit me. I was 'at the end of the trainline' and 'in the middle of nowhere', but of course it's only 'at the end' if you think of London as your centre; it's only 'nowhere' if you think of Wales as an empty landscape, ripe for habitation.

What I am trying to say is that, even if we can't talk about Wales as a colony, we can recognise elements of coloniality at work. Welsh-speaking Wales has a dual role in both resisting the ongoing linguistic 'colonialism' of its neighbour and acknowledging (and actively working to redress) its own complicity in the colonial project. It is possible to be both coloniser and colonised, and the field of Welsh-English translation – whether bureaucratic or literary – is where Wales' coloniality is most apparent. I have been quoting the poet R. S. Thomas throughout this essay; he wrote his own, more eloquent, pieces on the subject that are not at all easy to find unless you happen to be a member of a copyright library. He was an Anglican priest who learnt Welsh in adulthood so that he could better address the congregations of west and North Wales; he became an ardent critic of anglicisation, and saw English as a malevolent force, even though he wrote his poetry (somewhat begrudgingly) in English. He wrote: 'One must face the fact that major languages are aggressive, and whether deliberately or inadvertently they are likely to adulterate minor ones that are adjacent to them, as a large tree will enfeeble smaller ones struggling to maintain themselves in its shadow.'

The problem with R. S. Thomas' view or, indeed, the view of the boy at the Eisteddfod who refused to speak English, is that the battle against anglicisation is already lost. A monolingual Welsh Wales is not possible anymore: we live in a hybrid, multilingual country. Welsh and English exist side by side, each language enriching the other. What we need, then, is a different metaphor. In Robert McFarlane's recent book, *Underland*, he describes how what we thought we knew about trees 'enfeebling' each other to survive is, in fact, mistaken. The opposite is true. Trees give each other sustenance under the ground, sharing information and nutrients. They talk to each other, deep in the soil. Trees even grow together in a process known as inosculation, or en-kissing. Languages inosculate; they weave together. Tending towards plurality and complexity; they support rather than destroy. The success of Sian Northey's simultaneous translations – and her surprise that so many people read both the English *and* Welsh versions – is proof that a truly bilingual Wales is not only a possibility but a reality, one that will continue into the future.

BIBLIOGRAPHY

Aaron, Jane, and Chris Williams, eds, *Postcolonial Wales* (Cardiff: UWP, 2005)

Brennan, Catherine and Gramich, Katie, ed, *Welsh Women's Poetry 1460-2001: An Anthology* (Aberystwyth: Honno, 2003)

Conran, Alys, *Pigeon* (Cardigan: Parthian, 2016)
Pijin, trans. by Sian Northey (Cardigan: Parthian, 2016)

Evans, Gwynfor, *Diwedd Prydeindod* (Tal-y-bont: Y Lolfa, 1981)

Forns, Albert, 'Y brotest ddiderfyn', in *O'r Pedwar Gwynt,* Rhifyn Haf, 2018, trans. by Elin Haf Gruffydd Jones

Jones, J. R., *Prydeindod* (Bangor: Coleg Cymraeg Cenedlaethol, 1966/1991)

Jones, John Sam, *Y daith ydi adra*, trans. by Sian Northey (Cardigan: Parthian Books, 2021)

Thomas, Ned, *The Welsh Extremist* (Tal-y-bont: Y Lolfa, 1971)

Thomas, R. S., *Cymru or Wales?* (Llandysul: Gomer, 1992)
Wales: A Problem of Translation (London: Adam Archive Publications, 1996)

Stephens, Meic, ed., *Poetry 1900-2000: One hundred poets from Wales* (Cardigan: Parthian, 2007)

Roberts, Kate, *Feet in Chains,* trans. by Katie Gramich (Cardigan: Parthian, 2012)

Ros, Manon Steffan, *Llyfr Glas Nebo* (Tal-y-bont: Y Lolfa, 2018)
The Blue Book of Nebo, trans. by Manon Steffan Ros (Cardiff: Firefly Press, 2022)

Williams, Charlotte, *Sugar and Slate* (Aberystwyth: Planet, 2002)

8. SEEKING HAJAR: DECOLONISING TRANSLATION OF CLASSICAL ARABIC TEXTS

Sofia Rehman

In 2015, I attended an event held at the prestigious London School of Economics to honour the life and work of one of the pioneers of Islamic feminism, the African-American scholar, Dr amina wadud. I was joined by a friend who did not take kindly to Dr wadud's work but insisted he was open to learning, and so, somewhat hopefully, I agreed to him accompanying me. No sooner had the event started, than I could feel heat pulsing from his agitated and increasingly furious body, as speaker after speaker engaged language that he was unable to countenance. God referred to as She; women as Imams; it was absolutely disgraceful!

I was already intrigued at the gender contamination that occurred in his mind when God was referred to as She instead of He, and when the title of Imam (literally someone who leads the prayer) was being claimed by Muslim women, but nothing could have prepared me for what followed. A Shi'a speaker on the panel declared, "Five times a day, Muslims of all denominations stand in prayer facing the holy precinct of the Ka'bah in the holy city of Makkah. God orders us to pray facing this holy site, and yet buried beneath it is a woman! Hagar, wife of the Prophet Abraham who founded the city when she was abandoned there by him, with her infant child Ishmael. We not only emulate her in the rituals of our pilgrimage, but we also prostrate towards her final resting place when we turn towards the holy Ka'bah five times a day!" I heard a short sharp burst of air escape the lips of my friend. Did he just spit in disgust? True, I had not heard of this before, despite many years as a student of Islam, but the thought of any human being buried at the foot of the Ka'bah, whether man or woman, was discomfiting for me too, though also quietly revolutionary. I was determined to look it up.

It was an icy silent train ride back with my friend. Once home, I immediately got to the task of researching the claim about Hagar (Hajar as she is known in the Muslim tradition). I eventually arrived at the original Arabic version of Ibn Kathir's (d.1373) famed and highly acclaimed *Stories of the Prophet*. To my surprise, this orthodox Sunni scholar, esteemed as an authority by Muslims around the world, had written in black and white that Hajar was buried under what now falls beneath the precinct of the Ka'bah. I felt both vindicated and inspired at the possibilities this one seemingly innocuous sentence opened up to me, but before I could delve into that I rushed to find the English translation for this friend of mine. Seeking the relevant page in a popular English translation published by Darussalam, and hungry to get to the place where it would declare in plain English that a woman named Hajar, who found herself abandoned with a baby boy in a barren valley centuries before, had not only revealed the ever-flowing well of Zamzam, and founded the holy city of Makkah, but had also been honoured in her death by being buried under the Ka'bah. To my dismay though, when I arrived at the point where that should have been, I was met by a blank page. Who knew a blank page could feel so oppressive. Her burial site was erased from the translation. Wiped from the possibility of access for millions of anglophone Muslims. Hajar had been buried twice. I sat dumbfounded, hurt, and scandalised by the erasure. What or who is threatened by this possibility and the implications of its reality? I can only speculate at the cause for this erasure, because it appears to be an unaddressed issue in scholarly circles, but it aligns with a long practice of patriarchal marginalisation of historically powerful Muslim women whose narratives do not agree with patriarchal notions of what is an exemplary Muslim woman.

In a recent essay of mine, *The Gift of Second Sight*, published in *Cut From the Same Cloth?*, I write about a female companion of the Prophet Muhammed, called Khawla bint Khuwaylid. She became the inspiration of an entire chapter of the Qur'an after she disputed with the Prophet about how to resolve a marital injustice she was experiencing. After much emotional tribulation, the Prophet finally received revelation regarding her situation, an instruction on how it was to be resolved, eternalised in the Qur'an in the chapter entitled, a*l-Mujādilah* (She Who Disputes). In this essay, I refer to the story of a woman who sits so conspicuously in the Qur'an, and still I have received innumerable messages from Muslim women lamenting their Islamic education, both formal and informal, which deprived them of this narrative. It appears that the issue is not only one of translation, because in this case the story of Khawla sits squarely in the Qur'an and cannot be ignored in translation. The issue extends to what is brought to the consciousness of Muslims through their Islamic education; what is contained within curricula of Islamic studies, how the story is relayed, and who gets to engage with the story and build narratives and extract lessons from it. Regarding the latter, it has been an almost exclusively male endeavour, and one confined to scholarly elites.

Similarly, my work on the widely popular wife of the Prophet Muhammed, Aisha bint Abi Bakr, also exposes the ways in which a lack of women's engagement with the tradition has resulted in the marginalisation of narratives at odds with patriarchal ones, which could otherwise have provided women with deeply empowering stories and theological positions espoused by Aisha. Knowledge production, a part of which is constituted by translation, is never a neutral, value-free enterprise. It is political, and one seeking to engage in translation must repeatedly make the conscious effort of interrogating their intentions as they translate.

As a long-time student of Islamic Studies, engaging classical Arabic texts is a process I relish. When I embarked on translating the 14th century Arabic Islamic text, *al-Ijāba li-Īrādi mā Istadrakathu 'Ā'isha 'ala al Ṣahāba* (referred to simply as *al-Ijāba* from hereon), my supervisors told me confidently, "You need to write something about your translation methodology – it needn't be more than a few paragraphs." The few paragraphs soon became an entire chapter, as I realised that there was near to nothing written about translation approaches and methodologies with regards to the Ḥadīth, the Prophetic tradition of Islam. And yet translators make choices all the time; does one remain literal or not? How does one translate a language heavily gendered into one that is less so? What of cultural idioms? Does context of the source text take precedence or that of the audience for the translation? How does one convey a translation that is affective but does not obscure the language, culture, and context in which it was composed? These were but a few of the questions that remained elusive to answer regarding the translation of Islamic Arabic texts into English.

There were three issues I contended with when undertaking the translation of *al-Ijāba*. The first, the historicity and situationality of the text. My source texts are classical texts mainly of the 14th century but are heavily relied upon by Muslims around the globe to inform their religious praxis in the contemporary world they inhabit. I needed to consider how I could remain loyal to the intention of their 14th century authors, who in turn were quoting 7th century Muslims, in a way that was also relevant to the 21st century believer, without undermining the historical context of the 14th century. In particular, *al-Ijāba* is a text both radical in its time, and in the potential it holds now to contest some patriarchal interpretations which have become normative Muslim practices. It is a collection of over 200 statements made by Aisha bint Abu Bakr, wife of the Prophet Muhammed, in which she refuted, corrected, or corroborated the statements of invariably male peers. By the 14th century, the Islamic scholar Imam al-Zarkashi (d.1392) had already noted that many of her positions, which were in contradiction to those of her male peers, were being marginalised even though she was more senior and more knowledgeable than them.

The second issue is that of gender. Translating a text that is in Arabic and therefore gendered, into a non-gendered language like English means being sensitive to gendered readings of the Islamic tradition. This is particularly so with regards to reading expressions that are inherently gendered in a manner that could be misconstrued as lending religious legitimacy to sexist translations of the text, and thereby misogynistic interpretations of Islam itself. The third issue is that of orientalism. Islam has been systematically Othered via a variety of mediums – the media, arts, literature, education systems, academia, political discourse, to name but a few. It has been declared so deeply and utterly antithetical to the "West" that a "clash of civilisations" is a foregone conclusion in the imagination of far too many people, despite the record of history suggesting otherwise. We need only consider the extent to which the

"West" has benefitted from the mutual exchange of ideas with Muslim scientists, philosophers, artists, and even religious scholars. My challenge then becomes one of maintaining the distinction between the different languages, traditions, cultures, and times, without reproducing the Othering of Arabs and/or Muslims.

Perhaps the first challenge posed collectively by these three considerations is the question of how literal and equivalent a translation ought to be. I learned early on that a literal translation did not guarantee a loyal translation. With regards to the ḥadīth tradition in particular, I had to take into consideration their origins as an oral tradition, and all the expression and meaning making to be found in the expressive art of orality that is potentially lost when it is transferred into the written tradition. An example of this is in a tradition found in *al-Ijāba* where Aisha is described as sitting amongst a group of people, whereupon she hears a companion of the Prophet Muhammed, Abu Sai'd al-Khudri state that a woman is not permitted to travel without a male guardian. Aisha turned to the womenfolk around her and said, "Not all of you have a male guardian."[1] This statement has traditionally been read in a superficial and literal manner. It has been taken as evidence of Aisha's agreement with the restrictive statement, and as a warning to the women around her. But when we consider other Prophetic statements that contradict this one, Aisha's own practice of travelling without a male guardian, and an intimate understanding of her personality, we are led to a very different reading of her response. This was most likely a sarcastic incitement of the women around her.[2] A call for them to reject an inconvenient, impractical assertion that women should not travel unless accompanied by a male.

The transference of the oral to the written obscures meaning and context, which then have to be recovered by a panoramic re-reading of the Islamic tradition rooted in a deep understanding of the texts and

---

[1] *Sahīh Ibn Hibbān*

[2] Similarly, it is recorded in *Sahīh Muslim* that in another incident when another male companion of the Prophet Muhammed claims that a woman with braids must untie them before performing the ghusl (a bath which is a full-body ritual purification), Aisha responded with, "Why not tell us to shave our heads?" Certainly not a serious suggestion, but an extension of the foolishness of the original statement to lay bare just how ridiculous and arduous a suggestion it is.

their carriers. As such, whilst I remained committed to retaining the wording of the original Arabic, I also allowed some space to better reflect the context and ambience of the statement being translated. This approach to translation is captured beautifully by John Ciardi, in a note for his translation of Dante's *Inferno*: "When the violin repeats what the piano has just played, it cannot make the same sounds and it can only approximate the same chords. It can, however, make recognisable the same 'music', the same air. But it can do so only when it is as faithful to the self-logic of the violin as it is to the self-logic of the piano."[3]

Keeping in mind the historical context in which ḥadīth were being recorded and documented is vital to being able to translate the Arabic in a way that gives the text meaning in English, and the pedagogical force it is expected to have. As such then, it became important for me to ensure that the context and the characters involved in the Arabic text were well comprehended. Context is of great significance when attempting to understand both the Qur'an or the ḥadīth. Fazlur Rahman bemoaned the atomistic approach to understanding the Qur'an where piecemeal readings are done at the expense of attempting to engage in readings motivated by the overall *Weltanschauung* of the Qur'an—what he refers to as the "underlying unity" and objectives of the Qur'an.[4] This moral compass then should be what guides the reading and interpretations of the sacred texts of Islam. It was the view of Fazlur Rahman that the core messages of the Qur'an are the unity of God and the imperative to strive for the establishment of social justice. If the texts do not aid in the establishment of social justice, then either the sacredness of such statements must be questioned, or the process of interpretation that they have undergone must be scrutinised to identify the shortcomings and mistakes that have led an incongruous reading. Inspired by Rahman, it has become important for me too that my translation be guided by the dual objectives of the unity of God and the establishment of social justice. The implication of this is that a literal translation must sometimes be eschewed in order to convey the desired meaning and impact.

---

[3] Alighieri, D. (2003) The Divine Comedy Tr. John Ciardi. p.ix

[4] Rahman, Fazlur. 1982. *Islam and Modernity: Transformation of an Intellectual Tradition*. Chicago: University Press

This demand to remain loyal to the overall message and objectives of the Qur'an when translating the words of Aisha is made easy when I think about her own ethos. For her, a litmus test for deciding whether a statement could authentically be attributed to her husband or not was if it aligned with the Qur'an. One such example is when Abu Hurayra, a companion of the Prophet Muhammed, claimed that the latter said, "The child [born] of adultery is the worst of the three."[5] When Aisha heard this she said, "…there is no such statement of the Messenger. Actually, a man from among the hypocrites was troubling the Messenger of God, so he said, 'Who will relieve me of [this man]?' It was [then] said, 'Messenger of Allah, among his other [blameworthy traits] is that he is a child of adultery', to which the Messenger of Allah replied, 'He is the worst of the three' and Allah Most High states, 'No bearer of burdens shall be made to bear another's burden.'"[6] Aisha therefore challenged Abu Hurayra's claim, firstly by providing details about the actual conversation of the Prophet, and secondly by the Qur'anic principle that no individual is ever accountable for the sin of another; that no child bears the sins of its parents.[7]

Is this all not also a call to courage for the translator for, in the words of Walter Mignolo, "epistemic disobedience"?[8] For to acknowledge the positionality of the translator is also to eschew the normative colonial subject position of the all-knowing, objective, and impartial translator. For so long, the language of the dominant has been used to clip, reduce, and obscure the Other to fit the constrains of a language and paradigm that never imagined the possibilities in which the Muslim Other flourished. As Silvana Rabinovich wrote, "[Christopher] Columbus crossed the ocean to find the words…that his own language had, with ears closed to the unexpected, he could not understand those who

---

[5] i.e. Out of the child and its parents, the child is the most corrupt moral position before God.

[6] Al-Hakim, *Mustadrak*

[7] This was a particularly important point to make given that at the time of revelation it was common practice for a child to suffer the punishment for the crimes of his father, should his father wish to put him forward in his place. Islam abolished this practice. Abu Huraya's statement flies too close to a pre-Islamic attitude.

[8] Mignolo, W. 1010. Epistemic Disobedience, Independent Thought and Decolonial Freedom. *Theory, Culture and Society*.

welcomed him and there was no interpreter capable of guaranteeing understanding of the other…"[9] For me, decolonial translation of Islamic texts has to be guided by the Qur'anic moral, as well as an ownership of my role as translator that not only acknowledges my positionality as a Muslim woman – a product both of Islam and my British upbringing – but that also sees this standpoint as one that has something enriching to offer the translation process. To do anything else would be to fall short of the radical impulse of the original text.

But to commit to a decolonial approach also requires the rejection of patriarchal impositions on sacred texts. Sacred texts must not only transcend such systems of oppression but must also be catalysts for their dismantling. Barbara Goddard writes, "The feminist translator, affirming her critical difference, her delight in interminable re-reading and re-writing, flaunts the signs of her manipulation of the text. Womanhandling the text in translation means replacing the modest, self-effacing translator. The translator becomes an active participant in the creation of meaning."[10] As such then, the feminist translator allows for the lived experience of women and non-binary folk to inform the translation process and the language used, in order to dismantle patriarchy as the normative mode of life and living. The feminist translator rejects the erasure of themselves from the process of translation, abandoning any appeals to false idols like "objective translation" and "universal appeal." The very notion of universality acts as a wrecking ball of hegemony against the lived experiences, thoughts, ideas, cultures, and concerns of those excluded from the colonially constructed "universal being," which is in fact male, heteronormative, white, and middle class. As such, each translator would do well to accept that their translation is only ever one iteration of a text, and that translation is an ongoing process – "interminable," as Goddard said – where each person brings a different perspective and possibility to and for the text; none less enriching than another.

[9] Rabinovici, S. 2018. Resistance and the Sacred: An Approach to the Various Meanings of the "Right to the Sacred" in Mexico Today. *Open Theology*. 4(1), pp. 228-235.

[10] von Flotow, L. 1991. Feminist Translation: Contexts, Practices and Theories. *Traduction, Terminologie, Rédaction*. 4(2), pp. 69–84.

But before one can even begin to translate a text, a text must be selected. In order to dismantle the patriarchal canon, texts which centre the voice of women need to be translated. *Al-Ijāba* is a text that was almost lost. Whilst many of al-Zarkashi's texts were preserved, *al-Ijāba* was not as carefully treated despite his own pride in the work and his effort to ensure its longevity by teaching it to his students and his own children and having them memorise it.[11] In fact, *al-Ijāba* was recognised for its contribution to scholarship on Prophetic statements in its time and was heavily relied upon by other scholars such as Jalāl al-Dīn al-Suyūṭī (d.1505). It appears a rupture occurs and this particular text of al-Zarkashi's is given increasingly less attention until two separate manuscripts are discovered in the 20th century; one in 1939 by Jalāl al-Dīn al-Afghānī in Damascus, Syria and one in 1999 by M.B Arül in Istanbul, Turkey. Perhaps unsurprisingly, little attention was given beyond the conversion of the manuscripts into print editions despite both al-Afghānī and Arül expressing their excitement at their discoveries. As Audre Lorde put it so eloquently, "The master's tools will never dismantle the master's house."[12] Having the text brought back into availability was not enough for it to be engaged seriously because it poses too many challenges to patriarchally constructed interpretations of Islam. Even the selection of which texts get translated and critically engaged with is a vital element of decolonising translation. Works that challenge the colonial matrix of patriarchy and white supremacy are essential not only for the epistemic questions they ask of their reader but also what they demand from the translator.

For this reason, it is important that the translator not erase themselves from the process but allow the exchange of demands and influence between them and the text to be acknowledged. José Ortega y Gasset cautions against translators excluding themselves from the circle of those permitted to adopt a creative approach to language. He incites the translator out of shyness and into bold rebellion inspired by the source text. He calls for continual creativity with grammar and linguistic norms,

---

[11] Al-Zarkashi is reported to have asked his adult children to recite his books to him when he was on his deathbed, starting from *al-Ijāba*.

[12] Lorde, A. 2018. *The Master's Tools Will Never Dismantle The Master's House*, Penguin Modern Classic, 23

arguing that "To write well is to employ a certain radical courage." It is to not confine or domesticate an original text to the constraints of the language and cultural context into which it is being translated. He states, "The implication here is that the translator, in their effort to remain distant, objective and puritanically committed to equivalent and literal translations, interested only in the linguistic exercise and not the broader considerations of the text and its context, will be led by a 'cowardice' away from the rebellious and subversive nature of the source text relocating it instead into the 'prison of normal expression'."[13]

This warning by Ortega becomes particularly important when put into conversation with Ngugi wa Thiong'o's assertion that language is the purveyor of both communication and culture. For the decolonial translator, the ownership of positionality as one rooted in the cultures of both the source and target languages, as well as taking up the courage of engaging epistemic disobedience by permitting the creativity of the translator to be embraced, becomes essential. For far too long, playing by the rules of orientalist standards of translation has kept the texts of Islam locked in a language that seeks to provincialise it, with nothing valuable to offer to the 21st century, or indeed any time, to keep it locked in an oppositional dialectic with the "West." It is also to strip it of its own particular spiritual and ethical moral compass, its own worldview that seeks to achieve the establishment of justice and mercy on earth. And perhaps most violently, it is to confine Islam to the parameters of Eurocentric Christianity, moulding its language to fit a Christonormative lexicon, not so much to make it more like Christianity, but to prove how much it stands in opposition to it; to imply that it falls short intellectually and spiritually, and is therefore Christianity's inferior.

Coming back to my text, there are words in the original Arabic which I simply refuse to translate because they refuse translation. As other decolonial translators have asked, if a reader of the translation is not challenged at times by the translation, to think about the culture, context, historicity, and spiritual rootedness in Islam, coming face to

[13] Batchelor, K. 2017. Decolonizing Translation: Francophone African Novels in English Translation. *Transfer*. 5(2), pp.68–74.

face with the gaps in their own knowledge, then has the original text not been stripped of some of its most defining, informative and radical elements? In the words of Paul F. Bandia, "The practice of fluent translation effaces those culture-specific features which give the original its power and identity, and makes the English text a sanitised or watered-down version of the original."[14] One example of a word I find often problematically translated for the ways in which it is reduced by English translations, is تقوى *taqwa*, often translated as "fear of God," though it encompasses much more than simply fear; it includes mindfulness, consciousness, and an intimate awareness of being held within the gaze of God. It is to be mindful of God in such a way as to feel under God's watchful eye. Another example is the word محرم *Muhrim*, usually translated as pilgrim, but again the full scope of its meaning is lost in translation, for it is not only to be on a sacred journey, but to fulfil certain rites, to don certain clothing, to enter both physically and spiritually into a particular state, and to make the intention to enter into such a state at particular geographical points on the journey. Instead of offering a reductive or diluted translation, I explain the word in full as a footnote and then continue to use the original Arabic, allowing the reader to acclimatise to the Arabic. An example of this is the following statement of a peer of Aisha's who, discussing the laws regarding pilgrimage, said, "I heard Ibn 'Umar saying, 'That I should be daubed with a trickle of water is preferable to me than to be a *muḥrim* doused in perfume.' Then I entered upon Aisha and informed her of what Ibn 'Umar had said. She responded, 'I perfumed the Messenger of God, and he would visit his wives, and he would then enter into *iḥrām*.'" The words *muḥrim* and *iḥrām* are explained in detailed footnotes. The former could be translated as "pilgrim" while the latter is often translated as "sacred state." Neither fully encapsulates the connotations of the Arabic terms.

Anna Livia writes on the role of the translator, "In their dual role as linguistic interpreters and cultural guides, translators must decide what to naturalise, what to explain and what to exoticise."[15] When Muslims

[15] Livia, A. 2003. "One Man in Two is a Woman": Linguistic Approaches to Gender in Literary Texts. In J. Holmes & M. Meyerhoff (Ed.) *The Handbook of Language and Gender*. Oxford: Blackwell Publishing, pp.142-158.

approach sacred texts it is with the objective of enriching their faith and informing their praxis. When non-Muslims approach such texts it is with agnostic intentions which can vary from genuine fair-minded curiosity, to a desire to unearth some "evidence" that confirms their own prejudices. The translator cannot anticipate the full breadth of intentions with which readers will come to a text, and yet acting as a 'cultural guide' is about navigating the tension between keeping the distinctive qualities of the original text whilst not making it incomprehensible in translation. Similarly, though the term "exoticise" has been problematised for how it becomes another tool in orientalist depictions of Muslims and Islam, I understand Livia's use of the term as being less about exoticisation as a means of fetishising and further alienating, but as a neutral linguistic difference that requires effort on the part of the reader to understand the cultural context of that word. It is more about retaining those words in the Arabic language that refuse seamless translation into English. It asks of the reader to detach from their prior assumptions about language and to allow words to take on wider meaning that is informed by a Muslim normativity. It is an invitation to a "third space,"[16] in Homi Bhabha's words, a product of an encounter between different cultural, linguistic, political, and even theological positions. That is to say that the encounter of Western hegemonies and Muslim patriarchy upon classical Islamic texts is met with the agency of the translator who identifies both with the source text and with the intended audience for the translation and can create within the translation a third space. This third space rejects and exposes impositions of patriarchal and Christonormative translations, instead offering a translation that is sensitive to gender and remains loyal to Qur'anic and Prophetic ideals.

As a translator of a text that has the potential of opening new and important horizons for non-Arabic speaking Muslims (who, incidentally, make up the majority of the global Muslim demography), preserving a balance between retaining the unique historical and linguistic qualities of the text whilst also revealing its radical potential, all the while remaining loyal to the text itself, is at the forefront of my

[16] Bhabha, H.K. 2004. *The Location of Culture*. London: Routledge

translation praxis. Therefore, while it was desirable to translate *al-Ijāba* in a manner that allowed for readability in the target language, I have been careful not to homogenise the text into the culture of the English language. It retains its distinct historical and cultural location, one that most Muslims are familiar with. And yet, as the translator of the text, I am acutely aware that this does not mean the translation would be an exactly equivalent one. Instead, it creates its own particular text, reflecting those aspects of the original deemed most congruent with the possible intentions of the author, al-Zarkashī, the intentions and objectives of Aisha, the context and history of the moment, and the objectives of my own research—the recentering of the voice of Aisha at the epicentre of the Islamic tradition. A process that not only delivers those involved to a new intellectual space, but also transforms the subjects involved, including the reader.

Decolonising the translation of classical Islamic texts is one arm of the project of decolonising Islamic studies more broadly, as well as contributing to the discourse on decolonising translation more generally. It must be, as I have demonstrated, one that allows for Muslim agency and subject position to be trusted; to be acknowledged as having the ability to engage with the Islamic tradition and to produce valuable knowledge on its own terms. Importantly, this knowledge must not be contorted around whiteness or Europeanness by which Islam and Muslims are further alienated and Othered. It does not need to be squeezed into the language of Christianity, it can contribute to our existing vocabulary, and it can enrich and inform our definitions of existing words. A decolonial approach also requires a critique of orientalism that isn't reduced to the unveiling of biases and prejudices but that is cognisant of the constitutive interplay between power and knowledge. This means an embrace of translators who have hitherto been kept in the margins, excluded from engaging the texts and influencing the interpretive process, depriving the tradition of contact with a wealth of lived experiences. A decolonial approach to translation offers the opportunity of correcting epistemic injustices on our way to correcting social and theological ones too.

9. PROUST'S OREO

Layla Benitez-James

For the past few years, I've written and rewritten this line in journals and proposals: *literary translation is a tool to make more vivid the relationships between Afro-descendent people in the Americas and around the world*. I keep this sentiment close to my heart and imagine how disparate stories might be traced back and connected at a strong, central point. The quote comes from translator and poet Aaron Coleman, whom I interviewed for the Asymptote Podcast in 2018. He'd spoken on a panel with John Keene which inspired Keene's essay "Translating Poetry, Translating Blackness," and I set about interviewing the panellists to clarify my own questions about identity and translation. Keene's essay notes that were there more translations of Black writers into English, "we would have a clearer sense of the connections and commonalities, as well as the differences across the African Diaspora."[1]

In my first translation workshop at the University of Houston, we compared English translations of Proust's madeleine episode. My professor wanted to emphasize how we can, as translators, go too far in trying to make the translation fit a particular target language and context by suggesting how ridiculous it would be to make Proust's madeleine into a chocolate chip cookie or an *Oreo* to get at a U.S. version of nostalgia. As the only Black person in that workshop, Oreo landed differently for me. No one else batted an eye, but being a Black, mixed-race girl who had grown up in Texas and who was a bit nerdy, my associations with that particular cookie were that I had often heard

---

[1] Keene, John. "Translating Poetry, Translating Blackness." Poetry Foundation Harriet Blog. Originally Published: April 28th, 2016

it directed *at* me, meaning that I was Black on the outside but very white on the inside.

Oreo would often surface as a reaction to behaviour deemed "not Black" or "not Black enough," and I can't help but think that reading Proust or taking a translation workshop would both fall into that category. Once I got to high school, I remember one boy who was overly fond of the term *Oreo* would also sing, *white girl trapped in a Black girl's body* whenever we crossed paths in the hall.

You might think, as I did, that the madeleine's shell shape means it originated in a coastal town. France has so much coast that when I first started looking into the little cake's origins, I was certain I'd find its form inspired by the sea. I thought about making a little pilgrimage to the madeleine's birthplace, until I learned it came from Commercy and Liverdun, two areas of the Lorraine region that couldn't be more interior. The scallop shell is an abundant marker of the pilgrimage to Santiago de Compostela, and all over Spain you can see little shells etched in the stones on the sides of buildings or on flagstones on any one of the many routes. In French, scallops are called *coquilles Saint-Jacques,* named for a Saint who symbolizes one of the most important pilgrimages for Christians. The lines on the shell come from different directions at its edges, but they join at the top, just as many paths come together at Santiago de Compostela.

I first baked madeleines around 2003, and people often ask if I've read Proust. I used to nod, trying to acknowledge the connection without actually lying about having read the French tome. I must admit that I still haven't. I've tried listening to *Remembrance of Things Past* on audiobook and even listened to the opening in the original language several times on the occasions when I was definitely going to learn French, and it embarrasses me that I want people to think I'm fancy. In Proust's original, he talks about *ces gâteaux courts et dodus appelés Petites Madeleines qui semblent avoir été moulés dans la valve rainurée d'une coquille de Saint-Jacques (those short, plump little cakes called 'petites madeleines,' which look as though they had been moulded in the fluted scallop of a pilgrim's shell.* In C. K. Scott Moncrieff's translation).[2]

[2] Proust, Marcel. *Swann's Way: Remembrance of Things Past, Volume One.* Translated From The French By C. K. Scott Moncrieff. Henry Holt and Company, 1922. The Project Gutenberg EBook.

That UH translation workshop inspired a move to Spain in 2014, and while I really liked the poets I was working on, I also began wanting to find Black Spanish writers. I attended several festivals such as Afroconciencia in Madrid, and learned about an organization called Kwanzaa, a Black student union affiliated with Madrid's Complutense University where I had studied for a semester in 2009. In one Kwanzaa meeting, we went around in a circle to introduce ourselves and share experiences of the first time we felt racialized. We were in a huge, brick art space on the southside of Madrid called the Matadero, which had once been a slaughterhouse. A woman talked about being a bit of a nerd and being called a *coconut* by her classmates. In Texas, *coconut* was used more for people from South or Central American countries and made me remember reading comments from Native American and Asian American writers who talked about *apple*, *banana*, and *Twinkie* being used in this way, a literal centring of whiteness. Last year, I read Candice Carty-Williams' wonderful novel *Queenie*, in which the main character's stepfather calls her a *Bounty*: "White on the inside… Brown on the outside."[3] I had never heard that particular candy used like *Oreo* and it has inspired me to learn more about these kinds of phrases in a UK context, never mind all the other Englishes that exist.

In October 2020, I participated in a panel called *Softening the Blow: Translating Racialized Language* as part of the American Literary Translators Association's conference. I talked about translating the word "negra" ("Black" or "Black girl"), used as an insult in the nonfiction book *Ser mujer negra en España* by Spanish writer Desirée Bela-Lobedde. The title can be translated as *To Be a Black Woman in Spain* or *Being a Black Woman in Spain*, and the book traces Bela-Lobedde's experiences growing up in the 80s and 90s, then into her adulthood and having her own children. One chapter, "¡Negra!" (Black!), explores the first time she remembers "negra" being used as an insult against her. In the voice of her childhood, she wonders what could be so bad about being Black that other children would think to use it as an insult. Of course, *Black* can also be used as an insult in English, and in elementary school I definitely heard people say, "stop acting so *Black*" or "oooh, that's so *Black*."

[3] Carty-Williams, Candice. *Queenie*. Scout Press, 2019. page 251 ISBN 978-1-5011-9603-4 (ebook)

I found deep kinship in reading the book, especially in the opening pages when she says, "For the colour of my skin I've been Cuban, Dominican, Brazilian..."[4] as I have countless memories of people trying to guess "what I am," even going so far as to shout out nationalities while I'm walking in the street.

Finding myself in *Ser mujer negra en España* was comforting, making me feel less alone. Rather than being a translator and ferrying works into English for imagined readers, more and more I found myself seeking out projects that I needed to read myself. There is both compassion and humour running through Bela-Lobedde's book which feels tied to optimism and hope for a better future through difficult dialogues. It also made me think fondly of poet and translator Gregory Pardlo's essay in *The Art of Empathy*, "Choosing a Twin," which explores how we might build an affinity within the texts we translate. The idea of finding a kind of twin or long-lost sister seemed particularly fitting for this project.

I had a similar feeling of kinship with Madrid native Lucía Asué Mbomio Rubio's short story collection, *Las que se atrevieron*, and her first novel, *Hija del camino*, which I'm currently working on. In these works, she meditates specifically on her mixed-race identity which closely parallels my own, having a white mother and Black father. Watching a TEDx talk she gave in 2018 (¿Existen las razas? | Lucía-Asué Mbomío Rubio | TEDxManzanares), I was again struck by how fascinating I find food-based racial slurs in particular. While it roots me in a particularly painful time in my own childhood, Proust's madeleine also kept appearing to me as I wondered how best to translate these hyper-specific points of reference. Racial slurs and racialised language are often very localised vocabulary, even more so when we deal with food. I began to think about my use of "target" and "source" languages with Englishes, plural, in mind.

At the beginning of Mbomío Rubio's talk, she walks through the audience, passing out Conguitos candies, which are more or less M&M's with a history of deeply racist imagery that the company is still nowhere near ready to rethink. In an article, "Spain's Conguitos candy

[4] Bela-Lobedde, Desirée. *Ser mujer negra en España*. Plan B Penguin Random House Grupo Editorial, 2018. Page 21. ISBN: 978-84-17001-65-0.

pushed to rebrand 'racist' imagery" (still using scare quotes to talk about racist imagery, *El País* July 2nd, 2020), Mbomio Rubio is quoted: "The problem with the adorable Conguitos figure is that it is only adorable for people who are not black. There was a 'They called me Conguito in school too' Facebook group once and it wasn't exactly funny." In fact, one of the first images that appears in an image search for *Conguitos* is from a 2019 story about a footballer, Bernardo Silva, being fined roughly 58,000 Euros and having to sit out one game after tweeting a racist image comparing his teammate, Benjamin Mendy, with the racist Conguitos cartoon, which is still used on all its packaging and marketing (*El País* November 14th, 2019).

Bela-Lobedde also notes these candies in her discussions of various blackface practices still prevalent in Spain, and we get this jingle, which I've encountered in other Spanish texts, which is mockingly sung *at* Black children:

> *Yo soy aquel negrito del África tropical*
> *que cultivando cantaba la canción del Colacao*
>
> *I'm that little black boy from tropical Africa*
> *who sings while he is working the song of Colacao.*[5]
>
> (pg. 33)

While both Colacao and Conguitos have made small steps towards no longer actively using images of tribal people in their advertising cartoons, after sustained and intense pressure from various activist groups, the effect of their imagery is felt in many works I've encountered. On another panel focusing on the writing of Black playwrights in Spain in February 2021, I interviewed Silvia Albert Sopale and spoke about her short play *No es país para negras*, which I saw live in Madrid in 2016. I was excited to learn there was already an English version published with KRK Ediciones, but was struck by the force with which the food-based racial slurs had been rendered in English:

[5] Bela-Lobedde, Desirée. *Ser mujer negra en España*. Plan B Penguin Random House Grupo Editorial, 2018. Page 33. ISBN: 978-84-17001-65-0. English translation my own.

> "...una chocolatina, una chocolatina... joder, tío, es que yo no he conocido a una conguito en mi vida. ¿Y de qué se hable con los oscuros? ... ¡Qué yo no conozca a ningún negrata en mi vida! Así que me dio por pillar la enciclopedia." (pg. 41)

> "...a nigger girl, a nigger girl! Fuck me, I've never met *a little Congo girl* in my life and what do you talk about with nigger girls? ... I haven't met a nigger girl in my life, so I got the encyclopedia out." (pg. 41)[6]

Paola Prieto López, an Oviedo native and professor at the university, kindly offered her time to discuss these choices with me and explain the motivations behind ramping up the register of the language, while expressing enthusiasm for a translator or specifically a translator of colour taking on the project. This translation was made for Sopale's visit to Oviedo for EACLALS' (European Association for Commonwealth Literature and Language Studies) 2017 conference and was meant to serve as subtitles, not only for UK visitors but also using English as a bridge language for participants from places like Germany and Italy. López noted that she had several doubts about aspects of the translation, and a suggestion to heighten the violent impact of *chocolatina* and *Conguitos* came from a fellow professor who was worried that the force of the scene would not be sufficiently understood through these specific chocolate-based slurs alone. While I would move towards grounding the scene closer to the original, my Proustian question remains: would I try to gloss what these candies are and somehow allow a reader to glimpse the huge blackface lips and tribal spears of the original advertising? Could I explain in a footnote, perhaps even one with an image or link attached? Would I try to imagine these references as different foods? A key difference here is that whiteness is nowhere to be found in these Spanish slurs. Wildness and exoticism are placed on the human body in a comparison meant to emphasize the physical characteristics of skin, but it has nothing to do with contrasting the outside with the inside.

---

[6] Sopale, Silvia Albert. *No es país para negras.* KRK Ediciones, 2019. Page 41. Translation by Paola Prieto López. ISBN: 978-84-8367-648-6

At the Matadero, I talked about being called an *Oreo* and noted the distinction in different racial slurs between Spain and the United States. What I remember most about that meeting is that the next woman shared that she was really tired of Black people from the United States constantly bringing the focus back to ourselves. She was especially frustrated with hearing how happy we were to be in Spain and the way we talked about Europe as a refuge from our racist United States. She talked about the racial profiling that goes on in Spain, laws that require all foreigners to carry ID, which are, of course, not applied evenly, and how Black Americans fall into a special category of privilege. Her eyes held mine as she talked, and my face grew hot. I'd shared this sentiment many times. They might not be killing us on the streets as much, she said, but foreigners here are able to ignore the detention centres and are not targeted for profiling as much once they are heard speaking English. I was at least familiar with the special status of U.S. citizens in Spain after reading and translating a sample of *An African's View of the World from Eden* by Inongo-vi-Makomé. The presence of U.S. military bases in Spain from the 80s on meant that Black U.S. citizens got special treatment, and the sight of that blue passport would often transport someone into another category: "As if by magic, expressions of contempt disappeared from the officer's faces."[7]

After this initial, embarrassing spark, I noticed how much of Spanish discourse was centred on the U.S. as its point of reference. MLK, James Baldwin, Audre Lorde, Angela Davis, all of these important figures were translated into Spanish and held a place of importance within their discourse, and more recently Black Lives Matter has carried over, leading much of the vocabulary and strategy for continued efforts for equality and justice. Angela Davis often speaks at events in Spain (through an interpreter), and there is a sense that while these points of reference are helpful in many ways, Spain's own unique history means that a U.S. framework is not a cure-all for the specific issues Black Spanish people face. When I asked Sopale about this in our interview, she was quick to stress that Black Spanish people needed to constantly bring the focus back to themselves and their own unique situation, even

[7] "An African's View of the World from Eden by Inongo-vi-Makomé" My translation was published in Europe Now Journal on November 8, 2018.

as they honoured the work of outside influences. As a translator, I realised I must be more aware of how much I internalise this U.S. imperialist position.

I assumed I'd be able to use my own experience growing up in Texas to find the right words for my translation. That day in the Matadero was my first realisation that my background was also allowing me to make too many assumptions of shared experience and prompted me to ask, *How can I de-centre the United States or, at the very least, be more conscious of this centring when I'm translating between Spain Spanish and U.S. English?* What I'd like to figure out now is how to strike a balance between using shared experience to find common ground and making sure that I'm not pulling a text into my own preconceived path.

I must remind myself to trust the process of learning and embrace those hot moments when I need correcting. I was too focused on the pleasant promise of connections and commonalities without realizing that differences are often what help us learn most. In the case of Sopale's *No es país para negras,* I'd like to restore those specific chocolate references and allow English readers to adopt their meaning as they did the madeleine. Thinking of multimedia productions and digital editions, I'm excited by the idea of footnotes being more than mere words at the bottom of the page and expanding into YouTube links and a way for the reader to learn with the text. What will happen when these relationships between Afro-descendent people around the world are more vivid? I cannot simply seek to make my limited understanding of what I find here understandable to Black people in the United States, but deeply interrogate what I think I know before I render it into my English. I have come to understand literary translation not just as a tool that can make these relationships more powerful, but as an instrument I must take greater care to learn how to wield properly.

10. WESTERN POETS KIDNAP YOUR POEMS AND CALL THEM TRANSLATIONS: ON THE COLONIAL PHENOMENON OF RENDITION AS TRANSLATION

Mona Kareem

1

In 2020, an English translation of Yi Lei, a prominent poet who came of age in '80s China, was released by Graywolf Press. Tweets and headlines in the American press rejoiced, stressing how this Chinese Emily Dickinson has been brought into English by none other than the Pulitzer prizewinner Tracy K. Smith. They marveled at such feminist collaboration, our best woman poet and their best woman poet, meeting in verse. 'An encounter with Tracy K. Smith eased the late Chinese poet's emergence into the Anglophone world,' declared the *New Yorker*. The verb 'eased' struck me; like an unwanted pregnancy, her poems arrive in English—a 'second life' to use the article's Benjaminian wording. Tracy K. Smith has no knowledge of Chinese, and as such, I doubt that she knows enough about Chinese poetry and where Yi Lei stands among her generation, or the place of her poetics within their literary domain. In the introduction, written without the co-translator, Smith makes no mention of any other Chinese poets, nor does she contextualize Yi Lei's work. She describes her as a revolutionary voice, tells us about her brief friendship with Yi Lei, comparing her to one American master: 'she was huge-hearted and philosophical, on intimate terms with the world in the way of Walt Whitman, one of her literary heroes.'

Although Smith does not hide her anxiety at the nature of this work, she does not frame it as a non-translation, or perhaps an anti-translation: 'I accepted the fact that the music of the original, which I wasn't capable of recognizing in the Chinese, or gleaning from David's intermediary translation, could not be a component of my concerns as a translator.' After all, it is no strange phenomenon for Western poets, from Ezra Pound to Ted Hughes, to hire a linguist or a literary scholar to compose a 'rough translation' to then make an adaptation of the text. I hold no objections against adaptation as a form of translation, nor am I interested in guarding definitions of translation, rather I am interested in examining how such co-opting of literary translation speaks of a larger attitude toward non-Western literatures. Sometimes it is the author of the original text who partners in this process and, where not versed in the target language or its literature, this yields a collaboration distinct for its uneven power relations. In July 2021, Graywolf announced a new translation, or an adaptation, of Dante by Mary Jo Bang, another beloved woman poet of America. It announced in a tweet, 'Congratulations to Jo Bang on her release,' to which I couldn't help but respond, 'Congratulations to Dante!'

This phenomenon of Western poets calling their renditions translations has always baffled me. Everywhere else in the world, poets might commit the sin of translating a text via an intermediary language (a translation of a translation) but never would they hire someone to give them a rough draft of the original to then workshop the hell out of it! One can't help but wonder, if the resources are available for a rough draft, if the enthusiasm is present to 'ease' a text into a new language, then what stops Western poets and publishers from leaving the task of translating someone of the caliber of Yi Lei to a qualified translator? After all, Chinese is not some obscure language of the Norwegian outskirts, it's literally the largest language in the world when we count native speakers! In his review of Smith's adaptation, Andrew Chan writes about the state of confusion he found himself in, wary of the 'false conclusions' that Smith's 'unfaithful renditions' would leave the English-speaker with. Chan, who has read the poetry of both Smith and Yi Lei (in the original), is able to tell how Smith's renditions are decorated by an aesthetic contrary to Yi Lei's work, a musicality specific to Smith, a drastic difference in style and tone. What poets who are not translators fail to understand is that it is exactly 'style, tone, and content' that makes or breaks a translator. Chan too is aware of this phenomenon, offering examples beyond poetry, where the translator takes liberty in not only domesticating a text, but making it a 'loose' adaptation. It is indeed a form of textual violence.

As an Arab poet, I can tell you that stories of what Western translators do to our work make a favorite subject in literary festivals, late-night gatherings, and zoom events. One cannot miss the sense of 'guardianship' Western translators practice over us—how they filter us, make us lyrical, oblique, politically-correct, or appealing. A sense of paternity is at practice, by which the Western translator takes your hand and guides you into the darkness of the abyss, especially if you do not speak their language. Often, you naively believe in them, after all this is not a matter of ill intentions, the two of you work on the belief that it is a 'collaboration,' and as so, whatever it yields, might be worthwhile!

2

When writing this essay, I decided against using the term 'bridge translation,' commonly used to describe this phenomenon of monolingual poets claiming to translate via a 'literal translation.' Instead, I chose 'rendition,' as a suggestion that we divest from this metaphor altogether. In their essay 'She Knows Too Much,' Jen Calleja and Sophie Collins highlight the violent implications of such labels, and how they express and reproduce various hierarchies and divisions of labor within literary production. Similarly, in an interview for *Getuigen* magazine, Egyptian translator Samah Selim states, '"I am no longer interested in translation as a bridge, but as a form of radical knowledge production."' From another angle, one can take the colonizer's choice to describe their renditions or adaptations as 'bridges' to be a confession of complicity. Bridges represent the earliest human attempts to overcome and tame nature, they also represent Western capitalist expansion into indigenous lands across the world. A 'bridge' is inherently invasive, just as Western curiosity is, seeking unconditional access to other cultures and literatures.

I had thought that the phenomenon of Western poets building bridges to where they don't belong had vanished. I would argue that it did disappear for a few years from English, only to return at the hands of poets, not translators! Translation has become 'cool'; in some way its popularity speaks of the failure of a liberal intellectual class wrestling with the rise of Western fascisms. It rejuvenates their monolingual diction and imagery, it fits in the tenure dossier, it rescues the Third-World poet who is always imagined as a singular voice against the savage masses; as if the Cold War never ended or, God forbid, wasn't won by the United States. Translation today, as scholar Dima Ayoub argues, is seen not only as a necessity but also necessarily good. What makes translations a must? Where does this blind faith in translation come from? Doesn't translation act also as unconditional access, as surveillance, as an expanding force of the global capitalist market of literature?

This year, I was invited to review *Let me Tell You What I Saw* by Iraqi poet Adnan al-Sayegh. I had read the poetry of al-Sayegh in my teen years and can still remember his ability to amuse and surprise, through unexpected imagery, as well as playful renditions of Arabic texts, both canonical and modern. Al-Sayegh is a poet of the '80s, and this English translation is specifically excerpted from his epic-like poem *The Song of Uruk* or *The Anthem of Uruk*, first published in 1996. It was a blunt attempt by al-Sayegh to bring back the long-form poem, at a time when his contemporaries were moving fast and steady toward the condensed minimalist poem. He did not shy away from high lyricism, which for many Arabic poets feels undesirable in the intimidating shadow of Mahmoud Darwish. I took note that the co-translator of the text, Jenny Lewis, is a poet and theater practitioner who has a lifelong interest in the *Epic of Gilgamesh*. I thought it would be a perfect pairing, but the translation revealed otherwise.

Instead, I found myself again before a translation by a Western poet who had hired a native speaker to produce a 'rough draft' before workshopping the translation with the author for 'hundreds of hours,' as Lewis states in her afterword. The book makes the mistake of placing the original and the translation next to each other, as if to make stark the many basic wrongs committed in the translation. This layout highlights the very absurdity of adaptation as translation—the Arabic pages placed on the left, when the language is written right-to-left. As an object, it is confusing, a mass of papers shoved into a binder. I was anxious at the idea of such translation being the product of 'hundreds of hours'; I could only imagine what other useful work such labor might have produced. Lewis, a lecturer at Oxford, refers to her co-translator Ruba Abughaida—a Lebanese-Palestinian fiction writer—as her student whom she hired for the task. The English poet is unaware of the power-relations she draws for us here, a hierarchy between her and Abughaida. Her name appears on the cover without Abughaida's. The 'collaboration' brings me to raise an additional question: why is a native speaker assumed to be a translator?

In her notes on the 'translation,' which is not her first of al-Sayegh's work, Lewis compares the Iraqi poet to Andalusian poets, to Ibn Hazm; she speaks of her approach to bring al-Sayegh closer to Dylan Thomas! In reality, al-Sayegh might have come closer to T. S. Eliot, via the influence of Iraqi poet al-Sayyab, and his translations of Eliot. Al-Sayegh was hoping to write a contemporary adaptation of *Gilgamesh*, one to which the modern Iraqi reader can relate, to its subjects of war and repression, exile and love. In this attempt, he was in conversation with the voices of many Arabic poets, canonical and modern, sometimes hijacking their lines and completing them with his. This brings me back to what Chan said of Smith's translation: where are style, tone, and content? But I must add: where is intertextuality? Why is a text reduced to the singular, instead of becoming a tunnel, a little river to lead into the ocean that is Arabic poetry? Lewis has missed even the opportunity to put her playwright skills into amplifying the epic-like features of Adnan's poem, especially how it switches between the singular and collective voice, the protagonist and the chorus.

When reading the translation face-to-face with the original, I can say it's a literal translation that fails at the very task of being literal. The poetic compositions that, for Adnan's generation, often take the form of a 'construct case' are reduced to basic digestible images. The text opens with, 'On the balcony of vigilance I sit,' which Lewis makes into 'I sit on the balcony, alert.' Two lines later, the poem reads 'my lips are cracked like the trunk of a palm tree overlooking the river,' which Lewis turns into 'like the roots of the palm tree.' The latter image makes no sense, it fails to capture his contrast of the texture of cracked lips to the harsh trunk of a palm tree.

Another feature of Adnan's poetry is punctuation. In Arabic, italics and formatting are not a feature of literary writing, while punctuation, though present, is not a regulated business like it is in English. Adnan was known for his exploitation of punctuation as a way of switching between one voice and another within a single poem, or in other places, for spacing and repetition, to give a theatrical and lyrical affect to his verse. In the English, Lewis merely copies and pastes these features, missing the fact that punctuation too must be translated. What comes as an intervention in the Arabic poem must also be reinvented as such in the English. If brackets and dots do not resonate similarly in English poetry, they should be substituted with italics and formatting, to give one solution. This can be seen as well in the way he uses interpolated clauses (digressions), which appear aimlessly in English as is, or sometimes arbitrarily interrupting the very logic and flow of a verse.

The adaptation omits basic sentence parts, such as pronouns or adverbs and conjunctions, without which the narrative is lost. Lewis translates: 'In my name and yours / attached / to the skyline / is the arch of lazord,' when it should have been 'as the arch of lazord' referring back to the names. She adds: 'Tiresias laughs: love cannot be buried / yet Juno buries it out in the wasteland / leaving it half-covered, its penis exposed'; the use of 'it' makes it sound as if love, in the abstract, is what Juno buries, when in fact she buries Tiresias himself, or as the myth goes, she blinds him. Similarly, the translation struggles to catch the Arabic's easy switching between a human and their parts, from the total to the particular, sometimes misleading the reader into thinking there are two women being addressed in the verse, not the same one: 'Should we waste our days at the newspaper? / I am closed like a book / I stroke your eyes as you drowse. And she makes me slide between her breasts / as her breast bursts out of her dress / free as a runaway ghazal,' instead of 'As they [the eyes] let me slide through your cleavage / your breast bursts out of the dress / running free like a runaway gazelle,' the animal, not ghazal, the poetic form.

3

Now I must ask you, dear reader, do you think this level of work would slide with translations from French or Spanish? Would it be funded, published, praised, listed? Can an Arab poet in England use his Russian student to produce a rough translation of say, Maria Stepanova, then go sit with the Russian poet to produce a translation? The history of literature teaches us that in the East or the West, the pre-modern writer was necessarily multilingual; it was a given, not a form of genius only afforded to aristocratic writers of the likes of Nabokov. History also teaches us how the European nation-state brought upon us the illness that is monolingualism, and ever since, the gift of polyglotism has become exclusive to specialists who, unlike bilingual immigrants and refugees, are afforded the chance to study the other and translate him. I grew up reading Russian masterpieces translated into Arabic from the French, as I also read Mishima and Kawabata in Arabic translations from the English. I love these translations and still return to them; they are their own beautiful creations. Nevertheless, today in the pre-capitalist Arabic publishing industry, readers demand more, demand better, they devour re-translations and battle each other in evaluating one against the other.

Thinking of translation as a service for the Third World poet, as an 'easing' into the colonial language, as a championing, a celebration, or an unearthing, should simply not be tolerated. Translation into English today reflects a general mentality shared by Western writers themselves—that they know it all, have seen it all, and the only thing left for them to do is to take us under their wings. They do not see us as their counterparts, as their comrades; their savior-complex is clothed with polished words and self-described radical poetics. Their canon, which does not make even a third of, say, the Arabic or Chinese canon, somehow has more to draw from and fit into when they translate us. The establishment, the industry, the poet, the translator, come together in allowing a level of mediocrity afforded only to certain figures. The Third World poet too, fascinated with the West, with the wondrous machinery of Western publishing, sometimes surrenders to whatever the mud might make of their work. How can one any longer believe in 'collaboration' or in 'translation' without first addressing the power structures that cast their shadows over any two people working together? Today, translation has become so vicious that certain Arabic writers would prefer their work be published in English first, before the original Arabic. *The Guardian* would then declare him a best Arabic writer before even being read in his own language, as if Guardian critics know anything about Arabic literature. I am not arguing that a poetry translation might win you the Nobel or welcome you into the canon, but I am saying the textual violence disturbs my peace and pleasure alike.

BIBLIOGRAPHY

Al-Sayegh, Adnan. Let Me Tell You What I Saw. Translated by Jenny Lewis and Ruba Abughaida. UK: Serene, 2020.

Chan, Andrew. "My Name Will Grow Wide Like a Tree: The work of Chinese poet Yi Lei arrives in a problematic translation." 4Columns. October 30, 2020.

Jen Calleja and Sophie Collins. "She knows too much: 'Bridge Translations,' 'Literal Translations,' and Long-Term Harm." Asymptote Journal.

Lei, Yi. My Name Will Grow Wide Like a Tree: Selected Poems. Translated by Tracy K Smith and Changtai Bi. New York: Graywolf, 2021.

"Translating the Egyptian Revolution, on Translation, Testimony, Activism: An Interview with Samah Selim." Getuigen: Testimony Between History and Memory, October 2016.

Zhang, Han. "The Second Life of Yi Lei." New Yorker: May 5, 2021. https://www.newyorker.com/books/under-review/the-second-life-of-yi-leis-poetry

11. FREED FROM THE MONOLINGUAL SHACKLES: A MONGREL CRÔNICA FOR THE MUTT TRANSLATOR

Lúcia Collischonn

***crônica* – (pt) noun.** Portuguese-language short writings about daily topics, published in newspaper or magazine columns. Usually written in an informal, observational and sometimes humorous tone, an intimate conversation between writer and reader. Between journalism and literature, opinion piece and micro story. A mongrel textual genre.

As the mutt mixed-breed Latina translator that I am, I need to write a crônica here. This is my academic-essay-manifesto-crônica, a collage, a truly cur text.

WORLD LITERATURE IS NO *LONELY PLANET*

Who is afraid of the L2 translator? Many are. More specifically, many of the gatekeepers who have managed to take and keep their hold of the language: at the centre of the empire, at the centre of knowledge production, even now in the 21st century. The time of literary tourists or literary anthropologists who travel to far- off places, learn far-off languages and bring these into the centre of the canon may seem to be over, but are these times really gone? As Tiffany Tsao says in an interview for *Liminal Mag*, 'Ultimately, literature isn't a tourist guidebook'.[1] You won't open a travel guide and find the soul of a country within the list of authors deemed representative enough but also harmless, tame. A lot of what passes for World Literature nowadays is

[1] https://www.liminalmag.com/interviews/tiffany-tsao

still, however, tied to national boundaries, and not only those of nation but those of a national language.

Read all about it! Anglo-monolingual Man becomes the leading expert in Igbo literature without speaking a word of Igbo.

Hear ye, hear ye, another white anglo saxon person translated this very exotic piece so that all of us literary tourists can swim in this sea of "culture".

This other Oxbridge-educated translator spent six months in Brazil and now translates all of our diverse voices for your pleasure.

Our postcolonial stories and cultures are still an ethnographic subject at best, a stereotype for literary tourists at worst. Why must we accept that our literatures are written or translated by others, with little of our own voice to tell our stories to the world? I say 'to the world' because English is, like it or not, the lingua franca of the literary world: Translating into English confers power. So why can't we write in a different tongue? And more importantly, why then can't we translate outwardly as well? To gain access to hegemony we might need to reconfigure our practices, but can't we also shake their foundations and maybe start change from within? Must we always be outside?

In a paper about ethical communication in *Lonely Planet* guidebooks, Debbie Lisle (2008) offered an analysis of the problematic nature of these guides when talking about the specific case of Burma. The author foregrounds the colonial logic embedded in the humanist approach to these guidebooks and, most importantly, in the Good Tourist type that is part of the guidebooks' target audience. In her analysis, the books convey the idea that it is beneficial for tourists to visit places with ongoing conflict and power struggles because it helps the economy, when in reality this kind of thinking works as an uncritical, colonialist attitude to the countries visited. A similar mindset is at work in the much-criticised 'human safaris' in the favelas of Rio.

If literature is no tourist guidebook, why cling to the narrative of the white-saviour literary scholar who does all of us a favour and reads us, translates us, interprets us? They speak for us. In a language that they either forced upon us, to make us suboptimal, variants of the norm, or they charged us very high fees for Cambridge to tell us we can speak it. But don't let me, the angry mongrel street dog, scare you. I am all bark and no bite. I've been purified, assimilated, taught to be polite and agreeable and to not tell them the truth. My snout is properly muzzled.

INCOMPETENT *UNDER*LINGUAL SUBOPTIMAL BEING

While at a conference in Prague about translation into a non-mother tongue, one participant kept repeating, during different discussions about the practice and profession of translation: 'Yes, translating into a second language can be done, but it is always suboptimal.'

Suboptimal, suboptimal, suboptimal.

When translating into English, it seems these gatekeeping practices that put us in the realm of suboptimality are even more enhanced. Does this perhaps reflect the dire state of foreign language teaching and learning in many English-speaking countries? If native English speakers do not feel comfortable or able to translate in other directions, that is fine for them, but why must this rule apply to those who feel they can indeed work in different directions? In Brazil, where I come from, and in fact in many of the countries represented at that international conference, a translator is a translator is a translator is a translator. Some might need help in certain areas, but trained translators are able to translate in both (or more) directions. Such an essentialist idea of a translator's linguistic abilities also ignores the fact that language is not fixed, and a person's linguistic repertoire, especially in regard to a second language, is bound to change through the course of their life.

In academia, Translation Studies initially mostly ignored the issue of directionality; when the direction of translation comes to the fore, it is often shunned. Directionality itself has only begun to be studied at the end of the 20th century, and according to Alison Beeby Lonsdale, it was only 'when some scholars in countries where A→B translation is common practice questioned the assumption (particularly widespread in English-speaking countries) that B→A translation was the only viable professional option.' Before this, directionality was mentioned either explicitly or implicitly, but with a preference towards L2-L1 (or B→A) translation. In older proto theories of translation, authors such as Goethe, Schlegel, Rossetti, Pope, Erasmus, Voltaire would implicitly refer to the L1 norm in their writings about translation, by using words such as 'own language', 'native', 'domestic', etc. implying the translator would bring works from other languages into his own domestic context.

However, Leonardo Bruni, in *De Interpretatione Recta,* posits that a translator must serve both masters, so there is no preferred directionality implied in his writings. This is also true of other early Translation Theory texts. As Translation theories and studies progressed and the discipline started to evolve, the translator increasingly became an ideal subject, the 'perfect bilingual', still a monolingual-based ideal of a person's linguistic skills which holds no water in linguistic (or, more specifically, literary) reality. Whenever explicitly opposing or shunning L2 translation, authors bring to the ring concepts such as 'naturalness' and 'authenticity'. Translation Studies scholars such as Newmark (1988), Samuelsson-brown (1995), Chesterman (2004), Duff (1989) have all considered L2 translation to be on the 'unnatural' side of the spectrum or even blamed the interference of the translator's native language for the negative aspects of the target text.

But these, as well as the discipline (which has existed in its own right only since the second half of the 20th century), are recent developments. You can see in the years of publication next to these authors' names, that the prejudice against L2 translation has come hand in hand with the development of translation studies as a discipline. But what do I mean by 'recent', in this case? The creation of nation states in the 19th century together with the many independence movements of former colonies in the 19th and 20th century led to a monolingual, nationalist-based idea of languages. One nation under one God who speaks one language. Translation Studies being a child of European-based Linguistics and Language Studies, it is no wonder the subject itself has been based around communication between the major European national languages, glossing over or blatantly ignoring or othering realities such as dialectal variety, minority language communities, migration movements and languages of small diffusion, not to mention multilingualism in the continent and natural multilingualism in communities around the world, in Asia, Africa, the Americas and beyond. A similar central problem is faced by disciplines such as World Literature and Comparative Literatures, which both started as European cosmopolitan humanist endeavours and are now facing constant challenges both in name and scope whenever the category of 'world' is brought into question.

And further, Translation Studies as a discipline is extremely anglophone-centred, hence the forced monolingualism and supremacy/superiority of the native English-speaking world makes for rules and norms about what translation should be and who gets to translate what, which excludes those who do not fit easily and seamlessly in(to) the arbitrary lingualist categorisation and hierarchisation of an individual's L1 and L2. After all, can we really put our languages in order? These norms exclude, more specifically, those who cannot claim to be native speakers of English. Why let the English-speaking Translation Studies world lead us directly into the L1 norm?

Outside of academia, we often see, in calls for translators in workshops, courses, magazines and journal submissions, and even sometimes in contracts with publishing houses, not only the assumption but the outright rule that L2-L1 is preferred, or that the translator in question needs to be a native speaker of the target language. Funnily enough, the work itself comes second. One question, that comes to my mind whenever I am faced with such constraints is: if I didn't feel comfortable translating into English, would I pay three hundred pounds for a translation workshop with other English speakers just to feel out of place? Not that feeling out of place is a problem, but if a person is willingly taking part in something and feels fluent enough to submit, participate, or be evaluated by others in a learning or professional environment, surely the mother tongue norm does not need to come to the fore? Why not see the text the person produces, first of all? It seems that such gatekeeping practices are unconscious (or maybe very conscious) attempts at safeguarding the centre from the peripheries. English has many more L2 and L3 speakers than native speakers. Who holds the power? If native speakers are not protected, they risk being overtaken by all those 'savages', like us, ruining the purity of the English language and using it to our advantage.

In my life I have known countless translators whose language skills differ, depending on the language context. Vladimir Nabokov and Joseph Conrad famously had very thick accents when speaking English, yet their English *oeuvre* is part of today's literary canon. Every individual's linguistic background and experience and, most of all, expression, is different.

I am a published translator in my home country, Brazil, but in the Anglophone world I remain an emergent translator, a second-class citizen, an anonymous citizen. Suboptimal. All because my name has an accent.

In the UK, this English-speaking island where I find myself, my accent is a constant reminder that I am from elsewhere, I am not native, nor will I ever be. Suboptimal.

I am incompetent, lesser than, not monolingual, a bit multilingual, but rather underlingual, suboptimal, my *língua* is not enough.

Never mind my lingua materna, when will my English be enough?

Many ask themselves this. Many who have been colonised by the English, many of whom live their lives in varieties of English that do not confer proficiency. What language are they speaking then? The monolingual norm has served colonialism and imperialism, while going directly against innovation and multilingualism in translation. In fact, as David Gramling states in his book *The Invention of Monolingualism* (2018), 'indigenous people in the colonies were gradually de-competenced through a multilingual process of monolingualisation'. This means that our indigenous languages were taken away, erased, but our varieties of the coloniser's language are 'not good enough'. We were made to speak a European language and became the forever suboptimal speakers of someone else's tongue. So, what choice do we have?

In a normative monolingual society, to speak more than one language is also a form of rebellion. In a Western anglophone society that for centuries has pushed against natural multilingualism in colonies in favour of a European national language that was in its infancy, thus removing the linguistic capabilities and identities of countless peoples, to take the coloniser's language and perform in it is in itself a rebellion, a decolonising performance. With the hegemony of the United States, its cultural imperialism, and the UK's ongoing post-colonial supremacy as well as the two countries' close geopolitical ties, to break down the constant pull of monolingualisation in anglophone spheres is even more of a rebellious performative act. Obvious examples, albeit going in different directions, include Kenyan writer Ngũgĩ wa Thiong'o who consciously renounced English and switched to Gĩkũyũ as his literary language, and Nigerian author Chinua Achebe who defended his use of the coloniser's language in *The African Writer and the English Language.*

Mongrel, Mutt, Suboptimal, Multilingual, Monolingual, Postcolonial, World Literature. Inundated by terminology, lost in the rainforest of words to define our practice, I propose yet another one: Exophony.

EXOPHONY

Is literary translation not an artistic, linguistic performance? If so, why are people whose linguistic lives are a constant performance not able to perform different directionalities, different linguistic avenues, non-essentialist, non-naturalist, non-native? Exophony, *ekusophonii,* to step outside of your mother tongue, is an active, performative, creative stance we can take as L2, non-native, lesser-than translators.[2] This is why I call such a translator an exophonic translator. How can we step out of the cradle of our mother-father-aunt-uncle tongue(s) and into others? How can we perform this outwardness, and occupy a place which we were told is not ours, that can never be ours?

In my doctoral research, I have found both academic solace to defend my ideas about L2 translation and my own practice, and a lot of gatekeeping from translation theorists and editors/translators alike. There seems to be little dialogue between academia and the literary translation market, except to agree that 'one should translate into one's native language/mother tongue'. As Europe colonised and imposed national monolingualism on naturally multilingual communities, one could say that the monolingual mindset is inherently European, imported to the rest of the world. But Europe in itself, as a continent and as an economic bloc, is multilingual by nature. Are European languages just islands, separate but equal, exchanging ideals through renaissance

[2] My interpretation of exophony is directly related from the term as discussed by Yōko Tawada in her critical work, specifically the travelogue-manifesto *ekusophonii bogo no soto e deru tabi* (2003), and Chantal Wright's analysis of the term when applied to non-native writers (2008) and to exophony in translation (2010).

men, the *literati* and the *educati*? The anglophone historical amnesia that the monolingual mindset reflects points to its recent status and to a general ignorance or avoidance of Europe's multilingual nature. The UK, especially recently, seems to be on par with Europe when it comes to avoiding or denying multilingualism, but as it goes through the process of exiting the European Union, and thus renouncing its place in the continent's economic bloc, the UK also distances itself from Europe's many national languages in favour of anglophone supremacy by moving closer to the US instead. This denial also comes in the form of lack of funding and invisibilisation techniques within its own borders when it comes to language policies (such as the case of Irish, Welsh, Scots, Gaelic and Angloromani, among other indigenous languages in the UK).

The absolute authority of the native speaker and complete ignorance about people's actual linguistic backgrounds and practices that the 'L1/nativeness translation norm' reflects is also representative of this mindset. In fact, exophonic translators are in general more aware of these linguistic power structures, precisely because they have possibly grown up multilingually, or cannot easily or straightforwardly answer the question 'What is your L1?' Many names come to mind, though most of them are only just beginning to emerge from under the invisibility cloak of the monolingual paradigm, such as Anton Hur, Julia Sanches, and many more. Exophonic translators are slowly showing how their practice cannot be contained by the shackles of linguistic nomenclature, allegiance or an essentialist view of language and literature.

Thrown in the galleys of suboptimality, *underlinguality*, we are not allowed to advance unless we perform purity, mono, standard. Either that, or we must take a radical stance and wear our exophonic-outsider-suboptimal-mongrel badges with pride.

VIRA-LATA: A MONGREL PARADIGM

In 2020, a meme made the rounds in Brazil: when consultations began as to which iconic Brazilian animal should feature on the 200 *reais* bill, many on the internet suggested our very own breed of mongrel dog. *Vira-lata caramelo*. A caramel-coloured mixed-breed dog named after its main activity: turning over trash cans in search of food. Our very own mongrel dog is the result of centuries of unintentional mixes of the most varied breeds of dogs that came to the South American continent. Unlike some well-known hybrids, our vira-latas do not have a clear lineage and are not an obvious mix of two easily identifiable breeds. The vira-lata is the most easily found dog in any area of Brazil, and mongrel dogs make up the majority of household pets in the country. They are truly a symbol of our mongrel, mixed beings. Brazilians are old mutts, so widely and uncontrollably mixed that we can't quite put a finger on what makes us truly us. Some symbols come to unify Brazilians with a common feeling: that of being a mongrel.

Other former colonies of the Global South share this in-between, impure, mixed and matched sensibility, which not only defines us but puts us in perspective. This concept is not news, as one of our main national exports in the realm of literary and cultural studies is the concept of *antropofagia,* with its motto *Tupi or not tupi,* part of the Modernismo movement of the 1920s in Brazil, still widely studied by Latin Americanists and Postcolonialists alike. To be this savage who eats its enemies, members of their own human species, an anthropophagic manifesto by Oswald de Andrade written in the 1920s influenced Brazilian artists in the following decades to make Brazilian art but taking influence from Europe and America. It is in our blood and in our cultural heritage to consume the best of each other and leave out the worst, it is part of us to mix and match and use coloniser forms to make truly colonised, but our own, art. We are and have always been mutts by definition, by contact. Initially *criollos*, white Europeans born in the colonies, then *mestizos*, to now everything in between but still far from a racial democracy.

The word "mongrel" comes from the Old English and Proto-German, derived from mingling, kneading, the forcing together of two things to form a new one. Seen as derisive, derogatory, frowned upon, a mongrel is not a purebred. Is the monolingual the purebred pedigreed linguistic being, while the multilingual is a street mutt? Are we talking *Lady and the Tramp*? In the monolingual national discourse that permeates so much of cultural ideals around translation and world literature, the monolingual subject and reader is an ideal subject who lives in a vacuum. Even the most purebred of purebreds, the white European, is not really pure in any sense of the word. Have they forgotten the centuries and millennia of mixing that brought them here today?

The negative consequences of inbreeding are historically well-known. The Hapsburg dynasty is a cautionary tale. Monoculture crops kill diversity and lead to erosion, barren lands, deforestation. Science already knows that purity kills. Society knows that defending purity at all costs also kills, in a more violent way than the evolution. Defending purity over diversity leads to wars, to genocide, to ethnic cleansing. Hence, mongrels are the future. Our biological aim is to diversify, to shuffle DNA and create complex structures that will have the strength and ability to fight back diseases, invaders, enemies. Seeking to preserve a culture, or a language, is not a bad idea in itself. But tradition for tradition's sake, purity and closing oneself off to diversity is a runaway car quickly reaching a precipice. Will multilingualism only be truly seen as an advantage when a way can be found to capitalise on it? In the meantime, we are still paying Babel's price and being scattered among multiple tongues. And many of us dare to speak more than one.

EXOPHONY AS PERFORMANCE: A MANIFESTO

All the world's a stage, we are all performers, and all of us language speakers merely players. Language is playful. Language is performance, it is interior but overflows outwardly, externally. There are books that perform a kind of Multilingual Drag (Gramling, 2016), which sell themselves as multilingual fiction when they actually come from a monolingual perspective. If there is a multilingual drag, can there also be a monolingual drag? And, more specifically, a monolingual drag performed by exophonic subjects? And if that is the case, what would it involve? Would the aim of an exophonic subject be not to simply pass as a monolingual subject, but rather to perform their outwardness in language via this monolingual passing? How could we achieve that?

Firstly, I need to make clear that there is no possible consensus to define mono- and multilingual drag, as the connections between the world of drag and the world of language performance in literature seem to still be in their infancy. Many of the examples that come to mind could arguably be seen as passing rather than drag. I want to focus, instead, on the performative aspect and the mono/multi binary that the 'performative exophony' could help disrupt. When talking about drag, we need to bring Butler's *Gender Trouble* (1990) to the table. Butler proposes that drag performance disrupts the inner/outer perceptions and definitions of gender. Could we imply that a drag performance of monolingualism would disrupt the idea that an individual's monolingualism is both internal and external? Does an individual performing language drag disrupt expectations of the monolingualism/multilingualism binary? This remains to be seen. Queering the mono and multi prefixes also involves destabilising the very idea of a binary to deal with an individual's linguistic identities. This, in turn, would put forth another weapon against the L1 norm agenda, the monolingual paradigm.

Multilingual drag is also called by Gramling (2018) multilingual passing, translational monolingualism or semiodiverse multilingualism, or, in Yaseen Noorani's words: soft multilingualism (2013). Often when the works of authors of multilingual background sell and succeed in the publishing market, it is because they perform a type of soft multilingualism. Something that passes for multilingual, but is not necessarily breaking the mould, unsettling literary language and the readership who desperately need unsettling. It seems to me that many of the literary translators who are very comfortably found in the monolingual mindset but who know another language and translate from it into their L1, whom we could call 'monolingual translators', are enacting a type of soft multilingualism. Is such translation work breaking the mould or is it servicing the status quo? Through no fault of their own, as it is not easy to truly break away from a monolingual upbringing, are monolingual translators merely passing as multilinguals? Is this passing or could it be more of a performative act?

I would argue that this is not an easy question to answer, and generalising is never the researcher's cup of tea, but it is fair to say that openly defying a binary system, openly (and unashamedly) performing against the L1 norm and the expectations thrown against us by the monolingual and monocultural power systems at play in translated literature, is what the exophonic subject does, and what exophonic translation as a performance can embody.

Most of the translators I have interviewed in my doctoral thesis so far are also activists for decolonising translation and for seeing language beyond these binaries. To survive in the industry and to gain recognition, these successful literary translators, most of them multilingual, had to perform a sort of mono, rather than multilingual drag. Some are adamant: 'I translate, the direction does not matter'. Most, though, are largely unidirectional, translating in the so-called 'wrong direction', from L1 to L2 (or Lx). If taking the coloniser's language and performing in it is a type of rebellious decolonising translation practice, then couldn't we call this exophonic, or linguistic drag? Translator Anton Hur, when asked in a live streamed event for the National Centre for Writing, in the UK, about how to deal with impostor syndrome, or, more specifically, the invisibility syndrome that literary translators suffer from, claimed to see the act of translating as a performance and to 'try to project a kind of Nietzschean, übermensch charisma in that, yeah, I am a translator, I am a big deal, I know what I am talking about. And I say it with so much aplomb and confidence and, you know, fake it till you make it-ness, and at some point people started believing that.'[3]

So, in this case, upon a first look, what Hur is doing is precisely monolingual passing, as per Gramling's definition. But is he really only passing? Or is his performative approach to exophonic translation a performance that works to internally disrupt the binaries of literary translation? In the process of translation but also in the product, one would argue that exophonic translation involves a refusal of domestication, keeping certain words or phrases that may sound odd to anglo-monolingual ears, or refusing to italicise those words, but it can mean so much more, which is why these avenues of translational thought, practice and research must be opened to practitioners and academics

[3] https://www.youtube.com/watch?v=J8oFttUu2bI minute 52:00.

alike, so that exophony is rightly understood and practiced. But if we focus on process, or stance/attitude, instead of on the product itself, there are no set rules for what constitutes this linguistic drag, this performative act, but for now it seems reasonable to claim that seeing the exophonic act (whether writing in a foreign language or translating into a non-mother tongue) as a performance makes more sense and is more use than looking towards fluency, perfection, mastery, or any strict systematisation. The exophonic subject resists definition and, in fact, like the mongrel street dog, reminds us that the domesticating system fails us again and again. The solution is to be a reminder of this active performative self which defies binarisms and definitions.

While our post-monolingual world asks us to define a hierarchy of languages—L1, L2, a familial connection to language, mother tongue, father tongue, adopted tongue—we are expected to be essentially mono, unidirectional. Translators are, however, expected to transition between languages and cultures but to linguistically belong to one, to be loyal to one—their mother tongue—and translate into it. Following this line of thinking, how disruptive of this expectation is a translator being when they decide to perform their linguistic subjectivity, when they decide to go against the L1 norm?

I propose that we repurpose the mongrel concept as an aesthetic project. Like the anthropophagic cannibal who selects what will be used as reference, as influence, discards the rest and regurgitates a new mixed product, we need to perform our own lack of purity, our own suboptimality, make it visible, make it uncomfortable. That which defines us but does not limit us. Instead of hiding behind or conforming to norms, we should openly defy them. By constantly reminding ourselves and the readers of our work that the text they are reading is not a product of a single mind in a binary world, but rather the result of collective effort. A text which is *multi* in its very moment of creation cannot be put back into *mono* mode. Neither should the translator and translation. Of course, not all translation will be exophonic. But when we do have the option to perform our outwardness, our not-belonging, our exophonic selves, we should try to break the mould, play with language, destabilise norms, and challenge rules. Don't domesticate, do not hide foreign words and concepts, and idioms, let us make this all a bit uncomfortable. To not protect the reader from diversity. That's when we are truest to our mongrel core.

I propose that we make World Literature more receptive to multilingualism and the mongrel aesthetic of our postcolonial, post monolingual lives more visible. We should acknowledge the translation work, the translator, the collaboration that lies behind every choice to read a certain author, a certain country. World Literature should not be the *Lonely Planet*: translators of colour, heritage speakers, indigenous, queer, displaced, silenced, suboptimal in the eyes of gatekeepers, are ready to really show what meeting other cultures is all about. And we are far from alone. We each have a voice, and we are going to use it. To show you how uncomfortable and imperfect it can be, and how lack of perfection causes change, brings out beauty, and starts dialogues. Like that caramel-coloured dog who was ignored and teased for years, despised over other pedigree dogs, we can decolonise hearts and we will thrive. Together we can start this long and arduous process of decolonising the very centre of knowledge, art, history, and in turn decolonise the discourse and way of thinking which affects us all, in different but complementary ways. Just as former colonies fought and still fight for independence, we fight for a voice and for our space, but we also fight the colonial mentality, to free us all from the endless capitalist history of using others, of oppressing and silencing voices to preserve dominance. We can all speak if we take turns.

For my fellow mutts: be a proud mongrel, break the mould, perform your outsideness and let our non-fluent non-native suboptimal voices soar. No more muzzles.

BIBLIOGRAPHY

Beeby Lonsdale, A. 1998. 'Direction of translation (directionality)', *Routledge Encyclopedia of Translation Studies*. Routledge.

Bruni, L. 1992. 'Extracts from De interpretatione recta (the right way to translate) published in 1420', in Lefevere, A. (ed.) *Translation/History/Culture: A Sourcebook*. London, New York: Routledge.

Butler, Judith. 1990. *Gender trouble: feminism and the subversion of identity*. New York, Routledge.

Chesterman, Andrew. 2004. 'Beyond the Particular', in Mauranen, A. (ed.) *Translation Universals: Do They Exist?* Amsterdam and Philadephia: John Benjamins Publishers, pp. 33–50.

Duff, Alan. 1989. *Translation*, Oxford: Oxford University Press.

Gramling, David. 2016. *The Invention of Monolingualism*. New York, London: Bloomsbury.

Lisle, Debbie. 2008. 'Humanitarian Travels: Ethical Communication in 'Lonely Planet' Guidebooks', *Review of International Studies*, vol. 34, 2008, pp. 155–172.

Newmark, Peter. 1988. *Text Book of Translation*. New York, London, Singapore: Prentice Hall.

Samuelsson-brown, Geoffrey. 1995. *A Practical Guide for Translators*. Clevedon, Philadelphia, Adelaide: Multilingual Matters.

Noorani, Yaseen. 2013. 'Hard and Soft Multilingualism', *Critical Multilingualism Studies 1:2* pp. 7-28.

Tawada, Yōko. 1996. 'Erzähler ohne Seelen', in: *Talisman*. Tübingen: Konkursbuch Verlag.

Tawada, Yōko. 2003. *Ekusofonii: Bogo No Soto e Deru Tabi* (エクソフォニー——母語の外へ出る旅). Tokyo: Iwanami.

Tsao, Tiffany. Interview #154 – Tiffany Tsao, by Whitney Mcintosh. 16th November 2020. https://www.liminalmag.com/interviews/tiffany-tsao

Wright, Chantal. 2008. 'Writing in the 'Grey Zone': Exophonic Literature in Contemporary Germany', *Gfl- Journal 3*: 25–41.

Wright, Chantal. 2010. 'Exophony and Literary Translation: What It Means for the Translator When a Writer Adopts a New Language', *Target* 22 (1): 22–39.

12. WHY DON'T YOU TRANSLATE PAKISTANIAN?

Sawad Hussain

As a brown translator of Arabic, people always assume that I'm Arab – I mean, my last name doesn't hurt. When they find out that I'm Pakistani, the usually unspoken – though sometimes voiced – question is why am I not translating from Pakistanian? Another cause for distress is my American accent. Furrowed brows. Eyes squinting. What *are* you?

So what if the whiteness of the UK/US literary translation field makes you think of a snow bank? And we're not just talking about translators, but acquiring editors, book reviewers, award committees, etc. My mere existence as a brown body in this winter wonderland is an act of disruption in itself. Every. Single. Day.

Even before the callout for this anthology was publicised, I had been keeping a mental stock of the episodes I'm about to share with you. Only recently have I found a safe space, with other translators of colour, where I can talk about such things. I never felt comfortable asking my white counterparts if the following had happened to them, because honestly, I'd be willing to bet my lunch money that they hadn't. People usually describe me as sunny, positive, confident – and I am most of the time – but the sum of the experiences that follow have made me question if I really 'belong' in this profession, if I can keep swimming against the tide, when sometimes I'm just gasping for air. I have to clarify here that I am not talking about imposter syndrome – I am fully convinced of my creative abilities as a literary translator – but whether I am welcomed, understood, cared for in this space is another matter.

Disclaimer: The following episodes are as I remember experiencing them.

WHAT WERE YOU THINKING?

Reality: Sometime during the height of the COVID-19 pandemic, I was invited to speak alongside an author whose dystopian novel I had translated. The host for this event is a lauded literary publication in the Arabic translation sphere, and I was honoured to be invited, even slipping on some earrings for the Zoom call. I jotted down a couple of notes about my translation process and choices, as the novel had been released a while back, and I needed reminding about what I had done and why. As expected, the majority of the questions during the hour-long session were for the author. Two were for me, which I answered happily. As we were starting to wind down, the moderator asked, with a pained look on their face, "Why is there so much Arabic in your translation? It's jarring and makes some parts difficult to understand."

Translation: And you call yourself a translator? Did you just get lazy and forget to translate those words? Arabic has no place in an *English* text.

Commentary: At the time, because I was too scared to give ma réponse complète, I said that I had kept in les mots Arabes in order to stay authentic to the text. The book is heavily steeped in la culture de la nation, history and dialect – and in order to bring across some of the 'flavour' I kept in some Arabic words, which were always couched in context, or stealth glossed somehow. I also said that I wanted le lecteur to experience (because it is *that* kind of novel) what being in the country in which the novel is set would be like. Even Arab readers from elsewhere missed a lot of the references to shared cultural knowledge when reading ce livre, or didn't fully understand some of the political references, and yet, it has been a runaway bestseller in the Arabic speaking world. When you travel to un pays étranger and you don't speak the language, how do you make your way? You read facial expressions, body language; connect the dots. And that's what I expect of my readers.

But what I really wanted to say in addition was: I am challenging the language hierarchy in translation. In the previous paragraph, did the French words actually stop you from understanding what I was saying?

Did they bother you? More likely than not, you shrugged and kept on reading. Due to the historical, cultural and linguistic ties between England and France, keeping French words in an English text rarely raises an eyebrow. No one has ever said, "Why is there so much French in this translation?" I must stress that this is if you're a UK or US English reader. But if you were to sell your English translation stuffed with French words to, say, an Indonesian readership, it would be a different story. Maintaining العربية (in transliteration of course) may be unsettling for particular English or American readers, but for a reader from the subcontinent, it adds a layer of verisimilitude to the narrative (as I've been told by a couple of readers of my translations).

What I realized from this event is that, even if it makes you, the English or American reader, feel unsettled, uncomfortable, angry even – I still won't cater to you. I am going to translate this book being as respectful as I can to the source text, and that means you need to get on this train before it leaves the station.

ENTER COLUMBUS

Reality: I received an email from a publishing house that had acquired a novel I had pitched, saying they wanted to discuss an exciting opportunity over the phone. Sure, why not? I had already worked with this house on another book (granted, with a different editor), but I was intrigued all the same about this new development – especially as our prior contact had usually been by email.

"Sawad, thank you for making the time to chat today. We're in the process of launching this new programme that we thought your project would fit in with remarkably well."

"Thank you for thinking of me! I'm all ears."

"Well, we thought the book you're going to translate would be a prime candidate for this new mentorship scheme we're setting up, where a more experienced translator will guide an emerging translator through the process."

I hadn't envisioned co-translating this novel, but I'm open to it. Be open to it …

"We also thought that the mentor could share industry contacts with the emerging translator as well as help them be more conscious about their craft, whilst reviewing their work."

"Sounds great."

"I know, right! Well, the people we had in mind for you were X or Y."

Wait, what?

"Uh …"

"They're both experienced and we thought either of them would fit as a mentor for you."

HOLD THE PHONE! I'm the 'emerging' translator?!

"Okay. Just so I'm understanding this correctly, you'd like X or Y (*both older white men*) to mentor me whilst I translate this book." *This book that I pitched to you on my own.*

"Yes! That's it. Isn't it exciting that you'll get to work with the likes of them?"

"Was there something in my sample that you didn't like?"

"Oh, not at all. I loved the sample. I just thought that, you know, someone like *you*, might benefit from this programme. I mean they could introduce you to some other editors as well."

Both X and Y have worked with the same two or three presses over and over. Yes, they have more publications, but I have worked with over eight presses.

"Is my doing this book contingent on accepting this arrangement?"

"Well you know, with everything going on (*e.g.: Black Lives Matter, the world burning)*, we really want to be seen as doing something to help translators of colour, and I thought what a great opportunity, right?"

At this point, I am pacing back and forth, seething, trying to hold back my tears. I start writing down what she is saying to gain some sort of control in this warped situation that is quickly spinning out of control. I can – not – lose – this – book. Not now, not like this.

"Listen Z, I really appreciate this offer, I really do, but I don't think you realise how experienced I am. I look young but I've been translating for over twelve years, having worked with a number of houses from Hong Kong to India, to the UK and the US, and with over ten publications. I'm always happy to have someone interrogate my work, as it results in a richer text, but at this stage of my career, I wouldn't benefit from this 'emerging' translator mentorship."

"Oh … I see."

Translation: Hey you BROWN WOMAN. You must be inexperienced. I can help you. Let me do so, so I can check my CSR box, my diversity box, and my feel-all-round-good box.

Commentary: After this call, I cried. I yelled. Why could she not *see* me, like the other publishing houses I have worked with across the world? On reflection, I'm proud that I stood up for myself. And I appreciate the editors who do see me, who unreservedly repose their confidence in me, that much more.

CAMELS, PALM TREES, HIJABS, OH MY!

Reality: The head of a publishing house asked for my suggestions for the cover art of a short story collection I'd been working on for some time. I recommended a talented designer who also reads Arabic, and who would be able to capture the essence of the collection. Instead of following my recommendation, the head of this house came back and said, "We will probably go with a desert scene."

I was so confused, genuinely trying to understand why a desert scene would be his go-to option. Were there any deserts in the collection? No. Were any of the short stories based somewhere that could be misconstrued as a desert? No. It then clicked that because this was a translation from Arabic, it obviously had to be about deserts (even though the head of house had access to the reader's report and the blurb for the catalogue). Before answering, I took to Twitter to express my consternation and see how others felt. Within a few hours, I had over a hundred people who'd liked my tweet and written messages of support. That might not seem like a lot, but it was the boost I needed.

I wrote back to the head of house:

I completely understand about you not wanting to go with any of the covers [the author] suggested. However, having said that, can we please avoid a desert scene? The stories themselves aren't about the desert. Also there has been a lot of chatter about cliché covers, such as a camel, the desert, a woman with a hijab, for Arabic literature in general. As such, it's quite integral for us to steer away from this, otherwise I'm afraid it will turn off a lot of our target audience. Would it be possible to be inspired by elements of the reader's report or the blurb instead?

After holding my breath for a few days, a response finally came in that the head of house would scratch the desert scene and approach the designer I had suggested instead.

Translation: I am the head of this house, and even though I haven't read your book yet, I know what the cover should look like – I know better.

Commentary: Though the above does sound encouraging – after all, we avoided a disastrous desert scene – sadly other issues arose with the final cover, which made me realise that going forward I need to put a clause into all my contracts that says:

a) I must be consulted about the cover; and
b) I must be shown the cover before it is finalised.

PAS DU TOUT

Reality: Over thirteen years ago, I started out as a French literary translator, having studied French for much longer than Arabic. My major was actually French and Middle Eastern Studies, with my minor being Arabic. Bright-eyed and bushy-tailed, I had started translating excerpts from Mauritian novels, Algerian novels, pieces from outside of Metropolitan France that spoke to me. I applied for a workshop led by a star translator in the French-English field. I pored over the text, hope radiating off me. Even if I didn't get in, perhaps they would still critique my text. I found out in due course that I hadn't made the cut. But I still wanted to pitch the novel I had translated the excerpt from and let them know of my plans.

Their response was: "My advice to you would be to focus on translating from Arabic, which is very much a growth area. There are already too many translators from French and not enough work to keep everyone busy, especially translators with no track record from French. My feeling is that you need to develop your knowledge of French quite a bit if you really want to translate from it."

Translation: Stay away from French. This isn't *your* language. You don't belong here. You'll never be good enough – never.

Commentary: I really was stumped. How could I not be good enough to translate from French when I had a whole degree in French literature and had been speaking French since elementary school? Why was I more suited to Arabic, a language I only started learning in my first year of college? Was it because I'm brown and my last name is Hussain? To be fair to this translator, yes, the French literary translation field is saturated, but if everyone took their advice then there would be no new French translators – ever. And they'd all just die out. These days, I mentor Arabic-English translators, and translators in other language pairs. I know I am providing a much more nurturing environment than the one I encountered when I first started out. The above is just one instance of many.

SAY WHAT, NOW?

Reality: I co-curated a collection of short stories and was very excited to receive the edits and see what my acquiring editor – whom I respect immensely – made of my work. Unfortunately, it seems they were unable to edit my work due to life circumstances, and outsourced it to another individual (who, to my understanding, didn't work at the house). When I received the edits, it was an exercise in patience, having to explain over and over why things were the way they were. One example (the only context you need is that Abdel Samie and Fathia are refugees who are married):

Abdel Samie hurried to the classroom, ***where his aunt, Fathia's mother,*** *stayed, trying to get a hold of himself and the too-small flip flops he had on, to tell her that Fathia wouldn't be back today, and that her hairy legs were now the property of a gang, only to be seen again for an eye-watering amount of money.*

The words in bold were highlighted by the editor with the query: *This suggests Abdel and Fathia are cousins. Is this what the author intended?*

Translation: Whatever I read as an editor must fit into my view of the world. Anything which contradicts this is wrong and must be amended.

Commentary: Of course this is what the author intended! Cousins marrying one another is not only common in the Arab world, but in many other communities as well.

There was a barrage of this sort of queries, interrogating the customs, traditions, and way of life of people in an Arab community. I wrote a letter of complaint to the acquiring editor, stating that this stand-in editor needed to better acquaint themselves with the different ways of existing in the world.

* * *

Writing all of this was extremely cathartic, but also quite anxiety-inducing. I had a very different version to what you have read above, but decided to remove all identifiers of editors, publishers and other translators as I would still like to work in this field. At first, I felt so bold and brave writing all this down. But as the months passed, I grew weary and fearful that this would upset one person or another, and the point of this essay is not to hurt people, but rather to record what it has been like as a brown translator navigating the choppy seas of literary translation.

13. TRANSLATING THE INVISIBLE: A MONOLOGUE ABOUT TRANSLATING THE POEMS OF NAGRAJ MANJULE

Yogesh Maitreya

We were two friends
Carried the same attitude
Ready to die for each other
Lived with a single purpose
Had a single dream

Later on
He committed suicide
And, I write a poem[1]

In 2014, I watched *Fandry*, a Marathi film directed by Nagraj Manjule. Each frame in this film appeared to my eyes as a verse from a poem; poignant and demanding urgent and intelligent reading. The pain of life of an *untouchable* person, projected in each frame in this film, was part of a world whose contexts were missing for the larger world. They could see the pain but not its origin. They could *understand* the suffering of its protagonist but were far from *feeling* it. The ex-untouchable communities (now referred to as Dalits in the political sense), are part of caste society. They live in a caste society, but their lives hardly exist for the larger world except when it comes to exploiting their labour; *Fandry* deciphered the language of pain of those who are not visible to wider society.

A couple of months later, I discovered the poetry of Nagraj Manjule; I could connect both his poetry and his film to his unique poetic imagination. An artist perceives the world from his location; his art is the

[1] Translated by Yogesh Maitreya from the Marathi

product of his location in the world, in society, in the hierarchy. Manjule's poetry opened up a theatre of emotions in which I found my life at the centre stage. Whenever I imagined myself in the world, especially in the world of English language literature, I had always found myself at the margin and often *invisible* in it. Reading Manjule's poems confirmed my potential to change the way I think of myself and the world. While his poems were very much anti-caste in their consciousness and perceptions, they were starkly different from the entire body of poems from Dalit literature, which explicitly asserted itself as anti-caste. Because Manjule's poems, rather than addressing the oppression outside in the social structures, explore its impacts by looking inward. Rather than society, an individual becomes the focus for exploring the imagination of the new world in these poems.

I decided to translate Manjule's poems into English because he not only sharply metaphorised the life of a Dalit in its profundity, but also imagined him as a mind with limitless possibilities to create a new life. A Dalit as a mind is almost invisible in the eyes of the caste society. This is a pathological phenomena, an abnormal construction. The only avenue for his emotions and feelings is the language of poetry and translation; a literary process, I argue, is crucial to redefine our imagination of a man, his struggle and his existence in the world. The translation of Manjule's poems into English adds new sensibilities to English literature which were largely missing. If the world knows about India through the novels of Salman Rushdie, the poems of Agha Shahid Ali, the essays of Arundhati Roy or the political commentaries of Pankaj Mishra (all of them are Savarnas and privileged), then they need to read the poems of Nagraj Manjule in English translation to feel the disruptions in their understanding of India as a society.

* * *

The literary imagination of a person whose birth makes him carry the history of his persecution on his shoulders and in his mind, creates a history of emotions which is invisible in the dominant society that reflects the culture of its oppressor. In any society, where a person's history is that of being socially and culturally oppressed, his literary imagination can defy, subjectively, not only popular culture but dominant methods of conceiving literature. Therefore, it becomes increasingly difficult for a *language* (such as English), which is historically dominant over other languages, to capture and translate the tangible meanings of words sprouted from the minds of the oppressed. The most prominent reason why translation becomes difficult at this juncture, is the unverifiability of the oppressed person's history; the language of the oppressor has restricted itself from understanding the world and most importantly the human agency of the oppressed, from imagining their culture with respect and dignity. Literature in any world language, with translation being one of its facets, has always been a reflection of the dominant community. For the oppressed person to write in the same language is to change the way language and subsequently life is imagined by the oppressor. Our imaginations as well as perceptions are subjected to the social location in which we have been born and raised; these define our emotional and aesthetic responses and reactions towards the world. For the dominant language (the language of the oppressor and coloniser) to translate the imagination of the oppressed, is to translate the world of emotions, feelings, imagination, reason, logic and ideas, which never existed in it in the first place.

* * *

Dr. B. R. Ambedkar once predicated: foreigners of course know of the existence of untouchability. But not being next door to it, they are unable to realise how oppressive it is in its actuality. It is difficult for them to understand how it is possible for a few untouchables to live on the edge of a village consisting of a large number of Hindus; to go through the village daily to free it from the most disagreeable of its filth and to carry the errands of all and sundry; collect food at the doors of the Hindus; buy spices and oil at the shops of the Hindu Bania from a distance; regard the village in every way as their home – and yet never touch or be touched by anyone belonging to the village.[2]

---

[2] http://www.columbia.edu/itc/mealac/pritchett/00ambedkar/txt_ambedkar_waiting.html

This has not changed for centuries in India. Instead, the forms of discrimination and degree of oppression have changed and become more subtle. This is the epistemological backdrop of Dalit writers, regardless of whether they hail from urban or rural spaces. To translate such an intense life filled with visceral anger and anxiety, to break free from it, is to invent new vocabularies and consequently a new language itself. Therefore, the sound of the 'language in translation' changes as soon as the life of an oppressed person – who recently freed himself in his stories – asserts its arrival in it.

The world cannot live next to us as a neighbour, to experience or understand the caste-based oppression we face. However, if we go to them in the voice of the language which they speak, we can communicate our world with them, sharing the realities of our life, which were hitherto invisible to them. Consequently, we can make ourselves visible to the world into which our lives are freshly translated.

★ ★ ★

As Dr. B. R. Ambedkar elaborated almost a century ago, the nature of caste society and its everyday norms make *communication* between two individuals almost impossible. These two individuals can belong to the same caste but speak different languages. Hence, they are connected by their past but separated by language. Translation disrupts this separation. It is not only true between two individuals from the same caste, speaking different languages, but between any two individuals across the world who do not share the same language but share the same sensibilities. A reason to translate our stories from one language to another is to be connected; so we can expand the meaning of life from various locations, positions and hierarchies across the world, across societies; so we can put an end to our alienation, through which, despite all being human, we perceive each other as *foreigners*.

Translation can recreate what has been erased by us. In the domain of literature, what stories get heard or read and what stories remain mostly at the margins of readership across the world, is a matter of the hierarchical interests of a particular society in which the story is written. I don't know the native language of Kenya, which was a British colony like India. But English came to us as part and parcel of British colonisation. If a writer from Kenya writes in his/her native language about colonisation and if I write on the same subject in my native language, which a writer from Kenya does not know, then although our histories have been affected (albeit perhaps differently) by the same extremal power in the same period in the past, we still lack a medium to communicate with each other by the way of dialogue. Translation in a language we both understand, such as English, will open up a gate for us to enter into the domain of *active* dialogue. We were affected by colonisation but because we did not share the same language, we were erased from each others' minds. Translation in English recreates us as people who were, in the past, affected by the same external power: British Colonisation. It is only in translation that people who share the same histories with different languages expand their understanding of each other.

The translation of the stories of oppressed communities into dominant languages (for example English or Brahminic versions of any language in India) humanises the sensibilities of the dominant communities, whose language did not erstwhile even attempt to understand the world of the oppressed. Translation is the bridge between two worlds which have been separated by historical processes of alienation.

* * *

Despite caste-society being colonised for almost two centuries, not everyone had access to the English language; English in India is very much a language of the status-quo, dictated by Brahmins from literary fields to media to academic discourse. Hence we find English literature produced in India to be undisputedly elitist and Brahminical in nature; to understand English literature produced in India, one needs to know the politics of the English language here and the dominance of Brahmins, whose ideas of India as a nation stand opposed to the ideas and imagination of Dalits. In their words, a Dalit is no more than a subject of pity or a victim of oppression. In English literature in India, a Dalit has never been portrayed as a mind capable of thinking and imagining many possibilities of life.

The social position of a poet is greatly responsible for changing sensibilities, which is soothing for us, but could be irritating for others. For example, people with posh homes and an elegant ambience would love the idea of rain and observe it romantically, but people with rudimentary houses which leak in the monsoon would never feel romantic about rain, as it disturbs their already disturbed lives. When two such people write a poem about rain, their poems will be contrasting, defying each other's idea of and about rain. In India, the domain of English from the beginning has been dominated, controlled and dictated by people with posh homes containing elegant ambience (Brahmin, Savarnas). Hence, the world that understands India through its English poetry, can never understand the realities of this country because it is majorly constituted by people with rudimentary houses who cannot afford to romanticise the rain, as their survival during it is mostly at stake. It is not an exaggeration to say that whatever people from outside India know about the country, through the English language, constitutes very little truth about this society.

While reading English literature for more than a decade, I often ached to hear the sound of my life in this language. This was my subjective desire, but I was also aware of a need for the emotional education of readers, which could only be fulfilled through the process of translation. Translation could provide access to a world which was hardly *recognised* at an emotional and intellectual level.

But in India, the translation of literature by any author, into English, is determined by his caste location. The higher the caste he belongs to, the higher the chance of his works getting translated. Also, in India, translation is not a discipline; it is a vacation and done selectively; for example, if we lend a cursory glance over the trends in translation in India or try to understand the history of translation in India, we see that it is mostly dominant caste authors who have been translated from one language to another and from local languages to international languages. Authors from Dalit-Bahujan communities, who essentially uphold anti-caste perspectives in their literature, are hardly found in translation in international languages.

* * *

So translation in English for me is an act of asserting my *self* into it, and globalising my stories which were deliberately silenced, erased or mutilated to mere victimhood. This could be the reason why, when I began to translate Manjule's poems in English, I felt that I was translating the most significant part of my own emotional history, which is shared by generations of mine but which I had never found clearly visible in the history of the English language.

For example, take these two lines from his poem *'I'*:

I am living, being a deadly question,
I am eternally impregnated for the mother

In these two lines, Manjule explains the existence of a Dalit in this society; as a question, whose answer will destroy the oppressive existence of the caste society. In order to maintain and protect its oppressive existence, caste society repeatedly avoids this question because caste society knows that to answer it is to destroy its own existence. Yet, Manjule's poem travels beyond this immediate urge to be answered, to be recognised. His poem wants a Dalit man to discover his history, which is rooted in the history of humanhood, and not merely in the history of being exploited or humiliated. In this poem, mother is a metaphor for the origin of humans, humanhood and their roots. Manjule demands a man to move beyond all categorical identities and associate himself with the history of the earth in which we all are equal and human, in which we long to belong to our roots.

Translating Manjule's poems is like translating an entire civilisation. To read Manjule in English, is to expand the dimensions of truth about caste-society and its assaults on Dalits. For me, translating Manjule into English was to educate myself in imagining the local history in English, which had not erstwhile been readily available to me; to explore many possibilities of life in English, guided by the words of the poet's mother tongue (Marathi), and now it was for me to recreate my self in it. By this, I mean that the process of translation has helped me to kindle the spark of life in the darkness of the language in which I always existed but was made into an invisible entity. This invisibility of mine, as a Dalit and also of a poet here, was created in the language at the hands of

Brahmins, especially in English. And precisely for this reason, whenever a Dalit asserts himself in English, not as a victim but as a mind, through translation, it expands the scope of perceiving the life newly and freshly.

Oppression begins by imagining a language as per the brutal desires and intentions of the oppressor. I felt this phenomenon being disrupted while I was translating Manjule's poems. The poem *If I Did Not Have A Pen In My Hand* shows what I mean by disruption in the process of being oppressed by and in languages.

If I did not have
A pen in my hand
Then, it would have been a chisel
A sitar
A flute
Or a canvas and brush

I would have dug out
With whatever I had
The extravagant clamour
From inside the mind

A Dalit knows that 'language' as a tool has always been in the confines of the oppressor, who has, for centuries, been writing stories which justify his oppression, making the language almost redundant. History around the world shows us that oppressed people, for their liberation, have, from time to time, resorted to violent methods which stem from their need to survive, fighting oppressors, whose violence stems from the oppressor's will to dominate or suppress. Therefore, a Dalit, whose past has involved consuming the venom of untouchabililty, does not merely rely on language for his liberation. For him, whatever he has at hand becomes a tool by which he could draw the path for his liberation. A Dalit could sing or play or carve or draw in order to understand his oppression and possibly create a meaning out of it which consolidates his wounds and provides him with the courage and clarity to fight the oppressor in constructive ways, which is otherwise not always possible with violent methods. Since poetry is an uncensored response to our innermost instincts and suppressed emotions and feelings, it becomes a powerful way by which we can decipher the subtlety and depth of oppression.

As this poem shows, when an oppressed person resorts to language, as a conscious choice, to imagine his liberation, he changes the ways in which we have imagined that language so far. By writing about the oppressor and his oppression a Dalit rescues the language from its redundancy. Just imagine if stories in English were written only by British people and no one else had the right or freedom to write their stories in English; English as a language would have become redundant because it had restricted its growth by never allowing a home to different thoughts from different societies. This has happened with Sanskrit: the language of Brahmins in India. Brahmins never allowed any lower caste people to learn this language and as a result of this, over the centuries, Sanskrit has become redundant. Today, no one thinks in Sanskrit, therefore no one exists in India whose mother tongue is Sanskrit. In fact, Brahmins criminalised and penalised those lower castes and untouchables who heard the sound of Sanskrit by mistake. Molten lead was poured into an untouchable's ears if he heard the sound of mantras in Sanskrit. The history of India is filled with thousands of such examples. A language breaks the barrier of nationhood if the life imagined in it intends to fight oppression and humanise the oppressor. By this I mean that the language should explain what pain means for the most oppressed from the society, therefore humanising us all, so that we act consciously in our lives to put an end to that oppression, or cease to take part in the process of oppression from our end. Language puts an end to our alienation, which was created through distorted histories and stories written by the oppressor. Language has to change, and if it does not, it dies a silent death.

The translation of stories of the most oppressed people, who have not been imagined as subjects of stories in English, adds new and fresh sensibilities to a language that has hardly had them in its imagination. It is a rare sight to see a poet in the English language not romanticising the role of language in a poem while discovering the source of pain and dilemmas. *If I Did Not Have A Pen In My Hand* (in its English translation) introduces us to the ways in which oppressed people (Dalits) think about the role of language in their lives. Language is not romanticised in their lives, rather it is made into a tool to debrahminise and decolonise their lives.

★ ★ ★

For a Dalit who is conscious about his roots, to love or to be in love with a person from a higher caste in caste society is like being in a constant emotional tussle, treading vulnerable terrains, because of his attitude towards caste-society; he sometimes has to fight with his own beloved in order to prove the abnormality of caste and how pathological its norms and customs are. Yet, he cannot help but face disappointment in love with a person from a caste 'superior' to his. Because the person raised of and in caste is alienated from their human-hood long before entering a relationship, caste restricts a person to the world of his own caste, hence they cannot easily empathise with other castes; this also means that there is no fraternity in Indian society. Without this, how can one person understand the other at the same level? For a person who is 'untouched' by society, achieving this humanhood lies in sacrificing his immediate desire to be loved, as he instinctively knows that he has been *despised* by this society for centuries.

Our ability to overcome the grief of separation from our beloved, or any person, is the major factor which determines our imagination of the world. Elsewhere, I have argued that:

> in the tradition of love poems in world literature, poetry is often associated with the description of lovers in relation to nature and its beauty; or love in these poems is manifested intensely through sexual metaphors in which lovers' bodies are used as *objects*, subsequently producing a limited if not pathological poetic imagination. More than necessary, two major themes – romance and grief – recurred in love poems across the world. If the romance was often gently sexual, the grief was intense, drawing from the experience of 'separateness' from the lover.[3]

[3] *Singing Thinking Anti-Caste* by Yogesh Maitreya. 2021. *Panther's Paw Publication*

The theme of love and separation becomes differently visible in Manjule's poem, and, therefore, we discover the newest meaning of 'love' and 'separation', which did not exist in the world of the oppressors and never manifested through their literature. Talking about men who suffer but are unable to express their pain, bell hooks writes, 'much of the anger men direct at mothers is a response to the maternal failures to protect the spirit of the boy from patriarchal harm.'[4] How often do we witness a poem in which the strength to overcome the pain of separation from a lover is found in the enraging eyes of the mother who toiled to keep her children alive in the oppressive caste society of India? I am sure that a poem with such a sensibility is hardly written in the English language. But from time to time people refuse to obey the oppressive rules of the world and follow their instincts, only to humanise the generations. The translation of stories of oppressed people also humanises the body of language in translation, which hitherto failed to recognise their existence, emotionally and intellectually. Manjule's poem *Eyes of Mother* is an example of this; while I was translating this poem, I felt something in me changed forever. It took me a while to realise what this was; I had never read or witnessed a man (a poet or writer) write about separation from a lover while being so true to his history and his roots.

This brought my attention to the inability of love poems from India, written in English, to educate a man, emotionally, in a caste society which assaults his potential to freely love a person of his choice. In the history of the English language in India, there is not a single poem written by a Brahmin or Savarna writer which succeeds in portraying the problems of the act of love in a caste society. A Dalit man is often killed for loving a girl from a higher caste: a fact which has been given no place in the body of English poems in India. Manjule's poems and their English translation are crucial because they radically change how we look at the world around us; they are antithesis to the sexist-Savarna-male-gaze in India that has always sexualised women, never intellectualised them. 'Broken emotional bonds with mothers and fathers, the traumas of emotional neglect and abandonment that so

---

[3] *The Will To Change* by bell hooks. 2004. *Washington Square Press*

many males have experienced and been unable to name, have damaged and wounded the spirits of men. Many men are unable to speak their suffering',[5] writes bell hooks. The poems of Manjule are an achievement for they not only articulate the suffering of a Dalit man in Brahmincal-patriarchal society, but they also resist sexist oppression in the domain of a literature by resurrecting the idea of love which cannot be understood without fully acknowledging the pain of the mother, especially one who hails from oppressed communities. There is a reason for this:

> A quest for wisdom, compassion, or simply intelligence, was rarely sought through love poems…In the themes of 'romance' and 'grief' that dominate the genre of love poems, 'romance' appears as a profoundly elitist vision and 'grief' stands for a purely individual (human) feeling that stems from separation from a lover. Often, romance is exclusive, but grief is universal. In love, very few can afford romance. Grief is what most of us witness. Yet, 'love' is let loose from intelligence in our love poems. Not all of this was done intentionally. It was a result of the poet's inability to overcome their separateness from the world.[6]

In *Eyes of Mother*, Manjule triumphantly overcomes this separation and offers a unique perspective in which love is no longer purely emotional and personal, but has become historical and intellectual, mature enough to deal with separation from the location of *understanding* rather than the *power* of a man. I find this transition possible in Manjule's poems because he is not only a man in Brahmanical-patriarchal society but a Dalit (*untouchable*) man, and hence, he is subject to persecution and humiliation at the hands of Brahmins and Savarnas in multifold ways. This also means that he is vulnerable while confronting Savarna women who enjoy power next to their Brahmin men (their fathers, brothers and husbands). So caste society is not only casteist, racist and patriarchal, but also Brahminical, which means a Dalit is oppressed in the cruelest ways, which often are not visible to the world.

---

[5] Ibid.

[6] *Singing Thinking Anti-Caste* by Yogesh Maitreya. 2021. *Panther's Paw Publication*

Look/ how my mother
has furiously aimed at
deranged darkness
that comes upon running?
with the embers
of her pale eyes
if I did not look into her eyes
then, my dear
my moon and stars
would have fallen and been trapped
still, in your dense hair[7]

I fail to recall a love poem in the English language, at least from India, which explores the emotion of love using the poet's experience of their mother. I consider *Eyes of Mother* to be a remarkable poem, both in the original Marathi and in English because the lover in it offers the poet the desired romance, but the 'mother' in it is a metaphor for his social location, his roots – the history that is impossible to separate from him. The 'mother' is also a reminder of the assertion of the poet against the treatment he received as an 'untouched' in society. Even if his assertion against injustice, once manifested in a love-affair, has 'pale eyes', it is nevertheless capable of liberating him from the uselessness of the romance of a lover's 'dense hair', in which his dreams and aspirations, in the form of the 'moon and stars would have fallen and been trapped'.[8]

Readers in the English language would find it difficult to understand the context of this poem and the explanation that follows. This is because the world of the poet has not only been invisible to readers in English but also to his lover whom he loved: remember, each caste is a world in itself and people from two different castes in India are nothing less than foreigners to each other. Most people can never develop empathy towards a person from another caste, because their idea of life is restricted to their caste and they hold on to it until their death. This poem greatly helps in emotionally educating the entire generation of males who never succeeded in understanding love in its profundity and

[7] Translated from Marathi into English by Yogesh Maitreya
[8] *Singing Thinking Anti-Caste* by Yogesh Maitreya. 2021. *Panther's Paw Publication*

its historicity in relation to their identity. I feel that the English translation of this poem contributes in bridging the emotional gaps between males across the world who often get lost in the romanticism of love with their lovers and simultaneously alienate themselves from the contribution of motherhood, the highest act of love. *Eyes of Mother* by Manjule via its English translation provisionally adds fresh sensibility into the domain of English literature by putting the history of motherhood at the centre of the discourse on love.

The connection between society and one's private love life is not the dominant theme in poetry. The element of imagination, rather than dialectics, dominates the course of poetry rather than material dialectics. But an oppressed person knows that even the act of love is strangely political because it defines the course of his acceptance or rejection by the society. We do not often read such a love poem in the English language in which the idea of love is equally conceived with social equality and justice. But if there is no equality and justice, then there is no love. Those who are stung by the fangs of caste know how venomous it is to be in love with a person from an oppressive caste and constantly be misunderstood. As I translated this poem, I began to reconsider my own feelings and emotions, and I reconfigured them. The result: I started seeing injustice in romantic relationships in India, but at the same time I felt free because now I had a language to describe my emotional world in English, the language which is not mine but into which I consciously chose to recreate myself and my history.

* * *

On a subjective level, I feel much closer to the English language narratives of Black writers. For example I could identify with the portrait of his father as dark, as a Black man in James Baldwin's *Notes on a Native Son*; the explanation of his father's anger, his suspicion towards white people. On many levels, I found this in the life of my own father, a Dalit (ex-untouchable) man. I found the male voice in Langston Hughes' poems relatable, much closer to my context. I have never felt this chord of affection while reading English literature written by Savarna or Brahmin writers from India, although they belong to the same society. Translating the following poem, *Now You Are*, encouraged me, it guaranteed me the scope through which English can be reimagined in this divisive society. Through this process, translation can play an instrumental role for generations to come. The poem I am discussing is a testimony of Dalit consciousness; despite being hurt in his relationship because of his caste, the narrator intends to move beyond it because he needs to perceive and create life beyond earthly failure. This poem is the real beginning of a Dalit in the English language because it imagines a person beyond his failure and nurtures him for the future, by not discarding the past but making it the most intense souvenir of his dark part. The translation of this poem in English also translates the invisible – a Dalit – for the world:

> Now
> You are, for me,
> As if an old letter
> Of suicide

When I read *Now You Are* a couple of years ago, I knew that it explains the arrival of emotional maturity and intellectual honesty in the life of an oppressed person. An oppressed person in any oppressive regime is a human being who is constantly in search of humanity around him. Because *humanity* is his only ally. Because the oppressive regime, before enslaving him, erases or completely distorts his history in which he was a man with potential to create a beautiful world with his ability to love. His ability to love or create a world out of it, is a threat to the oppressive regime that wants to establish the kingdom of hate and rules. In order to protect himself from submitting to this kingdom of hate and rules, an oppressed person needs to develop a vision to look at life beyond failures in love with a person. In love, an oppressed person is intimately accepted and touched as a human. As soon as he is separated from his lover, he once again finds himself in the dark corners of the society where he instinctively knows that his existence will be rejected. But this is also the moment of transition for him, in which he could acquire the profound understanding of himself and the world: *my existence is not based on or validated by my acceptance by others, rather my existence is what I create out of my thoughts, feeling, and emotions, and how I resist the efforts of the society which intends to make me feel lonely and weak and lifeless all the time; I am my world and my instincts are maps of my existence.* In this poem, Manjule, being an oppressed person who undoubtedly followed his instincts, succeeded in imagining life beyond failures in love, with a person. The lover in this poem becomes "an old letter of suicide". He wanted to commit this act as he was emotionally so vulnerable. But he survived. His instincts guided him to life. His instincts not only emotionally strengthened him but nurtured him intellectually. An act of suicide is emotionally the most brittle state of the mind. Surviving this comes with the courage to digest the failures in life and use them as fertilisers to cultivate beautiful flowers and fruits on the vulnerable and infertile soil of a mind that is unable to imagine life beyond failures or pain. This unique poem not only establishes that a Dalit shares common instincts of survival and strength with all the oppressed people across the world, it also adds intimate sensibilities while talking about love and suicide, by creating a dichotomy between suicide and love, educating us profoundly in the domain of emotions. Reading this in translation, also educates a native reader of English about the emotional world of an oppressed person, and hence, both the poet and reader (people nurtured by two completely different languages) expand the human understanding of 'love' and 'suicide' with their words and silences.

* * *

After I finished translating Manjule's poems, the English language sounded very different to me. It was as though I could feel my own emotions in it and as though I could smell my own life in it. Translating them made me realise that the function of language is to create and recreate the endless possibilities of imagining life in its profundity. Despite the fact that while translating Manjule's poems into English I became increasingly convinced of the limitations of English as a language, to fully deliver the tangible meanings, essence and 'feel' of the original Marathi poems, the process helped me to discover the most rewarding consequence of the process of translation: to make the invisible visible in the literary imagination of people (oppressed) and subsequently and simultaneously involving them in contributing to enhance the meaning of the world of the oppressed, which once was *invisible* in the language of translation. The process of translating these poems has demonstrated for me the potential of translation to *humanise* the language. Translation re-humanises languages. I no longer perceive English as a foreign language. By translating my world into English, I feel closer to it, as close as I feel to my mother tongue (Marathi – with Vidarbhiyan dialect). A single poem can transform our views about the entire world. And the translation of such a poem into the dominant language (English), can re-humanise the language itself. For example, this poem:

> [...] the dreams you have conceived
> Will not sprout in this soil, and
> I have not agreed to be bonsai
> You take seeds of your dreams and leave,
> Search for a new fertile land,
> My barren land may someday become pregnant,
> Flowers will also bloom here,
> Dreams will come true,
> But until then
> I must turn my dream into fertiliser and water
> And I must bury myself
> For my suppressed people....[9]

James Baldwin in his book *No Name In The Street* writes, 'there is a reason, after all, that some people wish to colonize the moon, and others dance before it as before an ancient friend'. If the essential purpose of translation, irrespective of its political connotations, is to educate us about the mind which thinks in and speaks a different language to ours, making us conscious about the roots of humanity, which all of us share by the virtue of being a human, then its strength lies in inventing the vocabulary and consequently a whole new language in which the emotions and feelings of an oppressed person delivers its true meanings.

The oppressed person feels oppressed and discriminated against because he often sees himself as invisible, mocked, caricatured or

[9] *Singing Thinking Anti-Caste* by Yogesh Maitreya. 2021. *Panther's Paw Publication*

despised in the languages spoken around him. In languages, he senses the smell of his deterioration as a mind. Therefore, translation as a conscious and political decision and process, must reclaim the humanness of an oppressed person and make him a free man in the imagination of readers. But, the major portion of translation in English from India is unjust, hegemonic and dominated by Brahminical castes. Baldwin's words direct us towards the two poles within a man: one who wishes to capture and rule nature and hence destroys it eventually (injustice), but another who has already established harmony with nature and lives in peace with it (justice). *I must turn my dream into fertiliser and water/ and I must bury myself/ for my suppressed people.* The very sound of this poem, as soon as I translated it into English, felt to my mind like the sound of my own life, which I had never felt before while reading poems written in English.

If words make us feel closer to the life we live, so we can relate to them at the level of emotions, then words are doing their job: wiping the layers of ignorance, one at a time, from our consciousness. Translating the life of my people – Dalits – into English, has helped me feel much closer to English as a language of my emotions. This is one of the merits of translation: it introduces you to the world and the world is being newly introduced to you. Translation as a process carries the potential of redefining our imagination of a man, his struggle and his existence in the world.

14. DESASSIMILAR: DECOLONIZING A GRANDDAUGHTER OF ASSIMILADOS

Sandra Tamele

Being a daughter of the 8 of March Generation that built Mozambique post-independence and united the nation, I once failed to grasp the relevance of discussing – today – decolonization, a concept I thought was devoid of meaning in the 21st century. As fate would have it, months after I received the invitation to write this essay, a friend suggested two books that would shake my beliefs and change my initial approach to this piece. I'm at a loss for words to express my delight and surprise when I found Alexandre Pomar's Portuguese translation of *Black Skin, White Masks* (*Pele Negra Máscaras Brancas*, Paisagem, 1975) by Frantz Fanon, recently added to my to-read list, among my parents' old books, confirming once again their past as revolutionaries. A past rich in paradoxes. "White civilization and European culture have imposed an existential deviation on the black [wo]man" Frantz Fanon wrote, and I couldn't agree more. Both my country and I are in our forties. Both of us are doing our best to change how others perceive us, which is often in a detrimental, biased way.

* * *

Portuguese, instead of any of the 41 Mozambican native languages, is my mother tongue. I never gave this much thought until the other black girl in the book club I joined in 2014 asked me what my name was. When I answered, she insisted that she wanted to know my 'African', i.e. 'real', name. It was an awful feeling, standing there in my pantsuit with my relaxed hair, I felt like a pseudo-African next to 'Joy', Nthabiseng, towering over me in her traditional gown and afro.

In my family, Dad is the only one with an 'African' name, Matchovo. That was the name he was given in the spiritual naming ceremony, one that was deemed unsuitable and stripped off him on his first day at school. Aged 11 he needed a new, Christian name, they said. He chose the name Rachid, after the ob/gyn who assisted at his birth, his first of many rebellions against the Portuguese colonial regime.

I was born in Mozambique five years after the declaration of independence, to a southerner, Machangana father who, together with his companions, the proud 'utopia generation', was at 26 deployed to the north of the country as the Principal of the Industrial Training Centre, where he met my mother Abiba, a Kimwani student six years his junior. They were expecting their first born to be a boy, so it took them two weeks to decide to name me Sandra Marília, instead of Ingamo or Cina after my nanas.

My name and accent are a huge giveaway that I'm the grand-daughter of Assimilados.

Assimilado is the term given to African subjects of the colonizing Portuguese Empire from the 1910s to the 1960s, who had reached a level of "civilization", according to Portuguese legal standards, that theoretically qualified them for full rights as Portuguese citizens. While the British and Dutch, for example in South Africa, instituted apartheid, the Portuguese had a different approach to colonialism: to breed with the natives, thus creating the Assimilado status, which is unique to the former Portuguese colonies.

My grandpas were ambitious men who wanted to own land and become someone. To quote Frantz Fanon in *Black Skin, White Masks* (translated by Richard Philcox), "the more the black Antillean assimilates the French language, the whiter he gets – i.e., the closer he comes to becoming a true human being." I think that this is also true for Mozambicans and the Portuguese language and culture, and this seems to have been the driver in my grandfathers' decision to assimilate, and then impose white supremacy, patriarchy, and sexism upon their multiple wives and sons. Both my nanas' lives were hard. I wonder how they remained loving when they were refused an education and forced, at the tender age of 12, to marry and bear children of Assimilados.

Dad's generation was the turning point, guided by the writings of our first President, Samora Machel, who ruled based on a love ethics like the one I read about in *Salvation: Black People and Love* by bell hooks. My parents were the utopia generation; they were communists and socialists. Due to their indoctrination, they broke away from everything, including their religion. Those early years after independence, we weren't even able to worship the gods we used to worship. That generation lost their values and a little of themselves. They dreamed of national unity, to break free from the colonial regime, which had kept the people apart through tribalism. The post independence government, FRELIMO (Mozambique Liberation Front) proclaimed Portuguese as the official language, and it turns out that they did far more to promote the Portuguese language than the Portuguese rules ever did.

Because of this, my generation is also lost. My parents come from different regions and cultural backgrounds, which in theory would make us a multilingual family, but since they did not impart their mother tongues to their children, we don't speak any language except Portuguese. This has continued into the next generation with my nephews and nieces. We do have a very strong oral tradition in Mozambique, but all the oral culture from my grandmother has been lost. She used to gather her grandchildren around the fire to tell us stories and share traditions. I couldn't understand anything; we communicated through gestures and signs and touch.

This absence of a mother tongue left a void inside me that I tried to fill by learning foreign languages. Mom and Dad were both teachers, and they were readers, so books were present in our home, unlike the rest of our neighborhood. Some of those books were in English, I marveled at them, and at the age of 10 I started to teach myself how to read and speak the language. My entire education is from the public school system, which meant I could only choose between French and English as a second language. When I heard that the School of Architecture offered an Italian lecture free of charge, I enrolled immediately. Many years later, I set myself the goal of becoming fluent in German, Swedish, Mandarin, Arabic, Kimwani – Mom's mother tongue – and Mozambican sign language. These remain unaccomplished.

I've been translating since 2002, when I used to moonlight as an interpreter to pay the tuition for my degree in Architecture and Town Planning. I believe that I was fated to fall in love with translation because languages have been present in my life since I was in the womb.

Literary translation is so underrated in Mozambique, that I became the first published native literary translator in 2007 with *Eu não tenho medo* (*I Am Not Scared*), by the award-winning Italian novelist, Niccolò Ammaniti, an author introduced to me by my second Italian lecturer, Antonella De Muti, when she challenged the class to advance in learning the transalpine language through translation. I related to the narrative and made a daily mantra out of the title.

Seven years later there I was, an established translator/interpreter with a growing clientele and bottom line, but the profession's lack of visibility frustrated me. In Mozambique, translators are only put in the limelight if something goes wrong. Some translated literature omits the translator's name altogether. I decided to do something to change that. When I found out that September 30 was International Translation Day (ITD), the idea of an annual commemoration started growing in my mind.

In August 2014, I launched a call for essays titled "Why I Decided To Become a Translator" and posted it at Eduardo Mondlane University. Understandably there were only four or five submissions, but I decided to award the prizes anyway. The following year, I started sooner and this time, instead of an essay, I challenged the students to translate literature, just as my teacher once challenged me. I had recently read *Broken Glass*, Ellen Stevenson's translation of Alain Mabanckou's *Verre Cassé* and it seemed a good fit, thus the first chapter of the novel became the source text for what would be the first edition of the annual literary translation competition to celebrate ITD. The highlight of the competition is the award ceremony, which is held on or around September 30, at which a dramatic adaptation of the translated stories is shared with the audience. The event has earned the reputation of being the most innovative and inclusive cultural initiative with its dramatized readings by local young drama groups, and live sign language interpretation. In 2018, the organization and the drama groups worked together to present the first silent drama presentation of

Marguerite Abouet's *Akissi: ataque de chats*, making history as the first event bridging all the language gaps in this town. The competition is now in its eighth edition, with an unprecedented 250 entries, and has been awarded the 2021 International Excellence Award by the London Book Fair.

I was happy that I had started translating literature again and was promoting the profession among the youth, but three years into the initiative, I had still not been able to get the stories published. "Who is Alain Mabanckou?" asked the publishers I approached. "You not knowing who he is, is precisely the reason I'm translating his work, to make him known in Mozambique too." I replied to no avail.

This was when the competition evolved into a publishing company, Trinta Zero Nove (30.09), after ITD, dedicated to publishing authors from around the globe in translation in Mozambique. Languages such as Macua and Changana have significant numbers of speakers in Mozambique, but others are spoken only by 1% of the population. All those languages and their traditions are dying, to our great loss. 30.09 strives to make books affordable and accessible to all, but selling books in Mozambique is an uphill battle, 39% of our population are functionally illiterate. We run one of the few online bookshops in the country, going online to try and sell our books countrywide. Mozambique runs 2,500 kilometers north to south and 400 kilometers east to west, though the population is concentrated in Maputo, Beira, Nampula, and then scattered through many villages without electricity or water – and 30.09 aims to reach the readers there. The start-up publisher invested in translating into the main Bantu languages, Macua, Sena, and Changana, which are mutually intelligible with the other 41 languages spoken in the Northern, Central and Southern regions. I am often the bridge translator. I not only translate from English and Italian, I work with translators from other languages, such as Ruth Ahmedzai Kemp who is translating from Arabic, so I'm bringing in many languages. The works are translated into English, I translate them into Portuguese and then they are translated into Mozambican languages. There are many bridges to cross, like a relay. 30.09 has also been a pioneer in reintroducing audiobooks to readers, a strategy that we hope will earn us more readers by including people with no or low literacy, and the blind.

The other challenges 30.09 faces are the lack of a strong distribution network, and the too few and often unreliable booksellers that fail to pay for the books sold on consignment. Thus, the next step in the start-up's business plan is to open a brick-and-mortar bookshop. One that will also cater to low-income readers by running a parallel library service. I envision this as a place where women and girls can come, where they can buy, or just sit down and read or listen to books.

This decision was made in 2018, after I moved to Fafetine, a small fishing and farming village on the banks of the Komati River in Marracuene. The district of 262,000 people has a fair number of schools, but no bookshop and library, or place where children can access books, knowledge, and inspiration. The children are excited when I show them illustrated books or do storytelling in their language, Ronga, and women who can't read or write are happy to learn that they can listen to audiobooks.

Financial support for cultural initiatives like mine remains an unmet need. The Ministry of Culture here knows about our work but does little to support the initiatives. There are international funding mechanisms available, on paper. But when the funders come, they are only interested in holding a workshop and taking a picture. They focus on entrepreneurship, helping us to design a business plan for example, but it ends there. We know how to run a business, what we need is seed capital. Five thousand euros isn't enough to start a publishing company. Publishing is all about scale, the more books you print, the more affordable they become to readers, thus resulting in higher sales. But translation is a compounding factor, because it increases the cost of publishing a book. Funds are also needed to generate more jobs – at the moment I'm wearing too many hats, I do the quality control of all the books, the translation, the managing. I design logos and attend meetings. I don't want to do this alone, but people are understandably worried about earning their bread, and I don't expect anyone to work pro bono, like I often have to. But I don't have the funds to pay full-time staff. If I want to create jobs, if I want to train people, I have to tap into the funding that would be available to someone like me, if I were white and lived in Europe.

Unfortunately, when funding schemes for culture are available they are preferentially awarded on the basis of skin color, which maintains the status quo of white supremacy. It is assumed that white people are the writers, the translators, the intellectuals – that they hold the key to knowledge. We are the first generation of intellectuals. Prior to our independence, most black people were not allowed to study past 6th grade; only Assimilados were able to further their studies in colonial times. Today, we are witnessing the first generation of black people who have a degree; I'm the first person in my family with an MA. So we have the role of planting a seed for the coming generations.

Reflecting on reading Fanon and hooks, and the concept of decolonized minds, however, I came to think that decolonizing translation is not only about these practical aspects, it is also necessary to decolonize the translator as a person. A personal decolonization is needed through the de-assimilation of both the Portuguese language and culture, breaking free of the established color caste system, the decolonization of knowledge, along with south-north circulation of literature.

DE-ASSIMILATING THE PORTUGUESE LANGUAGE AND CULTURE

My translation of Ammaniti was published with a grant from the Italian Foreign Affairs Ministry, which dictated (or rather, it was 'suggested' by my teacher and the cultural attaché), that it should be readable across the Portuguese-speaking African countries (PALOP). Therefore, I should strictly use Portuguese from Portugal, the metropolitan matrix she deemed superior to the colonized variants. The innocence of youth coupled with my gratitude for the funding guided my choice of words when translating the novel. I did not question the guideline, thus my translation resembled that of a native European Portuguese translator. A white mask I used to pride myself on wearing, until repetitive remarks like "If I heard you with my eyes shut, I'd suppose I was talking to a white woman" by strangers and friends alike, left a sour taste in my mouth. I'm aware of the amount of work required to change the colonial mindset of many Mozambicans that anything intellectual and progressive must originate in the West.

Ten years later, I re-edited this translation and published it under Editora Trinta Zero Nove. I unconsciously unmasked my translation. Now the novel is Mozambican too, it speaks to readers differently, showing that we Mozambicans made Portuguese our own, like other African nations did to English or French. To the delight of our readers, the characters in *Eu não tenho medo* now play zoto instead of apanhada, and ride the machimbombo, instead of autocarro, to the nearest village. They are maningue adventurous, cycling in their burras though the grain fields.

BREAKING FREE FROM THE COLOR CASTE SYSTEM

I recently translated two projects that made me think about the internalized color caste system among black individuals in Mozambique. The first was a young Angolan writer's debut novel. The book was on my to-read list because I loved the Portuguese title, *Badass Babe,* in a free translation, and the cover artwork. I was excited with the invitation to work on the project; I knew very little about Angolan literature and was delighted that the writer I was translating was female. My happiness was short-lived. When I started working on the project, I found she had used a lot of Kimbundu words and idioms throughout the novel that both the editor and I read as inauthentic. We later found out that she doesn't speak the language at all, that she emigrated to Portugal at a very young age at the time of the independence war, and that she is mixed-race.

I was brought up in what I believed was a rainbow nation, free of any remnants of colonial segregation. I went to school with children of all races and colors, but at the same time, I grew up in an environment that perpetuated stereotypes and held prejudices against mulattos regarding their character and suitability for certain professions. Were these prejudices so internalized that they affected how I approached the author, her writing, and my translation? And the way the writer being mulatto – read whiter – initially treated me with some contempt and superiority? Not to mention the characters of color, who were caricatured as having no table manners, with little command of the colonial language and uncivilized habits. Did my bias affect the way I read her use of Kimbundu words, mistaking it for an attempt to Africanize a narrative to suit European tastes?

These prejudices are evident in day-to-day interactions too. I remember, one day I was chatting about musical preferences with a classmate at architecture school who was black, dark complexioned. Upon learning that I was dating a white man, he boasted that he listened exclusively to white musicians while I, come to think of it, listened only to black singers. He ended up marrying a white Italian woman who bore him mixed children, thus whitening his offspring and escaping the mulatto prejudice that will weigh on mine.

I then came to translate an illustrated story about a little girl who is dark as midnight and dreams of having a lighter complexion. The darker [than me] black author demanded a black translator and a black narrator for this children's literature project. At one point, I had to present photographic evidence of my blackness to her agents. I felt like an impostor. I wondered if I'd make the cut. How would I, often praised for having the choice of passing within reach, be seen by the author? Was she more mature than me in her understanding and upholding of Negritude?

DECOLONIZATION: CIRCULATION OF KNOWLEDGE

Recently, while attending the Cairo Book Fair, a Belgian literary agent put into words a concern of mine: the need for Western publishers and agents to understand that the literary reality of Africa is different. It is not just a question of asking for better deals, but of understanding that print runs are small, selling prices lower due to the weak purchasing power of the masses. She urged peers to accept token advances, and to adapt their sales reporting and royalty payment expectations considering the different banking policies that may make it more difficult to process transactions from Africa into the West.

There is also an internalized requirement by European institutions that fund literary and cultural projects that African applicants should cluster to be eligible to a fraction of funding available to single European individuals or entities (such as the EU's PROCULTURA, which requires applicants from the PALOP to form regional Consortiums, as opposed to its Central Europe grants of hundreds of thousands of euros to individuals).

In the process of establishing the first bookshop and library in my district, I have reached out to many charities that assist similar initiatives or provide books. They claim that they are all active in Mozambique's neighboring, English-speaking countries, forgetting that we too are part of the Commonwealth. Our speaking Portuguese should not constitute a barrier. Apparently, colonial-era maps still determine the limits of their intervention. A glance at a map of Africa will show that our borders are the product of colonialism. Johannesburg is just 300 kilometers and a six-hour drive away, but the reality is that the books published there will never make it to Mozambique. Knowledge doesn't cross borders. Now we've gone digital, why are those borders still so powerful that knowledge is not circulating? I wonder.

In addition to making rights available to the South, it is paramount that the West is open to publishing African voices. In the last few years, I have followed a vibrant generation of Mozambican writers and their publications. During this time, I read an article in CIOL's magazine *The Linguist* on the need and acceptability of bilingual translation, which gave me a boost to attempt translating prose and complete the translation of three poetry books: Hélder Faife's *DEsIGNS*, quickly followed by Mbate Pedro's *Voids* and Rogério Manjate's *Scar Incarnate.*

Bilingual translation, i. e. translation into and out of one's mother tongue, is still a controversial issue – particularly when translating poetry and trying to remain true to its structure, rhythm, and form – but one that cannot be brushed off easily, especially coming from a country that is a Portuguese-speaking island surrounded by an English-speaking community into which it tries to integrate, at least in theory. In reality, there is no circulation or cross distribution of books and literature within the region, nor overseas to the UK and US.

I had high hopes when a selection of poems from the three projects were featured in *Words Without Borders*' April 2019 issue and later pitched to a few publishers from South Africa, the US, and the UK. But I was told by these publishers that poetry was a hard sell, that they had a different editorial line and at the time were not looking for debut voices from Mozambique.

Literary translation is still underrated in Mozambique, and most writers, who paradoxically draw inspiration from authors they read in translation, do not share my view that translation can be a tool to find and perfect one's voice and writing. Nor do they share my view that it has a huge potential to impact and diversify the Mozambican literary tradition, as well as to bring gender and racial equality to publishing when almost every literary prize in Mozambique has been first awarded to white men and, despite the growing number of native, black winners, remain cis male centered.

"Black women face black problems and women problems," I once read. Well, I'm black and I'm a woman, and this doomed my pursuit of a career in architecture, scuttled by employers' sexist and racist perceptions and resulting objectification. But I have chosen a different path now, and this work is too important to me to give up.

15. TRANSLATION FOR THE QUAINT BUT INCOMPREHENSIBLE IN *PARSETREEFORESTFIRE*

Hamid Roslan

(Note: The editors who worked with me on this essay had different views as to how much context was required to understand it. There was one version that proposed providing more of the context upfront, for readers who might be unfamiliar with Singapore literature, or Singapore in general. Here's my dangerous compromise to that suggestion. My essay emerges from Singapore, a tiny nation-state with four official languages: English, Chinese, Malay, and Tamil; and a pesky English-based creole called 'Singlish' that scavenges scraps of grammar, syntax, and vocabulary from these official languages. A country with multiple tongues is also, therefore, a country with a multilingual literary tradition. I wrote my book in this thick linguistic mélange. My book, parsetreeforestfire, is courageously (or naïvely) parochial in its refusal to be legible for an English-speaking/dominant readership that has no knowledge of Singaporean culture and politics—much less of Southeast Asia, a geographical region better known for its travel destinations than its contribution to world literature. If you find yourself confused or perturbed by what appears to be a hazy entrance into this essay, please do not give up. Persist through the very linguistic environment that precipitated the book. You'll find your footing eventually, as is the case with any journey into a space that has flourished before your arrival.)

In July 2019, Ethos Books launched my debut book of bilingual Singlish and English poetry, *parsetreeforestfire*, at Grassroots Book Room, a bookstore located on the ground floor of a conserved shophouse along Bukit Pasoh Road in Singapore. As someone who is recognised as being ethnically Malay, and comfortable speaking English and Malay, I found it strange that the book was to be launched on a street that housed both traditional Chinese clan associations and neocolonial social clubs, and whose name I would only learn later was a corruption of the Malay word for 'vase', '*pasu*'. As outside, so within: Grassroots Book Room sold mainly Chinese-language books and other paraphernalia. Everything was in a script I could only half-recognise, from the smattering of Chinese I retained years after an attempt to pick up the language taught to the majority of Singaporeans. The audience who turned up that day were mainly Chinese Singaporeans. Though anyone could walk into Grassroots Book Room and purchase a book, it wasn't a space that made itself immediately available to a person of my linguistic background. The surrounding location was also close to Singapore's own Chinatown. The nearest establishments that consciously catered to a non-Chinese clientele were located a few streets away, at Singapore General Hospital. At least I got my choice of moderator: the well-respected figure of Singaporean letters Alfian Sa'at. He and I joked about being surrounded by all that had escaped us yet again as the audience settled themselves into the chairs before us. Two Malay people on an island of Chineseness. At least we all spoke English.

* * *

At the time, I called *parsetreeforestfire* a bilingual book of Singlish and English poetry. Here's the marketing copy, which I crafted: *parsetreeforestfire: a bilingual book of poetry in which poems in Singlish occupy one side of the book, and poems in English occupy the other. Conventionally such a book functions as a way for a person to learn a new language, but it remains to be seen if translation has successfully occurred, or if the book even intends to teach any reader how to speak either language.* A poet who read an earlier version of the manuscript during Sing Lit Station's Manuscript Bootcamp would call my poems Singlish poems and their English *transcreations*. Not translations. Transcreation is a local term for a poem written by an author who is not Singaporean, and in some cases, has English as a second, even third language. To ease their entry into the circles of Singaporean literary life, another author—often a poet—would take on the role of translating and editing first drafts of these poems, in conversation with the non-Singaporean author. The result is finely wrought, but also haunted by a Singaporean sensibility, hovering on the margins of the page. It is a precarious compact between two people of diverging circumstance and power but who for various reasons occupy the same island. I felt in the kernel of that remark the implication that I was, in Don Mee Choi's formulation in her essay *Translation is a Mode=Translation is an Anti-Neo-colonial Mode*, 'speaking as a twin'—except I had no good reason to do so. Wasn't I Singaporean? Was English inadequate? Was *my* English inadequate? Something was not quite right.

★ ★ ★

The intrepid reader expecting *parsetreeforestfire* to be a breezy read will be disappointed to find that the book doesn't guide its readers. The book's cover merely repeats the title vertically, making the reader awkwardly tilt their head sideways to read it. The contents page shows that each section in the book is titled after a word that makes up the title: 'parse', 'tree', 'forest', and 'fire'. In 'parse' and 'tree', poems are untitled and exist only in pairs by virtue of the book's verso-recto format: Singlish on one side, and English on the other, in accordance with its self-proclaimed bilingualism. Upon reading the first poem-pair, the reader will realise that the English poem doesn't actually translate the Singlish. Both poems address an anxiety about representing language in a standardised format, but each poem uses different techniques—the Singlish drawing upon cultural and historical references familiar to Singaporeans; the English opting instead for an unusual accretion of synonyms that veer dangerously close to nonsense. Translation only *seems* to have occurred, but the reader has to decide if it is present and successful, since the author-translator is absent:

Write statement for what? If write must sign. Must appear on TV say sorry sorry	*An axiom accents assumption, lends credence*
Ah Kong. Sotong. You think if you write you must follow other people. If they	*to charred dust, dialect administration &... basis to provide a blustering planet with*
makan potato you swallow starch—huh I cannot use starch? Should I cave in	*conventional approach: bitten apple, jargon arrangement doctrines, supplication*

to your force of habit, sight scanning
line swooning over turns & tricks?

Ok. Statement is metaphor for tuition,
for textbook, for discount sticker label

at Fairprice. Use your brain. If got formula
we sure export lah bodoh. Kan dah kena

bodoh. Don't ask me for footnote. When
you read English you look up. They always

tell you speak up boy speak up
now I speak up.

of prose-ethics, parching creation in
advance
& searing guidelines to the sound of a

found nation—in short...fundamentally
bankrolled & broiled with cooking method

to roast code, styled speech for vocabulary
regulation, not forgetting voicing
universes,

entrusting seething vale to word-truth &
shrivelled big blue marbles, loaning canon

to argot to world with protocol to
communicate
—which is to say: criterion, or rule, or

plunging dictum to conversation...or
dogma, diction or to
stake into discursive form a welt:
doublespeak.

The hijinks continue in 'forest', a series of numbered statements with accompanying footnotes that irresponsibly translate the text further up the page. In fact, the footnote of statement 2 in 'forest' explicitly *disagrees* with the premises set up in the section, potentially undermining the entire thrust of a quarter of the book:

> *2. This language is faulty for this present speaker because every time a word is spoken by this present speaker, that word, by its intent to speak as something otherwise, against, as deviating from a presupposed mean, is circumscribed to only one type of enunciation: I am not.*[2]
>
> [2]*Actually this one not my problem. I not this ang moh lang. This ang moh lang say when he talk he always must but actually is not like this one is actually like that. I where got I am not I am not problem. Where got problem want to say something. No need to say like this not like that. Just redirect & divert lah.*

Finally, in 'fire', the bifurcation that haunts the book is solved—visually, at least. Singlish and English are sutured into six pages of sentence fragments marshalled into a single column that ends in a sputter:

> *throat, securing future: YANG DI-*
> *PERTUAN NEGARA a mat*
> *significant, I'm possible, never*
> *again on seas, & final-ly-ly-ly-ly-ly*
> *ly ly ly ly ly ly ly ly ly ly ly ly ly ly*
> *ly ly ly ly ly ly ly ly ly ly ly ly*

The title on the cover doubling up as section titles; poetry appearing to float in a soup of its own meaning; and language-puzzle poetry that requires the reader's active decoding. The reader moves from one section to another and tries to make sense of a book that is obviously structured but will receive no indication that what they understand is the intended message. It is also assumed that the reader of *parsetreeforestfire* understands both Singlish and English. For those who only have knowledge of either language used, their reading experience would be drastically different. If one's linguistic make-up determines one's level of access to *parsetreeforestfire*, a degree of obliqueness is to be expected.

* * *

Reviewer and poet Jerome Lim would report in the *Quarterly Literary Review Singapore* a year after the book's publication that 'most people [he] surveyed told [him] they "especially liked the Singlish parts" over the "complicated parts".' 'Complicated' here surely a misnomer for the English that was written in an unnecessarily convoluted and excessively heightened manner. Common opinion was coalescing in that same direction: retired National University of Singapore professor Dr Ismail Talib offers a correction to my marketing copy in his round up of Singapore literature titles published in the same year in *The Journal of Commonwealth Literature*: 'bi-dialectal, not bilingual', as if to call my bluff. Oddly enough, no Singaporeans have commented that the *Singlish* is inaccessible. Certainly, it was a Singlish foreign to even a

Singaporean's ear. Even if the English-based creole was hewed from the Chinese, Malay and English, its texture didn't favour an audience with receptive bilingualism in either language. Some of the language is drawn from everyday speech. 'Due to unforeseen circumstances', used in a poem in 'parse', is a phrase commonly used in Singapore to announce unexpected changes at an event without divulging the reasons for those changes, a silence all too familiar to those who parry with Singaporean institutions and bureaucracies. Other phrases are only accessible to readers with a more than rudimentary grasp of the languages used in *parsetreeforestfire*. The word 'sotong', used in 'write statement for what', the first poem in *parsetreeforestfire*, is a Malay word meaning 'squid', but has a particular valence in Singlish as the image of someone who is dim-witted or gullible. An associated metaphor would be 'blur sotong'. On the other hand, the Malay phrase 'anjing tengok pantat' in 'we are majulah' would be translated as 'a dog looking at its own ass', but would only mean something if you understand Malay, since it has no specific valence as an image in Singlish. Chinese phrases used, though rudimentary and common to everyday speech, are similarly inaccessible to the Singaporean who is bilingual in English and a non-Mandarin language. For this reason, dictionaries, Google Translate, or one's token ethnic friend are unspoken, mandatory secondary resources for one's reading of *parsetreeforestfire*, if one was being sincere; or optional, if one wishes to skim to the last page. So many demands on the reader: to know multiple languages and cultural contexts; and to possess the knack of code-switching into the appropriate language, register of language, *and* cultural context with little prompting. Who was I writing or 'translating' for, then, if there was to be no objective location within the book to which a reader could orientate themselves? Conventional wisdom dictates that we should be able to comfortably extract the resources that a bilingual book, or any translation, offers to us. One usually builds that bridge of comprehension by translating that which deserves a *wider* audience, not a narrower one. It seems like I was going in the wrong direction. 'In [*parsetreeforestfire*]', writes Isabelle Lim in the *Cha Review of Books and Films*, 'translation presents then yet another complicating node in the already vexed relation between word and meaning'.

* * *

Perhaps I was wrong to stage what was plainly a faithless act of translation. Some readers have asked which arrived first—the English, or the Singlish—but the book didn't start out as a manuscript sliced into two halves that were then stitched together. The truth was much simpler: I started writing the Singlish poems first. I was in London in 2016, nursing my self-exile from Singapore at the School of Oriental and African Studies via a study abroad programme, that rite-of-passage available to Singaporean undergraduate students who were desperate to leave the country without cutting ties to it. The poems arrived shortly after, on a Facebook group that was then growing in popularity for its annual Singapore Poetry Writing Month (SingPoWriMo) challenge. Every April, hundreds of poets would respond to daily prompts on the group page. I wrote my first English poem and published it on that page. My first Singlish poems too. People warmed towards the English poems but loved the Singlish ones even more. I loved that people loved them. In the heart of Empire, I saw the outline of an escape hatch out of Anglomania. It was in the shape of its poorer English cousin. So, I pushed. I proposed a book of Singlish poems to my university as the culmination of my undergraduate education at Yale-NUS College. The then-untitled manuscript would be a riposte to my miseducation in Anglophone Singaporean society, written by someone who had grown up in Singlish and Malay, but was later forcibly introduced to the world in English. Singlish poems for an undergraduate degree taught in English. The university accepted my proposal—and promptly assigned me to a non-Singaporean advisor, Lawrence Lacambra Ypil. He could not speak any Singlish. What then, if not to begin translating my Singlish poems for that grading, English-educated audience?

* * *

I suspect that how Singaporean readers have approached my book and their affront at seeing my attempts at 'translation' have unintentionally revealed their biases towards official languages, and even other unofficial languages used in everyday speech. What is acceptable: that two languages must exist in separate and equivalent registers to be considered translatable in either direction. Less acceptable: that the whole range of registers accompanying each language, and the daily movements between those languages—a fact of life in a multilingual nation like Singapore—could also be recognised as genuine attempts at translation. It seems strange to question something that works, until one is made to understand the shape of one's code-switching and the beliefs that underlie it. Stranger still is the fact that Singaporeans are calibrated to respond to issues of race and religion with sensitivity and trepidation, but fail to question the languages they speak, why they have come to those languages and not others, and the daily linguistic commute between them.

⋆ ⋆ ⋆

Singapore is usually advertised as a multilingual country. An island-nation at the bottom of the Straits of Malacca, along one of the busiest sea trade routes in the world, it is home to four official languages: English, Chinese, Malay and Tamil, corresponding to its dominant communities: the Chinese, the Malays, the Indians, and 'Others' for everyone else. Malay is the national language for historical and political reasons, Singapore being a country nestled in the heart of the Malay-speaking world. English is the de facto bridging language because it is seen as a neutral, non-native language seemingly free of political valence. Chinese is an unofficial second by virtue of the size of its community. Signs in Singapore are translated into the four official languages; so are government notices and correspondences. Public free-to-air media exists in the four languages. Translation appears to exist on the streets, on paper, and in Singaporean mouths. Code-switching is not an alien concept; daily acts of translation take place. For a country that would almost certainly rely on translation to galvanise its multilingual society, there are, strangely, no government pronouncements on what translation should mean. What is available instead is the simplest desire, in the highest offices, for every citizen to speak at least two languages: English, for commerce, and a vernacular language or 'mother tongue'

(Chinese, Malay, or Tamil), for the transmission of cultural values. A buoy in a sea of internationalism tying untethered citizens to their respective parent cultures. It turns out Don Mee Choi was right: we were meant to speak as twins. Two languages in one body; two registers evenly split down the middle. There is to be no intermingling, linguistically speaking, between the public square and the private sphere. The 'four' communities in Singapore use a 'neutral' English as a bridging language, carefully ferrying their cultures, beliefs, and values across two separate rooms of the same mind.

★ ★ ★

There are problems with such a gross generalisation of languages. 'Mother tongue' is really a shorthand for language(s) that could comfortably encompass the major ethnic groups in Singapore, even if Singaporean Indians speak other languages besides Tamil and Singaporean Chinese speak other dialects than Mandarin—to say little of the other unofficial languages spoken on the island by all its inhabitants. The proximity of many disparate languages would later give rise to Singlish, that bogeyman of language in Singapore, doomed to continuous vilification. In his 1999 National Day Rally speech, then Prime-Minister Goh Chok Tong warned that the use of Singlish would leave Singapore 'quaint but incomprehensible' (I would later include the phrase as a dedication in *parsetreeforestfire*). No use building that bridge of comprehension amongst disparate communities if it is to end at the border. English, and only English, could be the reliable ferryman. If Singlish could enjoy notoriety in everyday, casual settings, it had to mask itself with standard English in official ones. After all, Singaporeans must communicate effectively to remain economically competitive and to be understood by other Singaporeans and English speakers around the world. There has been little change in this official stance: in 2016, Singaporean poet and literary critic Dr Gwee Li Sui wrote the *New York Times* op-ed *Do You Speak Singlish?* and was rebuffed by the press secretary of Singapore's Prime Minister Lee Hsien Loong for paying short thrift to the importance of speaking good English.

* * *

It is in the soil of the everyday, then, that Singlish is allowed to blossom as an unofficial marker of national identity. Phrases are commodified as advertising copy on food packaging, and billboards, and contemporary novelists rely on the creole to add texture to the dialogue and overall sound of their novels—Cheryl Lu-Lien Tan's *Sarong Party Girls* and Kevin Kwan's *Crazy Rich Asians* being its most commercially successful examples to date. (Philip Holden has done a wonderful job of drawing out the parameters for how other poets, playwrights, and novelists have used the patois in their writing in his essay *Always Already Translated: Questions of Language in Singapore Literature*, published in *Asymptote's* January 2017 issue.)

For a country with less than a century of contemporary history, and with much of its multicultural diversity drawn from parent cultures located elsewhere, Singlish, in its implicit role as an idiosyncratic blip in an otherwise highly regulated nation-state, is something that could only arise in Singapore. But this is only partially true: Singlish is notoriously context-dependent, relying on the languages shared between the participants of a conversation which uses the creole. There are, therefore, *multiple* Singlish-es, each incorporating its own mix of English, Chinese, Malay and Tamil. The Singlish in Cheryl Tan and Kevin Kwan's novels use a register of Singlish that incorporates more Mandarin and its dialects. This is a Singlish that is more easily understood and commodifiable to Singaporeans (and non-Singaporeans) because they understand, or at least recognise the languages being used. Singlish-es that incorporate Malay or Tamil are less legible since fewer people in the English-speaking world are aware that such languages even exist. In any case, my point here is that there is no 'neutral' Singlish that can comfortably map onto a multilingual Singaporean identity, since each person's linguistic heritage differs according to the communities they belong to, and what languages are spoken by those communities. Not for want of trying: earlier publications, such as *The Coxford Singlish Dictionary*, have attempted to 'translate' Singlish as a gift of self-representation within the public square to other Singaporeans who are told that Singlish is simply bad English; later ones, such as Dr

Gwee's *Spiaking Singlish*, and his Singlish translations of well-known texts (Saint-Exupéry's *Le Petit Prince* (*The Leeter Tunku*) and Beatrix Potter's *The Tale of Peter Rabbit* (*The Tale of Peter Labbit*)), operate under the same rubric in their attempts to prove that Singlish could be trained to *think*. *parsetreeforestfire* differs from this in that it eschews conventional ideas about translation by exploiting Singlish's context-dependence. Meaning emerges from the layering of multiple languages and cultural contexts. The resulting text would be rich and capable of accepting multiple, even contradictory interpretations depending on the languages that the reader knows. Looking back, I can now recognise that I was inspired not by earlier Singaporean print literature, but Singaporean plays, such as Paul Rae's *National Language Class* and Kuo Pao Kun's *Mama Looking for her Cat*. These plays present situations where languages exist on an equal footing, partial understanding is expected, and meaning emerges through juxtaposition, inference, and negative space. I decided then that if any translation were to occur in *parsetreeforestfire*, it would not be in service of becoming legible to an Anglophone audience. My 'translations' would not privilege any of the languages I knew. Everyone would have to begin from different linguistic positions.

* * *

I set some simple rules for myself when I wrote *parsetreeforestfire*. Firstly, if conventional translation believed in its possibility to provide a transparent window into another cultural context, I would prevent *parsetreeforestfire* from clarifying any of its content through paratexts such as footnotes, endnotes, glossaries or prefaces. *parsetreeforestfire*, therefore, contains no tools for the reader to clarify their understanding of what they read. Everything 'foreign' would depend on whatever proclivities the reader already had prior to their encountering the book, and not by paratext that would purport to tell the entire truth of the book. Secondly, I ensured that every 'poem' in the book could only be read in relation to another i.e. that each poem could only make sense in the context of its verso- or recto- twin; sections only made sense when all poem-pairs were related to the word that made up the compound title *parsetreeforestfire*; and the book only made sense as an accretion of its individual units, from poem to poem-pair to section to book. Readers may or may not catch on to the verso-recto format of *parsetreeforestfire*, so I requested my publisher print the section title twice at the start of 'parse', 'tree', and 'forest', to suggest that poems that faced each other were somehow related. The only exception to this was 'fire', which represented to me a frenzied suturing of an otherwise bifurcated voice.

Finally, I focused on ensuring that the aural qualities of the languages I used could provide some deeper, internal coherence as to what they were to mean. Using an invented register of Singlish meant that I was no longer bound to use it to only reflect the conversational texture that Singaporeans would be familiar with. I could instead surprise the reader at the level of both sound and form, whilst using the languages I knew well, and the ones I didn't. It allowed me to take advantage of Singlish's extraordinary effectiveness within a rudimentary syntax to make the poem 'I traffic rule hantam color color wheel', in which words could simply be added onto the end of the pronoun 'I' to become a pseudo compound-noun. I unintentionally released myself from a sanitised, lofty use of Malay and Chinese too. Similarly, the English I used was no longer bound to ensuring that it could speak for the Singlish. It could behave elliptically, gesturing at what the Singlish meant, or responding to it in its own peculiar fashion. A simple example of this would be the poem 'if say red:' in 'tree'. In this poem, each word that in Singlish might have conjured up other connotations appropriate to Singapore's socio-political context was destabilised by phrases that sapped it of such meaning:

If say red: The crisp skin of orchard fruit.

If say white: The powdered heart of Jungfrau.

If say lightning: One thousand two thousand three thousand—

The colours of the Singapore flag are, in fact, the colour of apples and snow. The insignia of the dominant political party in Singapore, the People's Action Party, becomes an instruction to count the number of seconds between what one sees (lightning), and what one will eventually hear (thunder). Causes and effects were expanded, but eventually aligned to the reader, who is the arbiter and final recipient of *parsetreeforestfire* according to their own linguistic proclivities.

* * *

Naturally, I would tell readers that how they approached the book reflected their attitudes towards reading, comprehensibility, expectation, and linguistic ability between the languages they could comfortably and uncomfortably command. None of this should be taken for granted. One is *trained* to read. If you did not like what you read, or felt suitably insulted or powerless with what you were unable to read, then what does that say about your attitude towards books that make themselves unavailable to your gaze? I think this is why people were so confused by *parsetreeforestfire*. It was seemingly the culmination of the worst of Singaporean language policy and translation. It imagined a vision of Singapore in which people were deracinated and disconnected from their 'mother tongues', lost at sea, and so could only use English to communicate with each other; Singlish making its way out from under the bed and into textbooks; and translations behaving badly, in contrast to the neat segregation between languages that people should be encountering in their daily lives. I don't seem to be saying anything new. In one of many biographies published by and about the architect of much of contemporary reality in Singapore, former statesman Lee Kuan Yew reflects on what a bifurcation of languages in the self has meant in *My Bilingual Journey*, a memoir specifically addressing language and language learning in Singapore:

> *Looking back, there have been two milestones in my thinking on bilingualism. The first came in the mid-1970s, when I decided that it was generally not possible for a person to be equally fluent in two languages. Most people can have only one master language – the one he thinks in and processes information with faster than any other. This belief continues to underpin much of Singapore's bilingual policy.*

This would surface years later, when I was asked what I thought of the languages I used. I said that English was the language I used to think, whereas Malay and Singlish were the languages I used to feel. Chinese was a language I had to learn in order to belong. I said the same to an audience who turned up for an Ethos Books' event: *This book is about the languages you know well, the languages you know less of, and the languages you wish you knew better.* And I wished, for a brief moment, to feel like my book and I could also belong to a place like Grassroots Book Room.

* * *

Before the book was published, I was invited to read some of the poems from *parsetreeforestfire* at an independent, non-government funded school in Singapore. Most Singaporeans end up within the public school system, so I found myself in a room of young students who were Singaporeans and non-Singaporeans. It was to be my first semi-public reading of these poems. I read them to a silent room. I was nervous. The teacher who invited me also invited other teachers to sit in for the session. One of them sat at a corner, growing visibly agitated as I read poems that I termed 'translations' of each other. I would later find out that her disdain for my poems was quite strong. She would tell me that what I was doing was wrong, these weren't translations, and that my misuse of language was going to ruin society. She felt insulted that I should feel confident enough to present my work in this way. The discussion I had with the students who attended my reading was less antagonistic. After I read my poems, the students spoke of their own experiences of the languages they knew, and the tug of balancing the languages they could command for the different parts of themselves. There was no compulsion to force these parts to cohere. Languages were allowed to live in bodies without needing to speak for their other inhabitants. In a classroom, beyond the reach of state expectation, and norms for how languages should behave, we found ourselves quaint and comprehensible.

16. WORLDS IN A WORD: LOSS AND TRANSLATION IN KASHMIR

Onaiza Drabu

As someone who draws their primary identity from their ethnicity, Kashmiri, it was a pity that growing up I could never speak the language. Only much later did I come to it, through a lot of luck, a little bit of effort and a rage inside me as a young, idealistic adult coming of age witnessing assaults on her people and culture. Although, for as long as I can recall, without speaking the words, I often took on the tongue in other languages – I borrowed phrases and structures. I took on its convoluted manner of illustration and its visual idioms, rooted in the physical landscape. I let its proverbs, laden with stories of lived experiences, seep into my English. All reminders of where they, and I, come from.

Recently, however, I have noticed that I often feel inadequate in my expression without an emoji. It feels impersonal, almost harsh, to use only words, and archaic to use full sentences when texting. I am unable to recall idioms, often resorting to internet slang and drawing this English into my other tongues. As a consequence, many expressions have slowly fallen out of my vocabulary and my sentences have become shorter, crisper, more hollow. If I were to follow the philosopher Wittgenstein's chain of thought, or Sapir-Whorf's hypothesis, I'd assume that with my shrinking vocabulary, my world has also shrunk around me.[1] Rapid texting, automated responses, and handy urban-dictionary-esque phrases have encouraged clichés, and limited expression for the world at large. Standard formulations, global in nature and laconic in character, are replacing careful constructions – wandering,

[1] Kay, P., & Kempton, W.. *What is the Sapir-Whorf hypothesis?* American Anthropologist, 86(1), 65–79. 1984.

winding, and delightfully delicate. And we as speakers are reduced to babel fish in a sea of nuance-less formalities; sacrificing the beauty of a language at the altar of efficient communication. What then of languages that come loaded with beauty? What also of languages – like Kashmiri – that struggle to live as much as to assert identities; that mark ethnicities; that political movements are tethered to? Does the sacrifice of language mean much more, beyond loss of a way of speech?

* * *

While researching for a book on Kashmiri folklore, I found folk belief and memory alive in the language. This wasn't something I'd paid attention to before, but now I noted down every instance, to build into a dictionary of memory – memory of the imponderabilia that seep into our lives and conversations. Examining it, I saw that what one is taught to classify as folklore here went beyond the idioms and stories I was searching for. Here, in my own culture, I found a way of life living in speech – the culture of people enshrined in the words that make up our language. Some would call it superstition, others a belief system, yet for us it is how we live, or rather how we lived. An ethical system now largely glimpsed through phrases that remain in our speech. Remnants of when 'scientific temper' and 'rationality' hadn't stripped us of the surrender to that which we don't know and a consciousness through which those before us tried to make sense of it.

We say, *Osa Ehsani?*, when asking after someone's health, 'Was there mercy?'. As though there is someone being merciful; as though someone is listening always. Today, we are more likely to use words off the shelf of global speak. *Sorui osa theek*, 'All was okay?', we say. It does what is intended after all – communicates an enquiry of well-being.

Idiom becomes less descriptive as the years go on. We lose the metaphor of body, and the familiar spaces our sentences were set in.

> *Mei chi vanij yiwan phatnas.*
> My heart has come to the point of bursting with longing for you.
> I miss you.

Mei chi vanij chawaan rath.
My heart is drinking blood.
It makes me so angry.

Raat chi kohistanas sumb.
The night is as tall as the peak of Kohistan.
The night is long.

There is a preserve of delicacy in the way we speak Kashmiri. A consciousness of others, alive in the language. The utterance of words that might invoke harm is discouraged. Even in a reprimand, we qualify it as being intended for our ill-wishers – to those who are our enemies.

Dapaan temis aes dushmanan kaambal.
They say, his enemies, had jaundice.
He had jaundice

For recalling a misery from the past, we don't forget the *wo na zahn*, the never again, now never again.

Yeli temis wunzah gai kaambal.
When he, never again, had jaundice.
When he had jaundice.

This sensitivity is not just an embellished figure of speech, but also signals a larger set of ethics and consciousness. Increasingly, I hear people substitute English or Urdu for the vernacular. I find they dismiss 'superstition', and watch idiom slip away in a quest for rationality. What was,

Dapaan, temin aaw ne yeti waar. Asli aeskih na aabedaani.
It is said, they didn't take to this place. Truly their grain and water wasn't destined.

is now,

Tim gayi na adjust *yeti.*

They couldn't adjust here.

The replacement of words is a replacement of emotions and a replacement of ethical and moral frameworks embedded in our everyday communication. Other words, from other worlds, now find a place in ours.

With a few million speakers of the language, in a politically disputed land, holding on to the culture as an ethnic marker against an oppressor is all Kashmiris can do. Faced with a weariness of inaction, and seeking to make their place in the world, the global onslaught on the language and culture could be the cause for the slow transformation of Kashmiri. With a loss of our language, though, if we speak the same tongue as the 'other', who are we and what do we stand for? In this tussle between the global and a local that lulls a diction into sleep by setting words and ethics against each other, how can languages thrive?

* * *

While many languages contend with the question of the global and local, for Kashmiri there are additional layers of complication. Its trajectory has been shaped by relations of power and polarisation. For seven centuries, various non-Kashmiri regimes governing the Kashmiri people, have pushed the language to the realm of the oral and shrunk its usage for little beyond casual conversation. The state uses the languages of rulers – Farsi under the Mughals and Afghans, Urdu under the Dogras, English for the British, and Hindi since last year, now that India is trying to re-write and erase Kashmir's pasts.

Post the partition of India and Pakistan, Kashmir became a hotbed of contestation. As both countries lay claim to the land, they also slowly began to export their culture through vehicles of the state, resistance movements, and religion. Given the years of oppression faced at the hands of rulers, only a handful of Kashmiris were literate – only six percent in the mid-20th century. The majority of Kashmiris remained unlettered in their mother tongue, yet the language and culture thrived in the oral sphere with a healthy dose of subversion. Much like how the remove of Punjabi from colonial institutions allowed for it to thrive in familiar forms,[2] Kashmiri survived in the oral sphere – in conversations and in satire away from the power's ears. This changed post the 1990s when the traditions our words were rooted in were replaced with those alien to us. Writer Farah Bashir, in her memoir of this period, documents lore and lifestyle, stories of faith and healing, ritual and language and writes of how they were erased in a mere decade of conflict. Visible forces changed a culture, almost unnoticed – the preparation for festivals was altered, the character of social gatherings changed, streets and street culture were painted with fear. With the change in life, the vocabulary shifted. Alien physical markers, imposed rituals, and the strange speak of war now found its place amidst us.

Over the past three decades, India's slow but steady imposition on education, culture and life has meant that Urdu and Hindi have throttled Kashmiri as much as global English has. As a counter to the resistance movement of the 1990s, allegiance to India became enforced in schools, in order to 'integrate' and 'assimilate'. A generation of urban Kashmiris were penalised for speaking in Kashmiri at school. Confined to their homes, watching Indian television, they took on Indian culture and language more than ever before. Thinking in Hindustani, translating to Kashmiri – young children unconsciously grew up betraying their tongues, while their parents struggled to live. As families grappled with their world rapidly transforming around them, they neglected to hand down rituals and idioms. When the dust settled, a generation of children couldn't answer back in the language of their ancestors, they hid trauma in this one-sided communication, hearing Kashmiri and answering back in lilted Hindustani.

Who is to think of the violence against our language and the power structures operating our pedagogy, when the streets burn? When families disappear and are exiled; young men killed and tortured; when psychological violence becomes a quotidian reality; when spirits are crushed, it is easy to forget that our language is slowly substituted and tradition wiped out. Each one of us, while complicit, is also equally blameless.

---

[2] Mir, F., *The Social Space of Language: Vernacular Culture in British Colonial Punjab.* Ranikhet, Permanent Black, 2010.

The exodus of Kashmiri Hindus (Pandits) from the region during the onset of the resistance movement led to hundreds of thousands being displaced. They lived in refugee camps as they sought rehabilitation from the Indian government. Three decades on, many of them have taken on the cause of Indian nationalism while still maintaining their Kashmiri identity, with the ferocity of every persecuted minority in diaspora. This stark polarisation doesn't limit itself to politics. In cyberspace, there are two groups that interact in Kashmiri – one that writes Kashmiri in Devanagari script familiar to readers of Hindi and one that writes Kashmiri in Nastaliq script familiar to readers of Farsi. The former the domain of Pandits, the latter, Muslims. For a language beautifully oral, this codification is doing a deliberate disservice. Increasingly, the rift is evident in the way they speak as well. A section of Pandits speak in a way that removes all Farsi from their speech and replaces it with Sanskrit. The idea that Kashmir was a thriving culture that Muslims invaded is pervasive with this group. Groups of Muslims, too, employ Arabic derivatives and the metaphor of religion in conversation. In the 1990s, the resistance movement had a markedly Islamic identity that has since continued; a resistance against a *kaafir* (infidel), Hindu-dominated India, its discourse peppered with Islamic vocabulary.

The more the political stances of Kashmiri Pandits and Kashmiri Muslims diverge, the more their speech does too. Each has subgroups that take on this re-writing of history as a cause – righting the wrongs of a history where all sides have been treated unfairly by a series of outside oppressors. As they do this, bystanders like me watch on, neglecting our language and letting it wilt and morph into a grotesque tribute to larger causes. Each cause shifting goalposts to an imagined 'authenticity' and in the process deriving entirely new tongues, mutually unintelligible to the two groups, whose almost indistinguishable ethnicity is tethered to a common tongue. In the midst of all this bickering, they're losing what binds them together.

Both sides are oppressed in their own way, trying to assert control over whatever they can. One faced with the trauma of a loss of homes, the other faced with threats to life every day – both helpless. Both use language and translation to serve what they think is an end. What can we say about these processes of translating a world, as they slowly change the fabric of our society?

★ ★ ★

Translators often invoke the cliché of being traitors to tongues when translating texts. '*Traduttore, traditore*', the Italian saying goes, 'translator, traitor'. Gregory Rabassa begins his memoir by examining this treason[3]. As speakers, we don't pay much attention to the betrayals of translation that we bring into everyday speech. We don't notice the shame associated with speaking a tongue in the presence of power. How we shrivel our tongues, and force the words to come out in the language of the powerful. We don't notice the disdain of 'superstition', the perceived superiority of rationality, and the self-censoring that ensues, cleansing our sentences of imagery of the other world. Our everyday tongue is slowly becoming globalised, bereft of the idiom that makes it aesthetically beautiful. We also don't notice what agendas we bring into our speech. What have we taken on and what have we forgotten? Our tongue, the very marker of who we are and what has kept us together and guarded us from our outside, is being used to polarise from within. In the process, it is also being lost – an unconscious loss for those that stand proudly guarding their home.

Where then should one turn to revive language, to relearn idiom? To literature, perhaps. But what of a language that lacks a repertoire of literature and ethical codes in writing, one that exists primarily in oral form? A mere twelve or thirteen novels are known to have been written in Kashmiri. There are short stories, but pitifully few. Its orality lent itself to rich poetry, but processes of creation are increasingly moving to other languages. Stories, songs, drama and proverbs are where the richness of Kashmiri lies, and if the language is shorn of these, how can oral literature survive?

Asav ne te lasav kith paeth

---

[3] Rabassa, G. *If this be Treason: Translation and its Dyscontents: a Memoir.* New Directions Publishing, 2005

If we don't laugh, how can we live?

An poshi teli,
Yeli van poshi
Food will thrive only
Till the woods survive

For a people facing a new calamity every generation, wise aphorisms pass down the generations as oral literature. Into these are packed ethical and moral codes – a need for resilience; environmental consciousness; affirmations of faith. It is also here that testimonies of lives of generations of women exist; women who embody these ethics, and own this language. Do we, ourselves, accord these the respect we would 'traditional literature'? Why did I go looking for novels in the first place – a genre so alien there isn't even a word for it in the language?

* * *

Famed Kaṣhmiri writer Akhtar Mohiuddin wrote in Urdu, won accolades across the years and only much later switched to writing in Kashmiri. He was afraid, he wrote, and wondered whether 'the Kashmiri language (would) be able to bear the weight of (his) emotions?[4]' To think that of one's first language is telling – there is little wonder few contemporary writers produce in Kashmiri.

Kashmir is reliant on the thriving publishing industry of a nation that has at its best been unfair to our people and at worst, an occupier. Articulations of occupation and even oppression are carefully edited and omitted from social media and in print. Kashmir, they say, is the litmus test of Indian liberals, and you see, veiled in their sympathy, claims to our land, our history and our language. They insist on translating us as a part of their national languages, in unionist anthologies, where Kashmir is just another feather in India's cap of diversity.

The choice of what gets published and how it is framed is not ours. Choosing what is translated from a particular language frames its

[4] Mohiuddin, A. *The World and A Tale*. Translated by O. Drabu. Asymptote Journal. 2021. Link: https://www.asymptotejournal.com/nonfiction/the-world-and-a-tale-akhtar-mohiuddin/

discourse. Verses on nature, love and spirituality are what one finds on bookshelves from Kashmir; not short stories set in the militancy, or during the time of partition; not radio plays, zeitgeists of the 70s and 80s; not manifestos, periodicals and pamphlets from the mid 20th century. The language is relegated to the realm of the exotic. Even there, poetry today deemed incendiary by the ruling dispensation, odes to a poet's *watan* – his country, are edited in translation; censored and translated as homeland or home, cleansing it of its nationalist overtones. A fair warning for the observant should be the case of Urdu – a tongue of thriving literature and discourse that has now largely been reduced to a token language of love poetry and floral flippancy.

Meanwhile, Kashmir's local publishing industry functions as an old-boys club. Many books are mere exercises in vanity, given the economics involved. An award-winning young Kashmiri writer had to self-publish and plead with bookstores to stock her work. Years later, those copies still lie on the shelf, largely untouched. Many young writers take to self-publishing rather than navigate the cobwebs of censorship and editing. There is little funding for literature, let alone literature in translation. When patronage is there, from the very state you resist; obsequiousness in word is expected and dissent punished. How can literature be produced when the readership is non-existent and engagement with texts doesn't move beyond restricted circles? Barring a few well done translations, the shame, the disdain and the lack of effort is visible also in the literary translations from Kashmiri to English. Those trained, don't translate enough, and even those who do, do it with a sense of duty sans the attentiveness the act demands. The translator, shy to carry the nuance of a lived experience, often ends up betraying the character of the text and subsequently of the language, and of words that conjure up a world. An ethical system lies lost in translation.

Threatened with erasure, both cultural and linguistic, the act of translating to and from the language and reading more in it, are all forms of activism. Simple articulations in our own tongue, and fearless interpretations, without the pressure to make it fit an audience's sensibilities, are acts of an activist. Isn't the reclamation of vocabulary an act of resistance in itself?

* * *

Ironically, the very global media that throttles the language of our home is also the one where active processes to keep it alive thrive. Groups of Kashmiris get together on Twitter, WhatsApp, and Clubhouse to revive one word at a time – through quizzes, through conversations, through sharing memes, and audio-visuals. Poetry, conversation, and humour help manifest a sleeping register of Kashmiri, awakening untranslatable words lying asleep in a corner of our subconscious. Speaking a tongue, invoking poetry, saying the words out loud gives the language a new lease of life.

The idea of making words live by reclaiming speech has slowly seeped into textual forms too. Kashmiri writers have begun to take charge of and pride in their language, spelling out Kashmiri names on a page the way they are spoken in the colloquial form, as opposed to the anglicised and Indian-ised way we are used to seeing them in print. These communities, active in cyberspace, bring together Pandits and Muslims; solidarity in cyberspace is the product of perceived persecution of their mother tongue. Yet the politics that brings them to this act of preservation is also something both groups avoid speaking of and skirt around in these spaces. The Kashmiri Muslims avoid speaking of India's oppression – an India that the exiled Pandits have found a home in and pledged a loyalty to.

Hearing some words over and over, reading them aloud also serves a more selfish purpose for many – that of conjuring up home. It is online that within spaces of superficial satire, the language and cultural production are seemingly and at least overtly free of traditional power dynamics. Space is democratized, a ready audience available and censorship doesn't restrict the creator. Even the economics might make sense, and the language lives in the form it knows best – oral. It is here, in the digital space, that we see the language and an oral tradition thrive and transform with the times.

Should we not engage in processes of decolonising translation through modes and media better suited to the language? If storytelling is alive in the margins, beyond the metropole, it is our shortcoming that we find the spoken word inadequate. Should we not, instead, adapt to formats we're trained to think of as non-literary? In other words, why impose the structures and genres of 'publishing' to a language in whose character it doesn't exist?

Verse, sung not written; dramatized folklore, performed not read. If a language is oral in its character, should we not translate it so? Can we, in this process of translating by adapting to orality, find ways to decolonise the language by ridding ourselves of the inherent superiority of the written literature? Can we give precedence to the oral – simultaneously translate performances or subtitle films, and through digital technologies – and give it a new lease of life? Through technology, we free it from the censorship of print, we remove the need for a heavy investment in publishing and distribution, and we find an audience that isn't limited by their ability to read the script. Is it not possible to translate and also address dynamics of power and polarisation?

* * *

Only one whose daily life involves an active engagement with the global and the local can actually pause to notice; can listen to local languages and appreciate their beauty, breaking sentences down and then lovingly putting the pieces back together in their minds and musings. I, like the nostalgic anywhere in the world, delight in details; in the tiny links Kashmiri has with Urdu and Farsi, in the word origins with Sanskrit. Often only to rudely realise that most languages have these peculiarities and connections. It could also be construed that projects like this, for preservation of languages and ways of being, come with a vision of an ideal past, and a dream of going back to the origins. Something that would make me no different from those I criticize. Yet, every time global language falls short at representing our local realities, I want to hold on to them lest they escape with each strange articulation.

Languages are mediums that both build and communicate the ethical landscape of a people. Forces – changing value systems, phrases, modes of communication – tug and push the language and in turn the ethics. These forces tug at our way of life – akin to a tapestry – where language, culture, morals, beliefs, ethics, are threads beautifully woven together which are now being pulled apart by global, national, and local agendas. They rip that which has been bound across centuries, putting it into silos, forcing labels on it. At the risk of enshrining or romanticising our language, I cry for help in angst at the state of affairs I find ourselves in.

When I see my language morph in front of my eyes, I see our world shrink. How long till loan-words colonise the language? How long till they invade sentences? How long till their presence is felt on the streets? The occupiers' gaze on our streets pierces, forcing us to speak strange yet familiar utterances in tongues we cannot even hold in our mouths. Our utterances end up making us look like the very clowns they satirize us as. With all that we have at hand, it is in orality that Kashmiri finds its due. In orality is our much sought-after autonomy. It is through orality that we can find a bridge between the fading old world and the devastation of the new.

17. TRANSLATIONS FROM ARMENIAN: REIMAG(IN)ING THE INASSIMILABLE

Shushan Avagyan

Armenian literature was introduced into English through the prism of the unique traumatic experience of the Armenian Genocide in the Ottoman Empire during World War I (including the events that led up to the Genocide, such as the Hamidian Massacres of 1894-96 and the Cilician Massacres of 1909). As the Irish jurist and politician Viscount James Bryce wrote in his introduction to the anthology *Armenian Legends and Poems* (1916), "interest in Armenia" and its body of literature was "awakened by the sufferings" of the Armenian people (ix). This historical event has left an indelible mark on Armenian literature in English translation from the late nineteenth century onwards—whether relevant or not, individual works have been read, interpreted, and translated as a reflection of this ineffable trauma. In other words, the texts that were chosen for translation either dealt directly with the subject of the Armenian Genocide or had nothing to do with the Genocide and yet were contextualized within the scope of this event through methodical strategies of translation, editing, prefacing, publishing, reviewing, reading, and teaching. Before delving any deeper into the topic, it appears imperative to introduce some key distinctions in approaches to translation.

(IN)FIDELITIES: METHODS OF TRANSLATION

In an 1813 lecture, Friedrich Schleiermacher classified two approaches to translation: "Either the translator leaves the author in peace, as much as possible, and moves the reader toward him. Or he leaves the reader in peace, as much as possible, and moves the author toward him" (Schleiermacher 1992, 149). Schleiermacher's identification of these alternatives reaches back at least as far as Cicero's distinction between "*ut interpres*" (word-for-word translation, like an interpreter) and "*ut orator*" (persuasive translation, like an orator) (Baker 1998, 163). Traditionally associated either with the literal and faithful or with freedom and creativity, this basic binarism reappears in more recent pairs such as "imitation" versus "metaphrase" (John Dryden), "literal" versus "paraphrase" (Vladimir Nabokov), "formal" versus "dynamic" (Eugene Nida), and "resistant" versus "transparent" (Lawrence Venuti). Many translation theorists have suggested a series of middling strategies, yet the dichotomy remains, and in this schema in which fidelity is understood as literal proximity to the original and its referential network, free translation, understood as more distant in meaning from the original, can only be read as betrayal.

As Lawrence Venuti explains, translation—throughout the history of the United States—has docilely served the "manifest destiny" project. Most pertinently, translation enabled the colonization, dispossession, and assimilation of Native Americans, and continues to support American political and economic hegemony across the globe. At the same time, it contributed to the formation of a definably "American" identity (white, Christian, heterosexual, male). So, for example, projects such as *A Key into the Language of America* (1643), a dictionary in the Narragansett language that aimed "to assist the colonist whatever the occasion be," symbolized the expansionist goals of gradually dispossessing and displacing the native tribes (qtd. in Baker 1998, 399). Nineteenth century projects, such as the fourteen-volume anthology of translations from European languages, *Specimens of Foreign Standard Literature*, edited by George Ripley, constructed a model that conformed to the cultural values of the elite intellectual minority, which subscribed to an Anglo-European canon and thus consolidated these values as fundamental to "American" identity. Methods of translation were determined by cultural hierarchies: literal or faithful translation was required when representing the expression of "civilized" cultures within the Western worldview, whereas less fidelity and expertise were required when translating "less civilized" texts. This principle is exemplified best by a notorious statement made by the English poet Edward FitzGerald, translator of the *Rubáiyát of Omar Khayyám*, in a letter to his friend E. B. Cowell in 1857: "It is an amusement for me to take what Liberties I like with these Persians, who (as I think) are not Poets enough to frighten one from such excursions, and who really do want a little Art to shape them" (qtd. in Lefevere 1992, 4).

American and British translators often shared translation strategies and standards based on cultural hierarchies, and a knowledge of foreign languages was not always considered necessary for the task of translation or making professional judgments about translations. Comparing American to early Soviet methods of translation, Lauren G. Leighton points to an odd tendency in American translation that "poets commonly convey poetry into English without possessing a knowledge of its original language" (Leighton 1991, 16). This method, usually employed in the translation of poetry, incorporated the work of two individuals, a translator (or the so-called "native informant") who provided an interlinear translation, and a poet who manipulated the interlinear text to recreate the foreign work in the target language. As I will show below, this method undermines the presence and labor of the native translator, without whom the translation would not have been possible in the first place. By contrast, the Soviet translation school not only emphasized "the integrity of the original text [as] sacred and translation [as] an art," and required that "a text be submitted to exhaustive analysis by an artist having the best possible command of both the native and foreign language" (Leighton 1991, 14), but also viewed the editor's and publisher's task as equally critical to the presentation of a foreign text. As Soviet critic Ivan Kashkin wrote in 1959, the editor "must perhaps know even more than the translator. In the first place, the language—or more precisely, both languages. This is axiomatic" (qtd. in Leighton 1991, 55). Another Soviet translation editor, Marya Lorie, contended that the editor must ensure that the translator has not omitted anything from the text and has not invented anything, as the task of the editor is "to bring the translation as close to the original as is possible, help the translator faithfully convey a foreign-language work in its unity of form and content" (qtd. in Leighton 1991, 55). Cautious of censorship, Lorie argued that the editor has no right to make changes: "Ideally, the editor must not touch a single word of the text himself, but only *point out* where the translator has in one way or another departed from fidelity to the original" (qtd. in Leighton 1991, 56). This view runs counter to the American school that not only assumed that "a poet's talent need not contend with linguistic nuances of a foreign poem" (Leighton 1991, 16) but also constructed a hierarchy of skills—the American poet as the master translator, and the "native informant" as the slavish assistant.

In Arshaluys Mardiganian's first-hand account of the Armenian Genocide, *Ravished Armenia*, for instance, the name of the Armenian interpreter does not appear in any part of the book, while the New York-based writer H. L. Gates, who knew no Armenian, appears as the interpreter of the text. Gates and his wife had also become the seventeen-year-old Arshaluys's legal guardians, which further complicated translation rights and royalty issues.[1] Another instance of the erasure of the native translator can be seen in one of the earlier translation projects of Armenian literature, the anthology *Armenian Poems* published in 1896 by the American suffragist Alice Stone Blackwell. The anthology presented classical, medieval, and nineteenth century Armenian poets to the English-language audience for the first time, functioning as a cultural emissary introduced in the context of the Hamidian Massacres of 1894-96. The volume was expanded and reprinted in 1917 as part of the fundraising and relief efforts during World War I. In her preface to the second volume, Blackwell reasoned that "the sympathy felt for the Armenians in the unspeakable sufferings at the hands of the Turks would be deepened by an acquaintance with the temper and genius of the people, as shown in their poetry" (i). A less-important reason for the publication was "the fact that Armenian poetic literature, while well worthy to be known, was practically inaccessible to English-speaking readers. Its treasures are locked up in an almost unknown language" (i). While Blackwell, who did not know

[1] The original text was published in English language first as *Ravished Armenia* by Kingfield Press in New York in 1918 and as *The Auction of Souls* in London by Odhams Press in 1919. It was retranslated into Armenian as *Hokineru achurte* [The Auction of Souls] by Martiros Kushakjian and published in 1965 in Beirut. For a detailed account of Mardiganian's narrative, see my essay "Becoming Aurora: Translating the Story of Arshaluys Mardiganian" (*Dissidences*, Vol. 4: Issue 8, available at: https://digitalcommons.bowdoin.edu/dissidences/vol4/iss8/13).

Armenian, acknowledged in her preface Ohannes Chatschumian and Bedros Keljik, among others, who had reproduced the poems in "literal translation in prose," she appears as the translator of the anthology (i). Such seemingly insignificant gestures nonetheless establish the imbalance between the "native informant" as a laborer without agency, a kind of subaltern, and the "translator" as a skilled and acknowledged "literary proletariat," as Emily Apter would have it (Apter 2006, xi). These gestures also institute the idea that literal translation should be less valued, as it requires less artistic talent, while they uphold free translation as a more inventive, and thus privileged, method. Ultimately, by obscuring the foreign presence of the native translators, Blackwell's volume concealed the numerous stages of the translation process (starting with the selection of authors and works, for example) and the conditions under which the translation was made.

In *The Translator's Invisibility*, Venuti examines the rhetoric of reviews by critics, writers, and academics who unanimously and consistently construct a dominance of *fluency* in English-language translations that renders the translator invisible. A fluent translation, according to Venuti, is easily recognizable, made familiar, "domesticated" so that the audience has an unobstructed entrance into the foreign text; the translator works to make his or her mediation "invisible," "producing the illusory effect of transparency that simultaneously masks its status as an illusion," thus creating a sensation of "naturalness" that obliterates foreignness or unfamiliarity (Venuti 1995, 5). The effect of transparency is produced by minimizing polysemy or the disruptive play of signifiers, and by pursuing linear syntax, univocal meaning, current usage, and linguistic consistency. Fluency thus results in an effacement of the multiple determinations and effects of translation. The translator's invisibility is further indoctrinated by the conception of authorship as individualistic, as an original and transparent self-representation, "unmediated by transindividual determinants (linguistic, cultural, social) that might complicate authorial originality" (6). In this schema, translation is, on the one hand, defined as a second-rate representation that is derivative and dependent upon the foreign text, which, in turn, is considered an authentic or true representation of the author's intention, and on the other hand, judged by its ability to efface its second-rate status by producing the illusion that it is, in fact, the original.

Through the illusory dictates of the translator's invisibility, the concomitant domestication of the foreign text and replacement of difference, translation then becomes an act of ideological violence, in which its aim is to bring back a cultural other as the recognizable and the familiar. The translator, Venuti proposes, must consciously try to move away from domesticating strategies and employ a "foreignizing" methodology, which he, following Schleiermacher, defines as "an ethnodeviant pressure on [target-language cultural] values to register the linguistic and cultural difference of the foreign text, sending the reader abroad" (20). The accentuation of foreignness—"receiving the Foreign as Foreign" (Berman 2000, 286)—allows for a disruption and revision of codes and norms that prevail in the target language and culture. This also extends to the very act of reading and otherwise engaging with translations, in this case—translations of Armenian texts—whereas developing critical lenses for reading against domesticating effects and discursive choices and locating inconsistencies that expose the translation as being a replacement of the inassimilable with assimilable images and characterizations allows for a more cognizant and complex process of reimag(in)ing the Foreign.

REIMAG(IN)ING HOW?

One of the earliest translations of Armenian literature into English appeared in the *Journal of American Folklore* in 1893, where the writer and editor A. G. Seklemian introduced American scholars to his translation of the Armenian fairy tale "The Youngest of the Three." Another tale, "The Wicked Stepmother," was translated and published in the same journal in 1897. The following year Seklemian published an anthology, *The Golden Maiden and Other Folk Tales and Fairy Stories Told in Armenia,* which was introduced by Alice Stone Blackwell who, as mentioned earlier, had collaborated with Armenian scholars on the translation of Armenian poetry. *The Golden Maiden* included twenty-eight tales and a tragic ballad about two young lovers, "Sia-Manto and

Guje-Zare," which was versified by Blackwell. Blackwell's introduction to *The Golden Maiden* was set against the backdrop of the Hamidian Massacres of 1894-96, as was the anthology *Armenian Poems* (1896), and aimed to draw attention to the plight of Armenians in Ottoman Turkey. In this context it is not surprising to read an introduction that says nothing about the literary merit of the tales, but rather offers an ethnographic summary of the Armenians as a "race." The introduction traces the origins and history of Armenians, testifying that "they are of Aryan race, and of pure Caucasian blood," and cites various travelers who "have been struck by the ability of the Armenians, and by the marked difference between them and other Oriental races" (xi). Blackwell quotes English explorer Isabella Bird Bishop who wrote, "It is not possible to deny that they are the most capable, energetic, enterprising and pushing race in Western Asia, physically superior and intellectually acute; and above all they are a race which can be raised in all respects to our own level" (xii). Such racializing descriptions not only rendered Armenians as inferior to Anglo-Europeans, but also indoctrinated irreconcilable differences between Armenians and other ethnicities in the region. In addition, it doomed the mixing between "superior" and "inferior" races, as is "evident" from the tragic union between the Armenian youth Sia-Manto and the Kurdish maiden Guje-Zare, which is strategically placed at the end of the anthology. An interrogative reader, however, might read against this translation that painstakingly portrays the Armenians as "a pure race," as Seklemian's preface, "The Story-Teller to his Audience," underscores the hybridity of Armenian culture as evinced in the folk tales:

> Although all the tales contained in this volume are taken directly from the lips of the Armenians, it will be noticed that some of them bear traces of Persian, Arabic and Turkish influence. This, of course, was naturally to be expected, as the Armenians have been ruled successively by these nations. (Seklemian 1898, xviii)

Despite Seklemian's recognition of foreign influences, Blackwell's construction of the "purity," as well as "physical and intellectual superiority" of Armenians, was a strategy for mediating the trauma befalling them, one that aimed to persuade the targeted American audience to become involved in relief efforts for the victims of the Hamidian Massacres who, being "the Anglo-Saxons of Eastern Turkey," were "like us" (qtd. in Seklemian 1898, xi). Hence, translation inherently meant reimagining and reimaging the Foreign in the image of the Self-Same. This strategy functioned as part of what Jeffrey C. Alexander calls "a complex and multivalent symbolic process" meant to convince an audience that it too had become traumatized by the experience (Alexander 2004, 12). However, Blackwell's assimilative reading of Armenians and their fairy tales muted the complex cross-ethnic relationships of the source culture at the same time that it set up an ethnocentric hierarchy that ensured the dominance of Anglo-Saxon culture over others. These strategic gestures not only reveal the domestic interests vested in Armenian-to-English translation projects at the turn of the century, but also helped popularize the Armenian cause through literature in the unique context of ethnic and cultural annihilation.

A wave of renewed interest in Armenian literature grew during the crisis of World War I and more translation projects were initiated or commissioned by individuals and groups who were involved in the organization of humanitarian relief. The anthology *Armenian Legends and Poems* (1916) was one such project in which the selection of works was motivated by topical proximity to the Genocide and the tradition of lamentation and elegy. The translator of the anthology, British-Armenian writer Zabelle C. Boyajian wrote in the preface: "In preparing this book of Armenian legends and poems my principal object was to publish it as a Memorial to an unhappy nation. The book does not claim to represent Armenian poetry adequately. Many gifted and well-known authors have been omitted, partly from considerations of space, and partly because of the scope of the work" (ix). In his introduction to the anthology, Viscount James Bryce, who was simultaneously involved in preparing a record of eyewitness accounts of the Genocide for the British Parliament, further constructed "the scope of the work"—a cultural rationale for humanitarian involvement:

> Few among us have acquired their language, one of the most ancient forms of human speech that possess a literature. Still fewer have

> studied their art or read their poetry even in translations. There is, therefore, an ample field for a book which shall present to those Englishmen and Frenchmen, whose interest in Armenia has been awakened by the sufferings to which its love of freedom and its loyalty to its Christian faith have exposed it, some account of Armenian art and Armenian poetical literature. (ix)

If Boyajian cast her translations as a mode of solemn commemoration, Bryce used the occasion to draw in a select group of Europeans ("Englishmen and Frenchmen") who were already familiar with the Armenian people through the crisis in the Ottoman Empire. In other words, the collection was not presented as a literary endeavor, nor was it marketed to a literary or a scholarly community, but rather promoted through the frame of the Genocide. The cursory survey of literature included hastily and indiscriminately arranged Armenian folk songs, medieval legends, and poems ranging from fifth- to early twentieth-century poets, as well as works *about* Armenia, such as the fourteenth-century English poet John Gower's "The Tale of Rosiphelee," with scant historical and cultural contextualization, which undermined the serious study of this body of literature. Blackwell's second volume of *Armenian Poems* came out the following year, in 1917, with an expanded list of works including contemporary socialist poets from Eastern Armenia, Shushanik Kurghinian and Hovhannes Hovhannesian.

That same year, the daughter of an American missionary, Jane S. Wingate, who had grown up in Marsovan, Ottoman Turkey, translated *The Fool* by the nineteenth-century Eastern Armenian novelist Raffi (Hakob Melik-Hakobyan), further building on this body of literature that was being framed through the singular context of the Genocide. Wingate grew up in a community of Protestant Armenians, where she studied Armenian and translated in order to improve her knowledge of the language. She devoted herself to the study of ancient and modern Armenian literatures, and commenced translating folktales, which she sent to the Folklore Society of England, of which she was a member. Several of these translations were published in a Boston-based journal, *Armenia*, in 1910, while others appeared in the British Folklore Society's journal, *Folklore*, in 1911 and 1912. However, her most widely read and popular work was the translation of *The Fool* (1917). Originally published in 1881, this short novel on the Russian-Turkish War of 1877-78 depicted the pogroms against the Armenians in Bayazet and their struggle against Ottoman oppression. Wingate may have selected this novel for translation because it portrayed scenes of atrocity in Armenian villages similar to what she was witnessing during World War I. She may also have seen it as an important text for understanding the historical context of the Armenians in the Ottoman Empire. Not only did *The Fool* show a long and continuous history of a state-endorsed program of ethnic cleansing that preceded the Genocide, but it also unleashed a scathing critique of the state of the Armenian Church and its clergy, and implicitly defended Protestantism. In this sense, the selection and translation of the text served as persuasive evidence for the necessity of American missionary involvement in rescuing Armenians from both the corruption of their own church and annihilation by the Turks.

Wingate's English version of the novel, however, included a variety of disparities that change critical scenes and "regulate" cultural, ideological, and political realities that were intentionally constructed as contradictory in the original. For example, the name of one of the characters Ստեփանիկ (Stepanik) or "little Stepan"—a male name—becomes "Stephanie" in Wingate's translation. While Wingate follows Raffi's description of this character as an Armenian villager's "youngest son" who resembled "Joseph, the beloved," she nonetheless hints at a discrepancy by choosing a feminine name: "The youngest son of Khacho was unmarried, being a lad of sixteen, who was called Stephanie [*sic*]" (Wingate's translation, Ch. 5). As a result, a crucial revelation in the novel is completely lost due to this free translation, for the character initially presented as the young man Stepanik, turns out, toward the middle of the novel, to be a young woman named Lala. The English translation thus erased the character's gender ambiguity, and diminished both the tension of the situation she found herself in and the impact of the exposure. Cross-dressing was not unusual in Ottoman Armenian households; Armenian girls were occasionally disguised as boys in order not to attract the attention of Turkish gendarmes, Kurdish tribesmen, or Circassian militiamen, who used systematic rape and forced impregnation as part of a campaign of ethnic cleansing. Later on, during World War I, this form of resistance was adopted by many Armenian women who applied strategies like cutting their own hair, rubbing coal or dirt on their faces, and wearing ragged clothes to appear unattractive, to avoid rape or "a fate worse than dying"—sexual enslavement (Bjørnlund 2009, 25).[2] In his construction of one such act of resistance, Raffi paid particular attention to his portrayal of the cross-dressed Lala, carefully dressing her up in masculine traits and passing her off as a handsome young man. Betraying her gender, in the context of the novel, literally meant risking her life and exposing her to a danger to which her older sister, Sona, had fallen victim:

> Sona's death left her father so oppressed with grief that he had a foreboding that his other daughter would suffer the same fate. His anxiety was not without grounds, especially in his country, where he had known of many and many a young girl carried off by Turks or Kurds. Consequently he wished to have Lala grow up as a boy till she became of age. . . . The secret had been kept most scrupulously. Outside the family only three persons knew the fact: the village priest, and the godfather and godmother who were no longer living. (Wingate's translation, Ch. 13)

In this passage and the following chapter, where Raffi further explores the predicament of the character as a cross-dressed woman, he stresses the "unnaturalness" of her condition through the main hero, Vartan, thus drawing attention to the normalizing gaze:

> Vartan had long known that Stephanie [*sic*] was a girl. He surmised, also, the reasons why her parents had been obliged to dress her as a boy, and to have her grow up as a boy. It was these circumstances that had attracted the attention of the young man to the unfortunate girl, and filled him with a heroic desire to rescue her from her unnatural condition. (Wingate's translation, Ch. 14)

The revelation that "Stephanie" *is* "a girl" in Wingate's translation comes as no surprise and doesn't draw attention to the "unnatural

[2] On gender-specific violence during the Armenian Massacres and Genocide, see Bjørnlund; Dadrian; Derderian; Watenpaugh.

condition," which Raffi tries to problematize in the original novel. Wingate's strategy to give Lala a female pseudonym, Stephanie, expunges the strangeness of the circumstances in which many Armenian girls and women found themselves and neutralizes the novel's turning point, which is marked by the gender revelation. Driven perhaps by a discomfort of having to deal with a cross-dressed woman or possibly trying to spare her audience the "gender trouble" caused by Raffi's destabilization of assumptions about gender identity, Wingate's domestication constructed a heteronormative anticipation of what Judith Butler calls a "gendered essence" (xv).[3]

Other discursive choices made by Wingate further misconstrue the Armenian text and its critique of parochial values and mores that, according to Raffi, were widespread especially in Armenian villages under strict Ottoman rule. For example, the original text employs a profusion of proverbs (such as "If you can't cut the hand of a villain, you must kiss it" (my translation, Ch. 17)) that perform the submission of Ottoman subjects to the duplicitous policies of the government. As the central character, Vartan, explains, "To talk with these people you must know hundreds of proverbs and anecdotes" (Wingate's translation, Ch. 17). Raffi strategically places three proverbs as epigraphs to the novel, which in their own way parody and negate the proverbial or metaphorical language of "the wise." The first two proverbs construct "the fool" as a troublemaker and a shrewd trickster: "The fool rolled a stone into the pit; a hundred wise men came to the rescue but could not draw it out" and "While the wise man ponders, the fool crosses the river" (my translation). And the last proverb "Խենթից—ուղիղ պատասխան" ("The fool will always give a straight answer," my translation) directly refers to Vartan's discourse, or the discourse of "the fool" as he is nicknamed in the novel, and is juxtaposed to the proverbial language of the Turkish authorities and the Armenian subjects who mechanically reproduce the language through which they are oppressed. While Wingate faithfully translates the first two epigraphs, she reverses the meaning of the last one, rendering it as "The replies of a fool become

[3] In *Gender Trouble,* Butler analyzes how heteronormative expectations and regulations concerning gender produce distinct "essences" that men and women are expected to reproduce through certain bodily acts of naturalized gestures.

the proverbs of the people," allowing for a slippage of the differentiation between "the language of the fool"—straightforwardness, frankness, literality—and other discourses. It further undermines Raffi's ironic overuse of proverbs, enlisted in the text to reveal the language of imprecise utterances and vague promises by authorities to reform the social conditions of Armenians living as colonial subjects of the Ottoman Empire.

In other instances, Wingate's choices can be described at best as arbitrarily unfaithful to the source material, as "մարդկային մարմիններ" ("human bodies") becomes "putrid bodies"; "պառավ տատը" ("old grandmother") becomes "old granddad"; "լարախաղացի օգնական" ("tightrope walker's helper") becomes "a clown or a juggler's assistant"; "անձնապաշտպանություն" ("self-defense") becomes "self-preservation"; "Նա իր զավակին հանձնեց ֆրերների միաբանությանը, իսկ ինքը անհետացավ" ("He left his son to a brotherhood of Frères and disappeared") becomes "He committed his son to a brotherhood of Frères, but he himself became an infidel"; "Եթե հավաքելու լինենք վերջին 20-30-50 տարիների ընթացքում կատարված փաստերը" ("If we look at the facts from the past twenty, thirty, or fifty years") becomes "If we collect together the proofs of this during the past thirty-five years," and so on. Other infidelities to the original appear to be motivated by an anti-socialist sentiment, as Wingate omits large sections of the novel on the socialist revolutionary Levon Salman, who is characterized by Vartan as "a skilled guide in life," and who, "apart from being an intellectual, is a very kind and honest man" (my translation, from an omitted section in Ch. 19). Finally, some of Salman's progressive feminist ideas, which are both original and far ahead of his time, are attributed to Vartan, the eponymous hero of the novel, who in the original seems less interested in women's emancipation:

> "It is necessary to draw on their strength which is confined within their four walls, then we shall surely succeed," Salman often said.
> "It is early yet," replied Vartan, "they need preparation first. [The following words belong to Salman in the original] No reform in the life of a people is possible without the assistance of women. If our people have remained static the principal reason for it is because

> women have had no share in public affairs. The strength, the energizing force which has lain abortive within their four walls has yielded no results." (Wingate's translation, Ch. 23)

Although this passage is inconsistent with Vartan's view on women's rights and appears contradictory to his character, Wingate may have wanted to construct Vartan as more progressive than he appears in the original novel to make him more sophisticated for the target-language readers (many of whom were prominent suffragists). Despite these inconsistencies, Wingate faithfully translates what is perhaps to her the most important message of this text (ironically, pronounced by the socialist Salman)—the uncanny continuity of the government-endorsed plan of annihilation in the late nineteenth century and of the Genocide during World War I:

> "We looked at the disorder, corruption and barbarity practiced, but we did not see the hellish machinery hidden beneath all this. We saw oppression, murder, forcible change of religion, all the wickedness committed by neighboring tribes. We considered all that as temporary and accidental and did not know that these irregularities were secretly encouraged and fomented by men of high degree. We blamed the government, considering it simply weak and unable to control its lawless subjects. We did not know that government officials themselves excited these barbarians against the Armenians, in order to destroy the Christian element. . . . Here the principal nationality that threatens the partition of that portion of the empire, is the Armenian. Therefore, in order to stop the noise of the European Governments [Turkey] must show them that no Armenians remain in Armenia." (Wingate's translation, Ch. 21)

In her attempt to alert the English-speaking world of the murderous crimes that she was witnessing in modern-day Turkey, Wingate turned to Raffi to show the continuous mechanism of ethnic cleansing that neither started nor ended with the Armenian Genocide. By producing a translation rather than a text of her own, Wingate was invoking the authority of Raffi's text and inherently drawing attention to Armenian literature, along with Seklemian, Blackwell, Boyajian, Bryce, and others, through the frame of the Genocide. Hence, translations from Armenian at the turn of the century unavoidably bore the mark of this historical event, and the humanitarian approach to translation clearly dismissed the developments of this body of literature throughout different time periods, beginning with the literary activity of the fifth century—the golden age of Armenian literature, and produced in different geographic communities writing in Eastern or Western Armenian. This foundational approach was to become the dominant pattern of most translation projects that followed suit.

Translation, as Lefevere argues, implies authority, legitimacy and, ultimately, power, and nations have always sought translators they could entrust with a faithful reproduction of their own values, ideologies, and traditions, which often means that trust in the translator has been more important than fidelity to the original (Lefevere 1992, 2-3). To Schleiermacher, for example, this meant that translators should only translate from a foreign language into their own, as anything else would be "an act that runs counter to both nature and morality" and would mean "to become a deserter to one's own mother tongue and to give oneself to another" (qtd. in Lefevere 1992, 5). From this perspective, where one is expected to remain faithful to his or her native language and cultural ideologies, it would seem impossible to remain at the same time faithful to a foreign text if its values and ideologies do not coincide with those in the translator's native culture. One would always be, if not consciously, then, unconsciously, domesticating a foreign text, which is evident, as I have shown, in Wingate's translation of Raffi's *The Fool*, where the translator remains faithful only to those elements that are not contrary to her own situated knowledge, ideology, and values. By "naturalizing" the gender ambiguities, for example, or by eliminating the socialist elements, Wingate created a fluent account that would comfortably fit into the dominant conceptions of heteronormativity and capitalism in the United States. Notions of fidelity, then, are always in constant flux and invoke different answers, depending on cultural dictates and the politics of the translator, to Roman Jakobson's famous questions: "Translator of what messages? Betrayer of what values?" (Jakobson 2000, 118).

BIBLIOGRAPHY

Alexander, Jeffrey C. "Toward a Theory of Cultural Trauma." In Alexander, Jeffrey C., et al. *Cultural Trauma and Collective Identity*. Berkeley: U of California P, 2004. 1-30.

Apter, Emily. *The Translation Zone: A New Comparative Literature*. Princeton UP, 2006.

Baker, Mona, ed. *Routledge Encyclopedia of Translation Studies*. London: Routledge, 1998.

Berman, Antoine, "Translation and the Trials of the Foreign." In *The Translation Studies Reader*, ed. Lawrence Venuti. London: Routledge, 2000. 284-97.

Bjørnlund, Matthias. "'A Fate Worse Than Dying': Sexual Violence During the Armenian Genocide." In *Brutality and Desire: War and Sexuality in Europe's Twentieth Century*. Ed. Dagmar Herzog. Basingstoke: Palgrave Macmillan, 2009. 16-58.

Blackwell, Alice Stone, ed. and trans. *Armenian Poems*. Boston: Atlantic Printing Co., 1896 (vol. 1), 1917 (vol. 2).

Boyajian, Zabelle C., ed. and trans. *Armenian Legends and Poems*. New York: Columbia UP, 1916.

Bryce, James and Arnold Toynbee. *The Treatment of Armenians in the Ottoman Empire, 1915-1916: Documents Presented to Viscount Grey of Fallodon by Viscount Bryce*. 1st ed. London: Causton and Sons, 1916; 2nd ed. London: Gomidas, 2005.

Butler, Judith. *Gender Trouble: Feminism and the Subversion of Identity*. London: Routledge, 2002.

Dadrian, Vahakn, N. "Children as Victims of Genocide: The Armenian Case." *Journal of Genocide Research* 5.3 (2003): 421-37.

Derderian, Katharine. "Common Fate, Different Experience: Gender-Specific Aspects of the Armenian Genocide, 1915-1917." *Holocaust and Genocide Studies* 19.1 (2005): 1-25.

Jakobson, Roman. "On Linguistic Aspects of Translation." In *The Translation Studies Reader*, ed. Lawrence Venuti. London: Routledge, 2000. 113-18.

Lefevere, André, ed. *Translation/History/Culture: A Sourcebook*. London: Routledge, 1992.

Leighton, Lauren G. *Two Worlds, One Art: Literary Translation in Russia and America*. Dekalb: Northern Illinois UP, 1991.

Raffi. *The Fool*. Trans. Jane S. Wingate. *Onlinebooks.library.upenn.edu*.

Schleiermacher, Friedrich. "On the Different Methods of Translating." In *Translation/History/Culture: A Sourcebook*. Ed. André Lefevere. London: Routledge, 1992. 141-166.

Seklemian, A. G., ed. and trans. *The Golden Maiden and Other Folk Tales and Fairy Stories Told in Armenia*. New York: Holman-Taylor, 1898.

Slide, Anthony. Ravished Armenia *and the Story of Aurora Mardiganian*. London: Scarecrow Press, 1997.

Venuti, Lawrence. *The Translator's Invisibility: A History of Translation*. London: Routledge, 1995.

Watenpaugh, Keith D. "The League of Nations' Rescue of Armenian Genocide Survivors and the Making of Modern Humanitarianism, 1920-1927." *The American Historical Review* 115.5 (2010): 1315-39.

18. BETWEEN CRIÉ AND ÉCRIT

Monchoachi
Translated from the French by Eric Fishman

"Migrant" comes from the Latin migrare, "to change dwellings," in which we find the Greek root mei, shared with the French muer (to molt). This small etymological detour reminds us that language is a dwelling, and as a result, that different languages establish different dwellings in the world, different lights and different gods, different works. "Man," writes the linguist Wilhelm Humboldt, "thinks, feels, lives in language alone" and "the diversity of languages is not a diversity of sounds and signs, but a diversity of views of the world."[1] In other words, language isn't first of all, or primarily, an instrument for communicating thoughts; if it was so we could easily *hear each other.* In this way, the same Humboldt, staying in Paris, wrote to the poet Schiller of his hopeless efforts to present Kantian philosophy to the French:

> The conference lasted five hours and went every which way ... We absolutely did not understand each other ... To hear each other, in a true sense, is impossible, and for a simple reason. They haven't the smallest idea, the smallest feeling for something outside of appearances: pure will, true goodness, the self, the pure consciousness of self, all this is for them completely incomprehensible. When they use the same words, they always take them in another sense. Their reason isn't ours, their space isn't our space, their imagination isn't ours.

Written just before the dawn of the 19th century, these remarkable words of Humboldt's concern neighboring peoples from inside the same civilizational air of Europe. It only makes the reach of his

[1] All Humboldt excerpts are translated from the French translations by Denis Thouard, *Sur le caractère national des langues, et autres écrits sur le langage* (POINTS, 2000).

reflection on the connection between language and visions of the world clearer. An important scholar of languages of America and Oceania, Humboldt's approach puts him quite certainly on the side of a Montaigne who three centuries before undertook a defense of the "cannibal-savages" of Brazil in the following terms: "It seems that we have no mark of truth and reason other than the example and idea of the opinions and customs of the country in which we live. *There* is always the perfect religion, the perfect government, the perfect and accomplished practices in all things."[2] He notes that he is naming "the marvelous distance" that the so-called savage languages open between their own humanity and Occidental humanity:

> They have a way in their language in which they speak of men as halves of one another; they had noticed that there were among us men who were full and gorged with all kinds of commodities, and that their other halves were begging at their doors, wasted by hunger and poverty. They found it strange how these needy halves could suffer such an injustice, without taking the others by the throat, or setting fire to their houses.

To pass from one dwelling to another, from one language to another, necessitates a molting. More precisely, "to pass into" is in itself a molting; as the Martinican Creole language rightly says, a "passage" is the rhetorical figure of metamorphosis—more than a place that fades, a spell that blurs, both incantation and password.

Passing from the crié (cried out) to the écrit (written), from speech to writing, the Creolophone must pass at the same time from one tongue to another, changing his horizon at the same time he changes languages.

This situation of the migrant writer is evidently not unwritten about. Leopardi points out quite rightly that "in the Late Period, the Germans and English were truly diglottoi (bilingual), or more precisely those who belonged to the educated part of these nations, who wrote in Latin, using it for correspondence, letters, etc, and already spoke a common language very different from written Latin."[3]

---

[2] All Montaigne excerpts are from "Des Cannibales," c. 1580.

Or again: "the civilized nations of Asia, after the conquest of Alexander, were truly diglottoi—that is to say, they spoke and wrote the Greek language not as their own language, but as a cultivated language ..." Further on: "among these diglottoi who wrote in a language that wasn't theirs, but who did it nonetheless remarkably, there was Lucien de Samosate. Examine his works, where he shows signs of his maternal language, etc."

If not unprecedented, this situation is nonetheless distinct from a straightforward bilingualism in that it results in a gap: like an immutable moon, a true heterotopia in which you can sometimes hear the unpronounced, the unarticulated, trembling, licenses, dissidences.

Yet from the strict demarcation of languages to their infinite mixture, the common background is the allegation that speech and writing are simply two modes of the same articulation. This goes without saying for languages which have lost all memory of authentic speech and whose speaking has for ages been reduced to *speaking writing*. In contrast, going straight to the absolute hostility of writing toward authentic speech brings us, on the one hand, to consider this in a completely different way than the habitual condescension toward languages without writing. On the other hand, it brings us to reposition the problem of the diversity of languages to a consideration of the different registers in which they are deployed rather than to privilege only one "variety of sounds and signs," which has as a consequence reduced the debate on diversity to a tiny spot, and enclosed it in the field of the unique language that the Occident speaks to say the same thing.

A few rare thinkers have had insights related to the implications of similar questions. Nietzsche first of all, when he exclaimed "the desert grows," noted elsewhere: "a man for whom almost all books have become superficial, who has kept nothing (and this for a small number of men from the past) except the belief that they had enough profundity *to not write what they know*."[4] Heidegger as well, who wrote:

[3] All Leopardi excerpts are translated from the French translations by Bertrand Schefer, *Zibaldone* (Editions Allia, 2004).

[4] Nietzche and Heidegger excerpts translated from the French translations by Aloys Becker and Gérard Granel, *Qu'appelle t-on penser?* (Presses universitaires de France, 1999).

> Socrates, during his lifetime, and until his death, did nothing but hold and keep himself in the wind of this movement (toward what pulls away). This is why he is the most pure thinker of the Occident, *and also why he wrote nothing*. Since he who begins to write at thought's exit must without exception resemble men who take refuge out of the wind because it blows too hard. This remains the secret of a still-hidden history, that the thinkers of the Occident since Socrates, without prejudice to their greatness, must have all been "refugees." Thought enters into Literature. These ones decided the destiny of Occidental science which, passing through the *doctrina* of the Middle Ages, became the *scientia* of Modern times.

We can approach writing and its fundamental hostility toward authentic speech through a story of fratricide from the Bible.

This murder interrupts the fourth chapter of Genesis: "Cain rose up against Abel his brother, and slew him."[5] The first two chapters are the creation of the sky, the earth, and enchanted existence in the Garden of Eden. The third chapter sees the first fundamental rupture, that with Nature, the simultaneous projection into the historical Time of humanity, who has captured the power of knowledge and is destined to the double providence of freedom and death. The fourth chapter precipitates us to the second fundamental rupture, the first murder in the history of humanity.

The first murder is a fratricide. Abel (Hebel, in Hebrew) is "vapor," that which disappears without leaving a trace, in other words, speech. Elohim "had respect unto Abel," since he himself, Elohim, is Speech, and creation is *criation:* "And God said, Let there be light: and there was light." Cain is metal, an artisan of bronze and iron, the builder of the city, otherwise known as the law and writing. He is at the same time cursed and inevitably protected by Elohim ("And the Lord set a mark upon Cain"), since it is from him that the human (after "The Births" that follow this chapter) can truly proliferate in the creature-imposture duplicity that designates him, history can truly begin, and the Book can *be written*.

The first murder not only adds a second rupture to the one with Nature: extending this last, it casts and fertilizes it all at once, *sets it on*

[5] *King James Version*, Genesis 4:8. All subsequent Bible excerpts are also from the KJV.

its way. Following the rupture with Nature, the passage from the *crié* (cried out loud) to the *écrit* (written), in joining writing and culture, simultaneously opened the perspective of historical Time as the required temporality, as mechanism or as *machine* (and as *machination*) for the deployment and infinite completion of one in the other, of one by the other.

A possible etymology of the name Cain is "the man of possession." There is assuredly possession in writing, like a challenge put to God and divine creation: the bet of *re-creating* the world, to make oneself "master and possessor" through knowledge. Writing and describing are ways of metamorphosing into *things* that which one offers to find the *cause* and, thus, if not ways of denying their existence due to divine will, at least placing themselves as *almost* equal to god ("And the Lord God said, Behold, the man is become as one of us, to know good and evil"), to be like him, by his side and at his height, in the *co-naissance* (knowing/co-birthing) of this world.

What does Cain kill in killing Abel? What does writing kill in actual speech? And, a subsidiary question (though not really subsidiary): what, in fact, is *actual* speech?

The name Abel, we are told, signifies "vanity, *inconsistance*" (inconsistence, crumbling). Inconsistent, that cannot hold itself together, what cannot hold itself together compactly, and from this, lacks solidity. The Latin word *consistere* from which it derives also gave us *consistory*, which designates an assembly. As for "vanity," hearing it not in the moral sense but in its proper sense of *vannus*, expressing the idea of the void, the desert, vanity is there for "the state of the void," *vannus*, from which descends equally *evanescere*, disappear, or again *vacare*, to be vacant, unoccupied. Hebel is in fact a nomad.

So speech wanders, or nomadizes, comes and goes, appears disappears, inconsistent and void, elusive Tao, "vessel usage will never fill," invisible, impalpable, fleeting, enigmatic ("welcoming it, one does not see its front, following it, one does not see its back"), it must be the "ancestor of gods," Lao Tzu interjects mischievously. Inconsistence and vacuity are necessary to welcome and gather the world, "join oneself into the universe" rather than "speak of it" with an eye toward grasping it. To be the "world's riverbed" and not to try and "mold" it. *Actual* speech is this "supreme vacuity" that apprehends that "it is by not-doing that one wins the universe" and that "softness and weakness are superior" to hardness and strength. This speech leads, therefore, to a wisdom that recommends to "restore the knotted cords and make use of them, to find one's own food delicious, to find one's clothing beautiful, to be content with one's home and rejoice in one's customs."

This speech defies the intelligence and knowledge that "trains the great artifice" and from which flows "strange products" as "the manufacturing intelligence." This speech, properly described, belongs to the "kingdom without things"; it is "the form without form and the image without image"; it can "open and close the gate of heaven," "see all and know all without using intelligence."

Cain, founder of cities, cannot in this way move through the world or live in it. He must each time leave his *mark*, his stamp, appropriate each parcel of earth, open in each place of the world an incision, a *graft*. This graft is *graphê*, writing. This writing-knowing, which, far from sheltering speech, keeps itself well away from taking it in custody ("Am I my brother's keeper?" responds Cain to Elohim when asked about Abel) and is deployed mainly *from* its fundamental hostility and from its *bad faith* ("And the Lord said unto Cain, Where is Abel thy brother? And he said, I know not … ") in regards to speech. Speech is the veil with which Cain must henceforth cover his face in addressing his god and that immediately falls forever over the world, rendering it opaque again, each time that in the way of the writing-knowing resolves to elucidate it a little more. Actual speech is naked. Alone with its body. Destined to dissipate.

Speech is at the origin of the world's creation, writing at the start of its negation. Between one and the other, a profound vertigo that disorients us, turns us, diverts us, throws us out, there where we endlessly sink into the devastation and growth where the writing-subject is formed, takes on *spiritus*, the writing-disaster, reduced to attempts to hold up the ruin, succeeding only in accelerating the loss, believing we are warding it off, deferring it through the constant grasping of illusions.

Writing, to paraphrase Marcel Duchamp, is speech put to death "by her bachelors, even."[6]

Writing is "what remains" of creation's celebrations.

CONTINUATION, ENTWINED

In an interview with Jacqueline Leiner, in honor of the re-publication of the literary journal *Tropiques* in 1978,[7] Aimé Césaire, pressed to explain his relationship to Martinican Creole, both written and spoken, was led to assign "levels" to the French and Creole languages, on a ladder intended to be hierarchical, which had significant contradictions, or even a certain incoherence, in particular as regards his surrealist convictions.

Asked about the possibility of publishing the journal in Creole, he responded that it was "a question that didn't make sense," that such a journal was "not conceivable in Creole"; "I don't even know if it could be *expressed in Creole*." Throughout the interview, Césaire kept returning to the following words: "For me, writing is connected to French and not to Creole, that's *all*"; "French is the language in which I've always *written*." In fact, all these assertions that seemed to "surprise" his interviewer, would not in truth have surprised any Antillean, for whom the asymmetry of speaking Creole/writing French seems completely *natural*.

On the other hand, it is surprising that Césaire justified this *inconceivable* with "the current state of the language," "the level of the language, of 'creoleness' (*créolité*), if you like, which is extremely low," and is explained, according to him, by the "Martinican cultural gap." All that remained for him, therefore, was to apply this system that led him to distinguish between an evolved French language, capable of "elevating itself, expressing abstract ideas," to create a "conceptual work," capable of "reflection," and a Creole language behind in development, situated at an "extremely low level," "language of immediacy, language of folklore, of feelings, of intensity." Asked then on the use of Creole, not even in writing, but in "spoken language … political speeches, for example," he responded with a pirouette: "for me, all my speeches are affairs of reflection, they are conceptual works, so, I must make them in French."

---

[6] Marcel Duchamp, "La mariée mise à nu par ses célibataires, même (La boîte verte)," 1934.

[7] "Entretien avec Aimé Césaire par Jacqueline Leiner," *Tropiques* 1, 1978.

One can, in reading this interview, speak of a profound failure. Even more so since later in the same interview, called to respond to an assertion of Sartre, who saw in "the image a degradation of knowledge," he came to oppose him (but as a *surrealist*) with the language of "immediacy and intensity," in other words, the imagist language that he had *just* rejected with his Creole hat on: "for me, the image isn't a degradation, *au contraire*! It's rather an enrichment." "In comparison to conceptual language?" insisted Jacqueline Leiner. Césaire:

> I have the sense that it's an *Occidental* idea; the Occident privileges the concept over the image and is wary of the second, privileging logical reasoning over analogic reasoning, over the *analogon*, if you like (the motor of the image is also analogy). All of European thought was a reaction against analogic reasoning, which allows understanding, and is by the way its greatest accomplishment. But it doesn't have only advantages, it also has inconveniences. We've made great progress in reasoning, but we've moved back at the same time, in poetry, for example. Everything that was won for reasoning was lost for poetry ... It seems to me that the surrealist conception of the image is the confluence! In this understanding, Europe makes a mea-culpa and comes back, in the end, to the *primitive* traditions ... *I find that it's the image that is rich, and the idea that is poor.*"

This sense of failure is reinforced by reading the pertinent remarks that Césaire made elsewhere about Frobenius:

> I was very interested in one of his ideas, namely that a culture is born, not when man *takes hold*, but when man *is taken hold of*. The world takes hold of him, and, in turn, he plays the world, *mimes* the world. ... He is *taken hold of*, in other words, he is *possessed*, exactly as in Vodou. ... You dance, you dance, and suddenly, the guy is possessed; he has moved on.

Well said. Only, as regards *being taken hold of*, the Frobenius detour is a striking and unnecessary addition, when you have direct access through listening to the Creole language.

Our current "defense and illustration" of Creole falls into the same linear vision, an obsession with writing the language. When it's *speaking*

Creole that must almost entirely call on us; when it's the Creole workshop of *criation* that we must get going again (but this would necessitate, it's true, the mobilization of *other authorities*). We would like, in effect, to give Creole access, by any means necessary, to the status of a language. By any means necessary, since it's obvious that Creole is, at the least, resistant. To see it in reality this exposed, at such a distance from the body and the mouth, one feels no connection. Does this come from the order of the written form? There is little doubt that alphabetic writing aligns with a certain organization of the world and of thought and that the question of knowing whether it *agrees* with Creole cannot be cast aside. Leopardi remarked, for example,—reminding us of the idea of representing a language with "another kind of signs"—that in Chinese,

> characters (independent of spoken language in Chinese) were not a habit or used by the people (above all in China where the art of reading and writing is so difficult), and retain their essential forms and meaning much more easily than do the words used daily and universally … by a population whatever its origin, its opinions, its nature, its ways of being and accidents of life. (On this subject, here is an excerpt from Voltaire ... 'Almost all the words that fall frequently into conversational language are much degraded and it is difficult to explain them, something that does not happen to technical words since their meaning is more precise and less arbitrary.') We also see this with Latin, whose spoken language we have lost and kept the written characters, the essential forms and their values. Same thing with Greek, etc.

In reality, the overuse of written Creole today is a backwards step: not only in the framework of a "faulty" writing system, with its blithe and highly dubious display, or when it insidiously and fatally tackles the dismantling and decomposition of the most symbolic part of the places' identities, their names; but also at the phonetic level, an essential and delicate aspect of the Creole word, the result of the long and prodigious activity of the Creole workshop of *critation* with the aim of fabricating that veritable marvel that is the *Creole word.*

All the regressive attacks targeting the Creole word contribute to this singular debility, to the lack of vigor, to the exhaustion of the Creole workshop of *criation* that we can observe today. The result is that French words that are integrated into Creole vocabulary are no longer "deformed" but enter without giving up taxes or rights. This "deformation" is not arbitrary or without consequence: following artistic rules, it's the product of acts of linguistic self-creation with the aim of continual formation and formulation of the language in its originality and its own character. Returning to the central role of phonetics in the character of languages, Leopardi (him again) noted the following, *a contrario*, about French:

> With their pronunciation, the French remove from innumerable words which they took from Latin, Italian, etc., that expressive sonority they originally had and which is one of the most important merits of languages, etc. For example, *nausea* in Latin and in Italian, with this *au* and this *ea*, marvelously imitates the movement and noise that a man makes when his stomach rises up and his mouth and nose contort. But *nosé* imitates nothing, and resembles those things that, bereft of spirit, of salt, of humor, of fat, etc., remain as inert residues.

BIBLIOGRAPHY

Becker, Aloys and Gérard Granel. *Qu'appelle-t-on penser?* Presses universitaires de France, 1999.

The Bible: Authorized King James Version. Oxford University Press, 2008.

Césaire, Aimé and Jacqueline Leiner. "Entretien avec Aimé Césaire par Jacqueline Leiner," *Tropiques* 1, 1978.

de Montaigne, Michel. "Des Cannibales," c. 1580.

Duchamp, Marcel. "La mariée mise à nu par ses célibataires, même (La boîte verte)," 1934.

Leopardi, Giacomo, translated by Bertrand Schefer. *Zibaldone*. Editions Allia, 2004.

Thouard, Denis. *Sur le caractère national des langues, et autres écrits sur le langage*. POINTS, 2000.

AFTERWORD: MONCHOACHI'S POETICS OF TRANSLATION

Eric Fishman

Antillean literature, as long as it has existed, has endured the obligation … of translating itself, translating its body …
–Monchoachi, "What language does the poet speak?"

The Saint Lucian poet Derek Walcott once observed the irony that the manifesto which launched the Martinican Créolité literary movement was written in formal French: "['Éloge de la créolité'] urges oralité in the solemn parentheses of the lectern, not of the vegetable market it wants us to understand."[8] A similar irony may seem to be at work in "Between Crié and Écrit," which argues—in an essay—that the positivism associated with, and caused by, written language is responsible for a desecration of language, mystery, and meaning. I could note, to start, that Monchoachi is adept at wielding Western philosophies and practices to his own ends. Yet a deeper look into Monchoachi's oeuvre suggests many ways his work—as a poet, as a translator, as a cultural organizer—offers generative paths for decolonizing translation.

Despite Monchoachi's prominence in the worlds of Francophone and Creolophone literature, outside of literary circles, many people in Martinique know of him more as a cultural organizer than as a writer. He has created a number of events focused on Creole literature and culture over the past decades. One of his most prominent projects was Lakouzémi (the zémi assembly), which supported both the publication of a journal, in which "Entre crié et écrit" was originally published, as well as triannual journées de rencontre (meeting days). As the Lakouzémi mission described:

[8] Derek Walcott, "A Letter to Chamoiseau," *New York Review of Books*, August 14, 1997.

> In order to leave the discourses that make us up, subjugate us, … there is un lakou [an assembly] where the idea is to open to reconsideration, in all domains, without restriction, the most accepted approaches. The Journées-Rencontres are a moment for debates and also a place for diverse performances: dance, music, theater, art, gastronomy and other modes of expression that take place in the symbolic location of the pitt (cock-fighting auditorium).[9]

When Monchoachi asserts, in "Between Crié and Écrit," that "it's the Creole workshop of *criation* that we must get going again," I think of Lakouzémi as one of these "other authorities" he refers to: a space where Creole orality and performance are at the literal and figurative center.

Monchoachi's work as a translator is also relevant, particularly his renditions of Samuel Beckett's plays, including "La ka èspéré Godot" and "Jé-a bout" ("Endgame"), which he published and staged in Martinican Creole.

When I asked what drew him to Beckett's work, he replied that the dialogue felt very Creole to him. "I felt that I had seen and experienced scenes like those … and I wanted the audience to wonder whether maybe it's from *here*." This is a fascinating form of subversive translation—transplanting "canonical" works from the colonial language and setting, "deforming" the French into Creole. His focus on (the performance of) Creole as a living, spoken language is central to his poetry as well—and he moves from the surface level of the language to the worlds underneath.

Although he maintains close relationships with many Caribbean writers, Monchoachi has never aligned himself with the literary movements of the Francophone world, most notably rejecting the Créolité movement initiated by Patrick Chamoiseau, Jean Bernabé and Raphaël Confiant in the late 1980s. As Monchoachi explained to me, he thinks that Créolité was not radical enough in its relationship with Creole language and Creole thought. He believes that Créolité "stayed on the level of using Creole words, without ever going to *the roots*, to consider what it would mean to truly listen to Creole, to find out what the language is *actually saying*."

---

[9] Lakouzémi, lakouzemi.blogspot.com, accessed April 17, 2022.

While Chamoiseau, Bernabé, and Confiant might disagree with Monchoachi's characterization of their movement, his critique provides one way to understand his own literary methods and goals. The rebellion of Monchoachi's poetry stems from the connection between his radical experimentation with language(s) and the astonishing array of cultural and philosophical sources that the poems take as their points of departure. As he asserts in "Between Crié and Écrit": "language is a dwelling, and as a result, different languages establish different dwellings in the world, different lights and different gods, different works." His poems attempt to explore how we got here through a poetic ressourcement, starting from the deep past ("la provenance du monde"). Language—the language of the crié—also provides possible paths forward, serving as an access route to ritual, mystery, alternate ways of being.

The relationship between Martinican Creole, French, and other languages in Monchoachi's poetry is multifaceted and has evolved over time. Monchoachi's first three poetry collections, published in the 1970s, were written in Creole. In the 1980s, he shifted to "parallel" volumes in which the poems appeared in French and Creole on facing pages. Monchoachi told me that he was trying to "prove that any poetry written in French could also be written in Creole." Yet *Nostrom* (*And Here is Man*, 1982), in particular, suggests a more radical relationship. The Creole title of the volume is not translated into French, and the Creole texts are written in bold, while the French is in a gentler italic script. Perhaps the actual question asked by this text is the opposite: can everything that is said in Creole be said in French?

> There is a euphony of ideas in the nature of the French language, whereas English, and Creole itself for that matter, have a euphony of images, of simile. This euphony of ideas creates polemic, the polemic of Fanon, of *négritude*, of Césaire and Chamoiseau. The euphony of images is something else.[10]

For a translator, this sounds hopeful in theory: maybe translating these poems into English could allow different aspects of Monchoachi's poet-

[10] Derek Walcott, "A Letter to Chamoiseau."

ics to emerge. But the reality of trying to translate Monchoachi's poems—particularly his later works—is fraught.

After releasing two poetry volumes written exclusively in French, Monchoachi began his ongoing, multi-volume poetic cycle *Lémistè* (*Myst'ry*). In each volume of this cycle, Monchoachi turns to a different region of the world: the Americas, Africa and Oceania, ancient Greece, ancient Judaea, ancient China. These recent volumes are primarily written in French, but Martinican Creole often rises up to break through the linguistic frame—along with occasional interruptions of Guyanese Creole, Haitian Creole, Old French, Latin, Greek, Hebrew, Chinese, English, and Spanish, among others. Through this movement between languages, Monchoachi aims to "create gaps, to jostle the reader."[11] The tension between these languages, and particularly between French and Martinican Creole, is central to the dynamics of these poems. Here is a small excerpt as an example of his translative poetics, taken from the poem "Les Imminences" ("The Imminences"), in the first volume of *Lémistè*.[12] For those without access to these languages, I've bolded words that are taken from, or inflected with, Creole:

Qui donc excellent encore à estropier les mots
Et à danser **lèsprit**

Nègues-fèilles comme ça sous son **gade**
Tout' temps tendus ferme aux quatre points **céomonial**
Tout' temps dans la façon laver-tête
Suyer-pieds **soucouer**-corps dans la façon
Vòyer oune coup'd zos monté

Tendu comme ça
Dans la façon où ça vous prend **blo**
Où **latremblade** vous prend **cé mouri-quitter**
Et vous escorte comme ça dédoublé
Ha **lézange**!

[11] Monchoachi, interview conducted by Eric Fishman, February 2019.

[12] Monchoachi, *Lémistè*, Éditions Obsidiane, 2012.

How should the relationship between French and Creole be addressed in translations of these poems? To me, this question is closely tied to a second one: who is the intended audience of these poems? A bilingual Creole/French speaker, or a monolingual French one? And by association: how challenging should the text be for the reader? For a monolingual, mainland French speaker, Monchoachi's later poems are not all easy to gloss, although the majority of the text would still remain accessible, given phonetic proximities. This is a literary question, but also one enveloped in questions of linguistic and cultural power.

One of my ongoing explorations in translating Moncohachi's poems is of potential analogs to the relationship between Martinican Creole and French. The Caribbean offers a multiplicity of linguistic possibilities. I've consulted with a number of people so far about this question, including Monchoachi himself, Martinican author Raphaël Confiant, and Creole linguists Lawrence Carrington and Lise Winer. One of the most promising possibilities is Saint Lucian English. Saint Lucia and Martinique share not only geographical proximity (fifty miles), but also colonial, cultural, and linguistic history, reinforced by a constant stream of migrants between the two islands. Saint Lucia passed back and forth between French and English control over a dozen times over the colonial period. The contemporary language continuum includes, at one end, a French-based Creole, and so-called "Standard English" on the other, with Anglicized French Creole and Creolized English in between. These varieties, therefore, might offer promising analogs for the Martinican Creole, and I have been experimenting with these in my translations.

But is it a mistake to try and find an analog at all? In a note accompanying a handful of translations from Monchoachi's *Mantèg* (1980), scholar and translator Brent Hayes Edwards critiques this approach:

> One might be tempted to carry over the relation between French and Creole in the neocolonial Caribbean context using a putative linguistic parallel: British English juxtaposed with Jamaican dialect, for instance, or US. English and African American vernacular. The problem with this approach, however, is that it assumes a homology between systemic racialized exploitation in very different contexts.

> It seems to me reductive to imply a parallel between the situation of the United States or Jamaica and the peculiar situation of Martinique (which remains politically a département of France, one that never acquired independence after colonialism).[13]

St. Lucia, which has been a sovereign state since 1979, might belong in this list of Edwards' "very different" contexts. But Edwards is discussing Monchoachi's early work, in which French and Creole versions are on separate pages. In the volumes of *Lémistè*, Monchoachi moves between languages within single lines, phrases, even single words. Ignoring Monchoachi's poetics of translation would feel violently reductive. As Edwards notes, the linguistic tension between French and Creole comes from the histories of power and exploitation on the island. Choosing a specific English-based Creole to work with could be important, therefore, in that it makes it clear that more is at stake than just linguistic wordplay.

But if it's impossible to find a suitable analog among existing English-based Creoles, would it be preferable to instead put English into an orthographic "deformation zone," pulling it closer to Martinican Creole? To create a sort of "shadow language" that destabilizes standard English, in a similar way to Monchoachi's destabilization of French? This is the approach that translator and poet Patricia Hartland takes, for example, in their chapbook of translations from *Lémistè*, noting that they worked to "privilege[e] proximity to Kreyol over French when it [felt] possible without losing the reader."[14] This approach is appealing in that it pulls directly from Monchoachi's original languages, and its flexibility can allow the translator to also maintain other important features of a poem, such as rhythm, rhyme, or wordplay. Yet I also feel concerned that this "shadow language" is not tied to a specific place. Attending to the relationships between place, language, and thought in Monchoachi's poems feels essential.

---

[13] Brent Hayes Edwards, translator's note for "From *Manèg / Manteca*" (Monchoachi, trans. Edwards), *Chain* 10, 2003, p. 137. I am also indebted to Edwards for discussing (in this same translator's note) the idea of a "poetics of translation" in connection to Monchoachi's work.

[14] Patricia Hartland, introduction to *Liberamerica* (Monchoachi, trans. Hartland), Ugly Duckling Presse, 2020, p. 15.

There are no simple answers here. In my work with Monchoachi's poems so far, I've utilized a combination of the above approaches, grounding my translations in the specific language(s) of St. Lucia when possible, and at other moments disrupting "standard" English to mirror features of Martinican Creole. In the end, Monchoachi is a poet whose work demands multiple translations, and I hope I will not be the last to explore ways to refract his work into English.

To return to the excerpt from "The Imminences": here is one attempt at a translation.[15] These stanzas also serve as a description of one aim of Monchoachi's poetry—to channel the experience of "*being taken hold of* … listening to the Creole language."

Those who excel at mangling words
                                        And dancing lèspirit

Nègues-fèilles, wild wise men   like this alert
Whole time outstretched   to the four céomonial points
Whole time how they wash-head
Shuffle-feet scrub-body how they
              Shoot the charm'd bones

              Outstretched like this
How you're taken   bram!
How the tremblin takes you   to a death-fall,
And escorts you like this   split
                                          Ha lézangels!

[15] The translation of "The Imminences" from which this is excerpted first appeared in *AGNI* 94.

BIBLIOGRAPHY

Walcott, Derek. "A Letter to Chamoiseau," *New York Review of Books*, August 14, 1997.

Lakouzémi, lakouzemi.blogspot.com, accessed April 17, 2022.

Monchoachi. *Lémistè*. Éditions Obsidiane, 2012.

Edwards, Brent Hayes. Translator's note for "From *Manèg / Manteca*" (Monchoachi, trans. Edwards). *Chain* 10, 2003.

Monchoachi, translated by Eric Fishman. "The Imminences." *AGNI* 94, 2021.

Hartland, Patricia. Introduction to *Liberamerica* (Monchoachi, trans. Hartland). Ugly Duckling Presse, 2020.

19. BAD TRANSLATION

Elisa Taber

Paraguay is the only Latin American country where most of the population speaks one Indigenous language. Macaronic literature burgeoned there in the nineties amid Alfredo Stroessner's dictatorship ending in 1989 and Guaraní becoming an official language in 1992. Contemporary proponents range from Jopara (Spanish and Guaraní hybrid) poet Susy Delgado to Portunhol Selvagem (Portuguese and Jopara hybrid) lyric essayist Damián Cabrera. However, Guaraní culture has been subverting mestizaje, which defines the aesthetic of Latin American nationalisms and colonization, since the sixteenth century Spanish conquest of what is now Paraguay.

The Guaraní linguistic world is preserved through its rendition in and alteration of the Spanish linguistic world. Literarily untranslated words communicate the incompatibility between languages, and footnoted cultural translations bridge Indigenous and colonial cosmologies. A historical outcome of rendering Guaraní myths legible in Spanish is that they capture settler colonialists' imaginations. These settlers make mythical world-making real by creating dystopias that displace Indigenous communities. The Land-without-Evil made Paraguay the site of multiple settler colonies. This Guaraní myth refers to "a privileged, indestructible place where the earth itself provides fruit and where one does not die" (Clastres 1995). It inspired the Garden of Eden founded by Russian Mennonites, which I describe in my fiction collection *An Archipelago in a Landlocked Country*.

Paraguayan **authors turn into translators** to write in Spanish. However, they refuse to translate some Guaraní words. These ñe'ẽs, or **"word-souls,"** are untranslatable because they conjure ancient mythical beings. For example, the Pombero is summoned by a tuñe, or whistle. Therefore, Guaraní word-souls are woven into their Spanish prose. I understand texts and cultures as webs of significance spun by human beings. The macaronic literary form is inspired by ñandutí, or **"spider's web,"** a Spanish lace whose weblike pattern represents Guaraní symbols. This textile technique illustrates how Guaraní culture exemplifies and subverts the mestizaje concept of mutually cannibalizing cultural codes and the baroque notion of decorazione assoluta in conjunction (Echeverría 1998; Adorno 1997). It is emancipated from its purpose, to decorate, and the colonial cultural forms are transfigured with remnants of the pre-Hispanic world.

The subversion of mestizaje defines **"bad" translation**: Indigenous linguistic and cultural codes are untranslatable into colonial ones, but not vice versa. Thus, Guaraní word-souls are incorporated into a Spanish vocabulary and possess readers of the latter language if they catch the mythical references. These **writers/translators turn into anthropologists** to culturally translate the literarily untranslatable terms in footnotes. They describe these mythical spirits in the context of a Guaraní cosmology. I call this **mythopoetizaje**, the recreation of myths (mythopoesis) born out of mestizaje. Unlike poesis, a creative force, mythopoesis is recreative, it offers a different way of being (ontology) within the existing world. Guaraní recreated myths are not facts from the past nor utopias for the future but serve as an imaginary and conceptual beyond from which to critique the present: this is true fiction.

Word-souls are "mythemes" (Lévi-Strauss 1963) or differential, relational, and plural constituent units of myth. The double vision required to recognize the soul in a badly translated word evinces another way of being in and understanding the world. This dual communication hinges on attunement, which I understand as speaking in order to listen to others, rather than eloquence, listening to yourself. The inclination of baroque mestizo writing to the act of listening can be traced to its origin in orality. The poet Elicura Chihuailaf (1999) describes oralitura (oral literature) in relation to the Mapuche concept of nüxam, as a conversation with one's deceased elders as well as a depiction of contemporary life, partly oral and partly written. The other whom you attune to can be your interlocutor or a word-soul. The latter weave a recreated mythical beyond which transcends "the willing suspension of disbelief" (Coleridge 1907). Thus, mythopoetizaje not only leads readers to imagine an alternate reality, but also to think differently and alter their behavior.

Inspired by Paraguayan bilingual authors, I propose a writing/translation/ethnography practice for conversing between other Indigenous and colonial linguistic worlds. The concept clusters I coined—**writer/translator/anthropologist**—and lyric terms—**webs of word-souls**, **"bad" translation**, and **mythopoetizaje**—constitute a model that others can practice. My concepts invert valuations and expand, not delimit, the identity and practice of my ethnographic interlocutors (contemporary Paraguayan writers), which I partly share as a Paraguayan-born writer and translator. Like them, I know to carefully handle webs of word-souls that gesture to ancient worlds because they are as fragile as they are complex.

The following can be considered an ethnography of a poetry collection. *Ita ha'eñoso/Ya no está sola la piedra Formerly and Again Known as Pyambu/Dream Pattering Soles* is a trilingual chapbook written in Guaraní by Miguelángel Meza (2021); translated into Spanish by Carlos Villagra Marsal, Jacobo Rauskin, and the author; and subsequently translated into English by me. *Pyambu* (Dream Pattering Soles), the original title, was replaced by the Spanish translators with *Ya no está sola la piedra* (The Stone Is No Longer Alone), whose literal Guaraní translation, *Naha'eñovéima ita*, was rejected by the author and replaced with *Ita ha'eñoso* (Solitude Abandons Stone). The transformation of the title, illustrated by the following diagrams and explained in the footnotes, demonstrates how my ethnographic English translation from Guaraní, via a Spanish bridge, draws out cultural references implicit in the original:

Ita ha'eñoso/Ya no está sola la piedra Formerly and Again Known as Pyambu/Dream Pattering Soles[1]

[1] The slashes between the Guaraní titles and their translations denote "and/or," and represent the resemblances and differences between the versions. Variation is due to the inequivalences between the syntax and vocabulary of the source and target languages. Similarity is due to the sequencing of the translations (i.e., the English could not exist without the Spanish bridge). They also denote line breaks and represent how each version continues where the last left off by expounding additional connotations latent in the original.

Ita ha'eñoso

Dream Pattering Soles

Ya no está sola la piedra

Pyambu[2]

[2] This diagram illustrates how the versions relate cyclically as well as sequentially. The English differs from the Spanish because it accesses the Guaraní directly and alters it, as exemplified by the recovery of the former title (*Pyambu/Dream Pattering Soles*). Revisiting the bilingual edition, *Ita ha'eñoso/Ya no está sola la piedra* (1985), thirty-six years after publication led the author to edit the original for the 2021 trilingual edition. Inversely, the English resembles the Spanish if it is truer to the poem's intention than the Guaraní, according to Meza, the author and Spanish co-translator. There are two bridges between the original and the English translation: Meza and the Spanish translation.

Pyambu *Ita ha'eñoso*

Dream Pattering Soles *Ya no está sola la piedra*

Pombero (Solitude Abandons Stone)

Attunement[3]

[3] This diagram illustrates the literal and literary or metaphoric meanings of the titles. The metaphors stand in for practices of attunement to other ways of being and beings in the world. The oneiric auditory image (*Dream Pattering Soles*) makes you aware of menacing presences, deities turned human—including the Pombero, a character from Paraguayan mythology. The affective visual image (Solitude Abandons Stone) makes you aware of multiple comforting presences, the humanity of the nonhuman—including a mineral.

Dream Pattering Soles is a contemporary counterpart to *Ayvu Rapyta* (The Foundation of Human Language), a collection of sacred Mbyá Guaraní myths transcribed and translated into Spanish by the anthropologist León Cadogan (1959). I untranslated the Guaraní terms that reference these myths, and expounded their literal and cultural meanings in the notes that accompany the chapbook. Meza creates a lyric flow between the ancient and new word. His writing/translation/ethnography practice consists of channeling word-souls. The slashes in the names of this practice and collection represent the interdisciplinary and interlinguistic mediation between realms. Accessing the imaginary and conceptual beyond requires altering language by incorporating word-souls.

Meza's central figures of speech are metaphors and metonymies used in conjunction. One thing substitutes another which is part of a whole. The attribute of a particular god is identifiable in a human, while that of any human is identifiable in an animal or object. The anthropologist Eduardo Viveiros de Castro (1998) claims, "Animism, interpreted as human sociality projected onto the nonhuman world, would be nothing but the metaphor of a metonymy." In *Dream Pattering Soles*, metaphors for metonymies topple the nature/culture/supernature triad and are replaced by literality. Animals are human and everything is sacred, immortal, cyclical. Paraphrasing the researcher Gloria E. Chacón (2018), the cosmos and the quotidian are symbiotic. This "thought as felt and feeling as thought" (Williams 1977) is encrypted in those words in that order; it cannot be restated but shows the reader how to become attuned to other kinds of realities.

The writer and researcher Mario Castells (2013) says of *Dream Pattering Soles*, "many words in avañe'ẽ [Guaraní] are micro-units of mythic narratives, ancient bridges that link Paraguayan society to their Guaraní ancestors." The phrase "Jasy ra'ýnteko ojovahéi hína" is a mytheme that references "The Myth of the Twins: Genesis of the Sun and the Moon." Its literal translation is "the new moon is washing its face" and literary translation, "torrential rain." It signifies that heavy rainfall and the first lunar phase are coinciding. The relationship between the moon and rain renders them parts of a whole, the natural world and Mbyá Guaraní cosmology. In *Dream Pattering Soles*, literality ultimately replaces metaphor, as attunement leads from being *with* to becoming yourself *in* an other: the lyric voice, the Pombero, or a stone freed from solitude.

Ayvu Rapyta begins with the myth of "The Customs of the Hummingbird." Ñamandú, the first being on the still barren earth, appears out of the shadows and is nursed by the primordial hummingbird. He then gains sight, literally translated as "divine wisdom," and hearing, literally, the ability to "hear-everything." The translated title of the collection, *The Foundation of Human Language*, implies that this being is animated by the word-souls that allow him to describe birth and name the original elements, the same words that compose this myth. *Dream Pattering Soles* begins with the poem "Apu/Aparezco/Appear," which thematically (though not stylistically) responds to the aforementioned myth. A disembodied lyric voice awakes in the shadows of what might be a womb or a lightless primeval world. This awakening resembles birth:

> Asẽ.
> Ajupi.
> Añakãrapu'ãsapy'a.
>
> Salgo,
> subo.
> Súbitamente levanto la cabeza.
>
> Emerge,
> ascend.
> Suddenly I raise my head.[4]

The lyric voice becomes cognizant of its body. Action is abstract and consists of single-verb lines. Darkness conceals the body that the voice describes in movement. This interconnected whole speaks for itself as well as for everything by morphing into different beings. The author is not veiled in the lyric voice and the chapbook itself is not fully autonomous, as it contains references to *Ayvu Rapyta*.

[4] The trilingual block quotes from *Dream Pattering Soles* intentionally interrupt the flow of the essay. They formally gesture to the absent presence of the Guaraní original and the Spanish bridge. In addition, they illustrate how the versions resemble or differ from each other.

The setting, which is as unimaginable as the body that the voice belongs to, is conveyed by single-adjective lines describing nothing but themselves, including the first line, "Dark…" This inhospitable landscape blurs the difference between origin and end-times. In this world, the *I* keeps vigil, guarding against an other's presence. However, the latter is denied by the final lines:

> Cheño gueteri.
> Cheño gueteri.
>
> Pero aún estoy solo.
> Aún estoy solo.
>
> But I am still alone.
> Truly alone.

The penultimate line in English follows the Spanish "Pero aún estoy solo" (But I am still alone). The English chorus literally translates the Guaraní, "Cheño gueteri" (I am truly alone), and differs from the Spanish, "Aún estoy solo" (I am still alone). The last line in English varies from the bridge, the original, and its own chorus, by omitting the pronoun "I" and the verb "to be." This omission gestures to the lack of distinction between the body of the lyric voice and the enveloping darkness, life and death, one and an other. Sometimes what rings wrong in translation is an invitation to think otherwise. The channel that the poem traverses must make itself felt in metatextual form through difference from the original. These instances in which the translator briefly transforms into an author will convey to the reader that they are reading a version; so these interventions do not damage but rather protect the original.

What is utterable and visible does not need to be interpreted as it constitutes the central metaphor, the poet's principal device. The creative linguistic function in relation to lines of light is explored in the poem "Ñe'ẽ reñói/Brota el lenguaje/Language Sprouts," which mirrors the myth of "The Foundation of Human Language," as they both analyze poesis. In *Ayvu Rapyta*, Ñamandú creates and is created by human language before the earth itself, amid primordial shadows, and before knowledge of things existed. In some versions, Ñamandú is not only kept alive by the bird, aforementioned in "The Customs of the Hummingbird" myth, but also becomes him. Then solitude leads Ñamandú to form the other gods, who together create the earth: Ñanderu py'a guasu, Father of Words; Karaí, Owner of Fire; Yakairá, Owner of Dew, Fog, and Smoke; and Tupã, Owner of Water, Rain, and Thunder. In "Language Sprouts," these four gods are conjured by invoking the elements they symbolize:

Ha ...
ojahúvo pytũre,
ohypýi tatatĩna pererĩmi.
Hendy ha tatatĩna pererĩmi.
Oñekũmberéi tatarendy
ha hyapúvo,
Oñe'ẽ tatatĩna.

Oikóma ñe'ẽ.

Y al bañarse de oscuridad,
rocía neblina delgada,
resplandor y neblina delgada.
A sí misma se lame la fogata
y al crepitar
conversa la neblina.

Ya se hizo el lenguaje.

And bathed in darkness,
fog falls as dew,
radiance and fog.
Fire licks itself
and crackles,
conversing with mist.

Now ñe'ẽ exists.

The Mbyá Guaraní elements differ from the Western ones of earth, water, fire, and air. While the Spanish repeats "neblina" and the Guaraní "tatatĩna" three times, the English alternates between "dew," "fog," and "mist." This inclination towards specificity and succinctness when naming the nonhuman is counterbalanced by the fact that all three forms of condensation are one insofar as they are Yakairá. The gods are not named but the closer the translation comes to the elements they symbolize, the more their omnipresence is rendered. What the voice and the Guaraní elements share is humanity. The world comes into existence with the appearance and transformation of the voice into stone.

"Ñe'ẽ," in the last line of the block quote above, is translated literarily or metaphorically as "language" in the title of the poem, untranslated in the body, and translated literally in an accompanying note as "word-soul." If "ñe'ẽ" had only been translated literarily as "language," the words as well as the collection as a whole would have been stripped of their anima and poesis. In addition, the references to mythical characters and the shadow text, *Ayvu Rapyta*, would have been expunged while their potential to affect and alter the conduct of readers would have been dismantled. This term can only be conveyed through cultural translation, by which I do not mean describing the skills and habits of a society, but rather introducing a concept that invites the reader to think differently about language in general. Only by understanding this term and all others as potentially animate, can this poetry collection be truly read. Beings like the lyric voice or Ñamadú always exist but are never born, and they do not die but hide temporarily. What precedes and succeeds them is not pitch dark but twilight.

After the loss of solitude and acquisition of language the speaker is conflicted between attempting and refusing to communicate. This internal tension is externalized through the emergence of light or sound so darkness or silence recede but only to reemerge. In "Mimby/Flauta/Flute," one of twenty-two poems from the original bilingual collection excluded from the trilingual chapbook, the voice becomes wind traversing underground tunnels and the perforated earth, a flute. The breath attempting to emerge through holes in the soil calls out:

che jopy, che jopy, che jopy.

me oprimen, me oprimen, me oprimen.

I am oppressed, I am oppressed, I am oppressed.

This slip of the tongue in the English and Guaraní versions, subtler in Spanish, is intentional. The odd word choice reveals that the orifices of the musical instrument are not blocked, but freedom of speech is repressed. This poem was published during Stroessner's dictatorship. Censorship is represented by and enacted on the author in this necessarily subliminal message. The socio-political context is understood and transcended by a mythical Guaraní order of being, as differences between the player, instrument, and air become blurred. The voice explains:

Chepype aikéva. Chejehegui asẽva.

Soy el que entra en sí mismo, el que de sí mismo sale.

I enter myself. I emerge from myself.

The self and context are indivisible. The voice enters itself in order not to witness but cannot cease denouncing. He is like the earth, its wind instrument, revealing the traces others leave on its surface be it litter on a sidewalk or tracks in the mud.

The promise of companionship takes the form of a deity turned human or the humanity of the nonhuman. These opposing ways of warding off solitude represent various dichotomies: the individual and society, Western and Amerindian cosmologies, and the origin and end of the world. What lies blurred between them are the concessions survival entails. The deity turned human haunting my translation is the Pombero. This character from Paraguayan-Guaraní mythology, also known as Chopombe, is described as red-haired with the body of a small man but the face of a devil. If those who enter the forest leave him tobacco and moonshine, he becomes their protector. If they do not, he becomes their enemy; he sexually assaults the women and claims their children as his own. His victims are his only witnesses. This myth is common throughout Paraguay, Argentina, and Brazil; the media still reports sightings of him in the rural Triple Frontier region.

The Pombero appears throughout the collection but is only named and described physically in "Mboriahu/Pobreza/Poverty." His presence becomes conflated with one of the few human characters in the collection, an unnamed homeless man asleep next to his dog in the shade of a queen palm. The lyric voice accesses the Pombero through sounds that verge on language. First, he takes aural form in the dreamer's moans and then, in pacing footsteps, which may occur in reality, his memories, or dreams:

> ¡Oikytĩ pirĩ tuñe'ẽ!
> Heñói kerasy.
> Chopombe
>   oguata
>   okupére.
>
> Un silbo corta el calofrío.
> Aflora el quejido al sueño.
> El duende
>   trajina
>   detrás de la casa.
>
> Piercing whistle erupts goosebumps.
> Moaning nightmares surface.
> Chopombe
>   paces
>   out back.

Instead of following the Spanish version by translating Chopombe as "duende" (elf), the English leaves the Guaraní untranslated. Naming him retains his characteristics from Paraguayan-Guaraní mythology, which are described in the notes. I also refer there to his depictions in newspaper articles and oral narratives that continue to circulate. Looking briefly past the potential for cruelty, there is desperation in the astuteness of this character. In this poem, Meza denounces the experience of need bluntly but without morbid details. "Poverty" left me asking: What kind of escape do myth and poetry provide one in material need?

The Pombero never speaks but emits unintelligible noises. These auditory images are cinematic because they are narrated in the third person, and sound is transformed through the imagination into sight. "Whistle" and "dream pattering souls," eponymous with the collection, are word-souls associated with the spirit of the Pombero. They appear in "Ñasaindy/Plenilunio/Full Moon" and "Y'ita pererĩ/Delgada piedra de agua/Pebble," and are culturally translated in the notes. The lyric voice describes the Pombero's visits to sleepers. The nearly comprehensible sounds emitted by dreamers, moans, and the mythical character, the whistle, along with their joint status as absent presences blurs the difference between them. The physicality of the sleepers and the nighttime events are indicated by miniscule or astronomical details. In "Full Moon," the reader is told that the sleeper's "Legs shrink," but it is unclear if he is curling up or transforming into the Pombero, given his short stature. As night ends, even the absent sun is implicated in what took place:

> Oipykua mbyjápe jasy
> ha oho ho'a, oguejy, oike, okañy.
> ... otĩ vaicha
>   iko'ẽ hag̃ua yvy ári.
>
> La luna sujeta las estrellas
> y se va cayendo, desciende, penetra; se oculta
> como si se avergonzara
>   de amanecer sobre la tierra.
>
> Moon ties stars to sky
> and falls, penetrates, hides
> —as if ashamed
>   to dawn on earth.

The embarrassment of the dawn cements that something occurred which oversteps the oneiric threshold, even if spirit possession was involved.

The poems in sequence tell the story of gradually discovering everything is alive and then dying or dead. "Mainumby/Colibrí/

Hummingbird," the sixth of ten poems, marks the shift towards death. The bird, unlike the Pombero, does not provoke a becoming that renders events unsayable and unseeable but, instead, more sensorially available. The lyric voice maintains its distinct character while morphing into another. The name of the primordial bird, Mainumby, is untranslated in the body of this poem. This proper noun restores its humanity. As its wing almost imperceptibly grazes the lips of the embodied voice it begins to tell Mainumby's story:

> Nde juru puku mboy'úpe,
> rehasávo yvytu
> che ãhóre reje'o;
> ka'aguýpe
>   embokua.
>
> Con tu largo pico libador
> perforas el monte,
> y al cruzar el viento
> te sellas en mis suspiros.
>
> Your long sipping beak
> pierces
>   the forest,
> and traversing the wind
> you seal my sighs.

In its flightpath an "aleph" (Borges 1998) opens, a point in space that contains all others. The voice witnesses a group of men turning into a stream, and the forest collapsing into itself and immolating. The poem ends with the hummingbird growing to a supernatural size and coming to resemble a crow. In the last two lines, its wing grazes the embodied voice's cheek and the *I* falls, a reference to "The Man Who Resembled the Sun." In the myth, an owl impregnates the first woman by grazing her head with its wing. Here, the same action provokes what can be interpreted as death or loss of all-knowingness.

Narrative, like ethnography, lends itself to description. The characteristic concision of poetry strips renditions of reality to their essence, akin to a ghostly presence. The visual image of an apocalypse in miniature and the almost tactile image of the bird becoming part of the disembodied voice portray a world as real as the presence of the hummingbird. However, this intangible reality can only be alluded to through metaphors for metonymies, never revealed in its entirety without neutralizing its potential to affect. In the same way that possession makes a becoming visible, atmospheric poetry makes a being with, in suspension, experientially available. Such a poem renders the feeling of being nothing and everything at once; essentially, connected.

Meza's poetry collection traces a lyric arc from nothing to nothing, only the flicker of an unfulfilled promise of companionship between birth and death. The collection ends with the poem "Y'ita pererĩ/Delgada piedra de agua/Pebble." The title in English mirrors the tendency towards concision in Guaraní, which cannot be achieved in Spanish. The literal translation of the Spanish title, "Slim Water Stone," is lyrical but sacrifices specificity. Opting for naming over description may recreate the micro-unit of myth in another language through translation, a sort of summoning. The epigraph reads "End times;" not only does the voice enter the void and the collection conclude, but so does this world. He finds himself alone but with his soul. This separation between the physical and spiritual is present in all the poems, but now it is the body that speaks. As the wind razes, he becomes mineral:

Ojehýi yvytu,
mbegue ojepyso.
Ipohýi ã itaky sarambi.

Hormiguea el viento
y lentamente se propaga.
Pesa este roquedal disperso.

Tingling wind
sprawls slowly.
Dispersed stones anchor.

Darkness reclaims the human language of the lyric voice. First, it becomes an intelligible sound: a whistle rising from a swamp that means "hear how it hurts!" Then, in the last line, it exclaims:

Ama'ẽ arasẽre ha oke,
oke … arasẽ.
¡Mamóiko ko'ẽ rekañy … !

Miro el Naciente y está dormido,
está dormido el Naciente.
¡Dónde te has perdido, amanecer!

Look East, it is asleep,
sun asleep.
You lost yourself, dawn!

The same sun that was ashamed to dawn is now lost. Losing the ability to see and ceasing to exist come as a relief to the voice, equivalent to the anguish of awakening. Earlier in the poem, the last line appears as a question, "You lost yourself, dawn?" As an exclamation, it reproaches some(thing/one) lost in a game turned serious. Not only life and death but the good and harm done to survive are staked in light and dark. The chorus, "Soul alone," which echoes that of the first poem, "I am truly alone," also feels like a question. The promise of companionship lingers behind this collection.

The opposite of being alone is having another within you or everything around you being animate. *Dream Pattering Soles* operates partly within a Western cosmology and partly within an Amerindian one, especially when in dialogue with *Ayvu Rapyta*. Viveiros de Castro explains that "the manifest form of each species is a mere envelope (a 'clothing') which conceals an internal human form" (Viveiros de Castro 1998). In both the threatening and consoling instances of companionship, the lyric voice acts as a medium attuned to deities turned human or the humanity of the nonhuman. A serious language game animates these spirits beyond the pages of the chapbook. It is unclear whether the collection ends with the world or whether this is a wink to the reader, as if it will now become real. *Ayvu Rapyta* creates a narrative arc from creation to apocalypse to recreation, so the cycle recurs.

Meza's *Dream Pattering Soles* is essentially untranslatable. The poems in this collection refuse to abide by the rules of the target language because they do not obey those of the source. The ungraspable essence, embodied by the italicized words that root the book to its origin, is a personal language. The untranslated terms summon myths, but there are many more words that evoke memories for the author yet remain inaccessible to the reader. However, words pushed to the limits of becoming sounds briefly bridge not only linguistic and cultural gaps but also the distance between individuals, creating a sense of connection. When I spoke to Meza on the phone, he began describing the silence of Luque, where he lives, then stopped so I could hear a traveling salesman calling his wares and, after he passed by, a cricket. This auditory image offered a return to the sincerity encapsulated in his poems. Lyricism does not allow for distance; one feels what the words express before fully understanding them. Bad translation requires true faith to recreate the aphoristic essence of a poem, while remaining under its spell.

BIBLIOGRAPHY

Adorno, Theodor W. 1997. *Aesthetic Theory*. Translated by Robert Hullot-Kentor. Minneapolis: University of Minnesota Press.

Borges, Jorge Luis. 1998. *Collected Fictions*. Translated by Andrew Hurley. New York: Viking Press.

Burrows, David J., and Simon O'Sullivan. 2019. *Fictioning: The Myth-Functions of Contemporary Art and Philosophy*. Edinburgh: Edinburgh University Press.

Cadogan, León. 1959. *Ayvu Rapyta: Textos míticos de los Mbyá-Guaraní del Guairá*. São Paulo: Facultade de Filosofia, Ciencias e Letras, Universidade de São Paulo.

Castells, Mario. 2013. "El uso de la metáfora en *Ita ha'eñoso / Ya no está sola la piedra* de Miguelángel Meza." Buenos Aires: Taller del Grupo de Estudios Sociales sobre Paraguay (GESP).

Chacón, Gloria E. 2018. *Indigenous Cosmolectics: Kab'awil and the Making of Maya and Zapotec Literatures*. Chapel Hill: University of North Carolina Press.

Chihuailaf, Elicura. 1999. *Recado confidencial a los chilenos*. Santiago de Chile: LOM Ediciones.

Clastres, Hélène. 1995. *The Land-without-Evil: Tupí-Guaraní Prophetism.* Translated by Jacqueline Grenez Brovender. Urbana: University of Illinois Press.

Coleridge, Samuel Taylor. 1907. *Biographia Literaria.* Edited by John Shawcross. Oxford: Clarendon Press.

Cornejo Polar, Antonio. 2013. *Writing in the Air: Heterogeneity and the Persistence of Oral Tradition in Andean Literatures.* Translated by Lynda J. Jentsch. Durham: Duke University Press.

Echeverría, Bolíivar. 1998. *La modernidad de los barroco.* Mexico City: Ediciones Era.

Geertz, Clifford. 1973. *The Interpretation of Cultures: Selected Essays.* New York: Basic Books.

Greetham, D. C. 1999. "Ontology: Being in the Text." *Theories of the Text.* Oxford: Oxford University Press.

Jeppesen, Travis. 2019. *Bad Writing.* Berlin: Sternberg Press.

Kohn, Eduardo. 2013. *How Forests Think: Toward an Anthropology Beyond the Human.* Berkeley: University of California Press.

Lévi-Strauss, Claude. 1963. "The Structural Study of Myth." *Structural Anthropology.* New York: Basic Books.

Malinowski, Bronislaw. 2019. "The Language of Magic." *The Importance of Language.* Edited by Max Black. Ithaca: Cornell University Press. 72-90.

Meza, Miguelángel. 1985. *Ita ha'eñoso / Ya no está sola la piedra.* Translated into Spanish by Carlos Villagra Marsal, Jacobo Rauskin, and Miguelángel Meza. Asunción: Alcándara Editora.

Meza, Miguelángel. 2021. *Ita ha'eñoso / Ya no está sola la piedra Formerly and Again Known as Pyambu / Dream Pattering Soles.* Translated into English by Elisa Taber and into Spanish by Carlos Villagra Marsal, Jacobo Rauskin, and Miguelángel Meza. New York: Ugly Duckling Presse.

Viveiros de Castro, Eduardo. 1998. "Cosmological Deixis and Amerindian Perspectivism." *The Journal of the Royal Anthropological Institute* 4 (3): 469–488.

Viveiros de Castro, Eduardo. 2015. *Cannibal Metaphysics.* Translated by Peter Skafish. Minneapolis: University of Minnesota Press.

Williams, Raymond. 1977. *Marxism and Literature.* Oxford: Oxford University Press.

20. CONSIDERING THE DYSTRANSLATION OF *ZONG!*

M. NourbeSe Philip and Barbara Ofosu-Somuah

For 24 hours on December 10th, 2021, M. NourbeSe Philip gathered writers, artists, storytellers, academics, and griots for a durational live stream— REVRRB/ORAshuns. Through offerings and conversation, readings and performances, attendants mourned, honored, and defended *Zong! (2008)*. A book-length poetry cycle, *Zong!* unbends and reshapes the text of a British legal case, Gregson v. Gilbert, to tell the story of the drowning massacre of 133 enslaved Africans over 10 days in 1781. For 24 hours, we held each other virtually and carried the work in all its forms.

Central to the gathering was naming the dystranslation of *Zong!* by the Italian publisher Benway Series and the many forms of violence it upholds. In a conversation with Setaey Adamu Boateng that Philip shares on her website, she outlines the myriad injustices of this translation, which include a failure to inform her it was happening, a failure to respect form in, for instance, her representation via word clusters, and absolute neglect of underlying intent. Others who had previously attempted to translate *Zong!* into Italian had noted:

> In an attempt to translate *Zong!* into Italian, the book presented some insurmountable problems, concerning its untranslatability. The idea of untranslatability came along little by little: the more we tried to translate it into Italian – in the etymological sense, trying to translate both language and experience across the postcolonial borders – the less we felt at ease translating a book that does not want to be read. We felt challenged when we tried to grab this language and catch a minimal sense in order to achieve a coherent translation into Italian.[1]

Yet, Benway Series dismissed Philip's focus on reparation and healing as "identity differences" and "presumed essences." Philip writes: "At least five people, including representatives of the Canada Council which funded the translation in the amount of some $13,000, have been involved in this Italian translation of *Zong!*, all of whom are white, and yet no one thought it necessary to consult with me, the Black and African-descended author of the said work, which engages with the transatlantic slave trade and which, as plainly stated on the cover—as told to the author by Setaey Adamu Boateng—involved Ancestral voices." Central to this violence, in my opinion, is the extension of colonial assumptions of ownership. As a Black woman translator of works primarily written by Black Italian women, I was struck by how *Zong!*'s translation became yet another site of unapologetic colonial claiming.

I came to *Zong!* at the start of the Covid-19 pandemic in 2020. Grieving a dying world and drowning in the sorrow of unknowing, *Zong!* and other texts by Black women writers became anchors. For months I returned to it. Looking for meaning in the empty spaces of the text, I hoped that its constant breaking, remolding, and disfiguring of language as a form of mourning would help me deal with the compounding losses wrought by the pandemic. Though not always understandable, the book's poetic form—an ululation and an expansion of grief through repetition—gave me space to carry my own sadness. Like many readers since its publication in 2008, reading *Zong!* meant healing and breaking, gathering language and being gathered.

In February 2022, two months after the gathering, NourbeSe and I met virtually once more. Over a two-hour conversation, we attempted to unravel questions of erasure, racial violence, death of empire, permission, and silencing.

– Barbara Ofosu-Somuah

Barbara Ofosu-Somuah: You have said in interviews that *Zong!* is meant to be untranslatable. It's supposed to be unintelligible. Each reader makes their own journey through the book, keeping in mind both history and current context. The dystranslation of *Zong!* and the conflict around it, for me, is yet another example of Italy's inability to acknowledge its colonial past. So, when incidents like this happen, some Italians can't step back and say, "this is a real and lived manifestation of that history." Rather, everything becomes, "This is a one-time thing. There's no history here. There's no lineage here." So, let's start with Italy.

M. NourbeSe Philip: Yes. It's quite poignant and ironic because I've said for the longest while that my soul city is Rome. There's something about it that really pulls me. The light in the city is like nothing I've seen before. The other aspect of Rome that called to me was being among ruins, particularly the ruins of empire, which I find comforting. On one trip, I was feeling depressed, I don't remember why. I left the hotel room and took a bus to that area—the Via dei Fori Imperiali—and after walking down that broad avenue and seeing those ruins, I felt as if my heart and my spirit had lifted—something had lifted off of me. And on the most superficial of levels, what comforts me is the fact that one can see—I could see—tangible evidence of the end of empire. And that gives me an assurance that this too shall pass—all that we live with now, what Ngũgĩ wa Thiong'o calls the American Imperium. The Roman Empire ended, the British Empire came to an end. I recall during the days of Margaret Thatcher's right-wing rule in Britain, I used to love going to Roman ruins in Great Britain and thinking, "Yes, that ended, and this too shall end."

So, what has happened with the "dystranslation" of *Zong!* is even more poignant because I have such fond and strong feelings about Rome, my soul city. We're still in COVID times and I haven't traveled at all, but I do wonder if I'll ever go back there, and how I'll feel when I do.

Barbara Ofosu-Somuah: Thinking about Italy and the idea of an empire ending, and about Rome, a place that is a tangible and visceral example of that end of empire, and then *Zong!,* which is about empire starting or empire being built. Can you speak to the book?

M. NourbeSe Philip: I think the book exists in the interstices of the Roman and the British Empires, which no longer exist but continue to throw long shadows. Latin, the linguistic legacy of the Roman Empire, still proliferates English in the sciences, in Christianity, and of course, in the law, which is where it connects with *Zong!*. Law and religion were two of the forces greatly at work in the transatlantic trade of Africans. Latin terms and expressions from both those areas of life weave themselves throughout the text. Though contemporary Italy only came into being some three decades after the end of slavery in the British Empire in 1838, it entered the colonial game in the 20th century by acquiring colonies, namely Somalia, Libya, Ethiopia, and Eritrea. While acknowledging that the Vatican is an independent city-state, we have to recall the power of the various Popes who, through the mechanism of the Papal Bull, justified, condoned, and encouraged stripping Africans of every vestige of their humanity, their beingness in the colonization of the Americas. I would argue that the Vatican's role in worldwide colonialism continues to reverberate alongside the very real history of Italy's colonial past. Those reverberations, I believe, are felt throughout Italy and have a direct bearing on its relationship with its Black and African-descended populations.

Barbara Ofosu-Somuah: And how does that history show up when thinking about the book and its dystranslation?

M. NourbeSe Philip: Benway Series took a page straight out of the colonial handbook. Within the context of the racist hierarchy developed by European scholars like Arthur de Gobineau, the Italians, not being Aryan, are considered less white. But we also know that many aspects of Italian culture, such as opera, are highly valued as part of European culture and that Italy is, indeed, a part of the European family and shares a colonial history with it. When Europe, including Great Britain, began making violent inroads into Africa, Asia, and Oceania, alongside the extraction of raw materials and destruction of the culture, they appropriated aspects of the various cultures, including words, foods, clothing, etc.

Regarding Africa, in addition to the kidnapping and transporting of millions of Africans for forced labor to the New World, the products of the plastic arts themselves—masks and other artifacts, for instance, as well as the aesthetics of those practices—were appropriated, resulting in a revivifying of Western art and leading to what we call the modernist art movement. But as we know, spirit was always an integral part of those practices in Africa. These carvings were always designed and intended to honor something more significant than humans, be it a god, an ancestor, or a cultural idea. So the aesthetics were taken, more often than not, literally, as in the plunder of artifacts which, as someone once corrected me, are beings made manifest, but the spirit inherent in the "object" through ritual or ceremony was impossible to translate or appropriate. And indeed, one of the emails from the publishers says something along those lines: "Benway claims validity and legitimacy for the book, both in terms of poetic restitution and in terms of the graphic rendering of the text, which, moreover, has been elaborated and produced with the utmost care."[2] The emphasis is on the production of the "graphic rendering of the text" with the "utmost care." But what the publishers, Benway Series, and the translator failed to understand was that it wasn't simply about the graphics. The graphics are in service of something more significant, as with carvings and sculptures from various African cultures. Those forms were in service of something much larger than the physical form itself. So too, what they call the "graphic rendering" of *Zong!* is in service of something larger than the appearance of the text itself, which, I must add here, they did not even get right. That something else has to do with honoring the drowned and murdered, which the text performs and manifests in its appearance. So, to summarize, what the publishers and the translator did regarding the so-called translation of the text was a reprise of that age-old colonial strategy of theft and appropriation under cover of law, which Benway Series also used to justify this travesty. I say under the guise of law because in one of their emails, they write that: "[t]he Italian edition of *Zong!* is the object of a publishing agreement between Benway, who bought the rights, and Wesleyan, who sold them." The echoes of contract law of insurance, which the ship's owners used to justify the massacre of the "cargo" of enslaved Africans on board the Zong, are almost too loud to bear.

Barbara Ofosu-Somuah: There is a thread here about erasure: the erasure of Italy's colonial past, your story, your work, your Blackness. You are a Black woman writer who wrote a story about enslaved African people, and your work was mistranslated by a white Italian translator and a white press without your consent. Without apology. There is persistent erasure of your voice. Can you speak to the implications of this perpetual and cyclical erasure?

M. NourbeSe Philip: One of the things I want to get out of the way is the accusation made by Benway Series on their website that my objections to the translation were based on the fact that the translator was white. This is untrue, and they know it to be untrue. If one looks at the correspondence between myself and Benway Series, it is clear that when I first get the information that the book has been translated, apart from my anxiety about whether or not they got permission to do it, there's no concern expressed about the person being white. In fact, I thank them on my behalf and on behalf of the ancestors. That was before I saw what they had done with it. Further, two of my books, *She Tries Her Tongue; Her Silence Softly Breaks* and *Harriet's Daughter* were translated by white writers, the former into Spanish, the latter into German. There is a discussion to be had about whether the race of the translator is relevant, particularly with a work like *Zong!*, but that was not the issue here.

I see the evasion or erasing of Italy's colonial past playing out in the translator's correspondence with me. Morresi focuses on the migrant crisis that Italy currently faces, and she draws equivalencies, shockingly and inappropriately to my mind, between the trans-Atlantic trade in enslaved Africans and the migrant crisis. Of course, there are links and resonances when we consider the effects of the depredations of colonialism and how it wreaked havoc on the continent of Africa and the Middle East, but to my mind, she didn't grasp what that centuries-long horror and trauma that was genocidal in intent and effect, what I call the Maafa[3],was all about. Beyond the obvious consistencies—Black bodies being the subject of trade, Black bodies on board boats, Black bodies in the sea—and despite the historical links created through the many and variously exploitative colonial projects, the differences are enormous. From Morresi's point of view, the purpose of *Zong!* was to enhance and elaborate—in effect, to add to the issues pertinent to the migrant crisis in Italy.

> As I wrote to you some time ago, the premises of the Zong massacre are still active also here in the Mediterranean, with thousands of lives lost to the blind politics of the European Union and to the fascist sentiments periodically resurging in Italy. (Sep. 1, 2021, email from Renata Morresi)

In that sense, *Zong!* is subjugated to the needs and demands of Morresi and the publishers and what they consider to be the issue. I say that because when I explained to her that there are reasons why the words in *Zong!* are placed the way they are and that the placement honors those who drowned on board the *Zong!*, she replied that her arrangement was based on the observations of a helicopter pilot observing bodies in the Mediterranean:

> ...the pilots involved chose the floating body of a woman dressed in vivid purple to function as a reference point (in Italian it's called "punto nave", literally "ship point") to give coordinates and assistance to the rescuing team below. So, I treated the clusters not as points pinned on the page, but as floating points in relation to each other, which could provide a form of help in this moment of danger, even after more than 200 years. (Jul. 1, 2021, email from Renata Morresi)

She writes of "points pinned on the page," which is not what is happening in the organization of the words—it's all about the words and, therefore, text needing to breathe. Morresi's arrogance is astonishing, and the result is yet another level of erasure that you name so well—the failure or perhaps refusal to understand the specificity of the history that *Zong!* comes out of, and her refusal to accept my own explanation. Not to mention the horrific objectification of the woman's body. Who was she? Surely not only a body floating in the Mediterranean Sea.

One of the things I've learned as a writer is that universality comes out of the particular—so I do understand how *Zong!* can be instrumental in looking at what we're living with today—the migrant crisis, for instance—but its specificity, particularly to form, must be respected. *Zong!* is also doing another kind of work that addresses spirit, something larger than who we are and which I think is really necessary for us, particularly the descendants of the Maafa, or the trans-Atlantic trade, on both sides of the Atlantic.

I think *Zong!* functions best within community and with a collectivity of voices, which fundamentally goes against the grain of this individualistic, capitalist society. It is profoundly about relationship—at its most basic, the relationship of the words to the spaces in the poem, which I think are the most critical activity happening on the page, if you can call a space an activity. But if we understand that one aspect of those spaces is breath, you can see how the space becomes active. It's not the words, it's the spaces, the lacunae, which are doing the work.

And what do they, the spaces, mean? I don't exactly know myself. I sometimes think of them as spaces of potentiality, spaces of the future, spaces that represent the erasure of the past, spaces that function as musical rests, as spaces of fugal amnesia—all that and more. But in its entirety, the work is about relations—the "poetics of relations" as Édouard Glissant describes.[4] If, for instance, you take any page in the book, you can draw these networks of lines between the individual words and fragments across those breathed spaces of potentiality, creating nets and networks of relations. That is what the translator and publishers missed as they focused on the "graphics" and misinterpreted breathed space and relationality as "pinned points." If you'll excuse the metaphor, they were utterly at sea in their understanding of this text.

What I am very clear about and what I was very conscious of when I was writing *Zong!* was the deep, rigorous inner structure of the work, to the sections that come after the opening section, "Os." The scholar and poet Faizal Deen describes this as a spiritual architecture. The structure arises from the requirement that no word, fragment, or cluster of words can come directly under another. They must always seek the space above to breathe, which is integrally linked to the massacre by drowning, in that they, the words, are seeking the space above to breathe, as the Africans who were thrown overboard were not able to. Therefore, the words and spaces above and below are in a context of relationship—shifting relationships. Each word or fragment is breathing

Zong! #

uncommon case

great weight new trial

great weight

new trial uncommon case

new trial

uncommon case great weight

uncommon weight

great trial new case

great trial

new case uncommon weight

Zong! #1

w w w w a wa

w a w a t

er wa s

our wa

te r gg g g go

o oo goo d

waa wa wa

w w waa

ter o oh

on o ne w one

w o n d d d

ey d a

dey a ah ay

s one day s

wa wa

Zong! #21

is being is

or

should

is is

is

be

being

or

been

is was

is

should be

or

have been

is there

into the space above. That is non-negotiable and is described in the accompanying essay, "Notanda": "[E]very word or word cluster is seeking a space directly above within which to fit itself and in so doing falls into relation with others either above, below or laterally. This is the governing principle and adds a strong visual quality to the work."[5] The translation failed to observe this principle of organization. The text is working around breath and can be seen to foreshadow the deaths of African American men such as Eric Garner and George Floyd, who cried out that they couldn't breathe as they were being murdered by law enforcement officers. If this work is ever translated again, it might look somewhat different in another language because word lengths and so on differ, but I am not committed to the appearance of the text as in the original edition. However, the text must breathe and live in the breaths of those who died and for whom we now breathe. What I'm committed to is the work that the text is doing. The text is simultaneously performing and allowing a pneumatic function to happen; in our reading of the text, which can be said to be arranged pneumatically, we are carrying out the act of breathing for those who couldn't breathe at an earlier time. Perhaps we can say it is a pneumatic text lodged in the poetics of breath. Morresi did not understand this requirement when she did the translation, and refused to accept it when I explained it. She writes in another email: "I could work on a reviewed edition where the main concern is spacing. I will have to reconsider lines, then, and pages." (Sep. 1, 2021, email from Renata Morresi) Morresi misses the point entirely—the main concern is not spacing but the spaces—the words must breathe into the space above, so there must be a space above to allow them to breathe. This means that they are always in relationship to the words above and below. As happened in the translation, you cannot have a word or phrases come directly under another. There are very few things in my life that I'm this categorical about, but this is one of them. And so, their failure, not just failure, but their refusal, their adamant, arrogant refusal to listen to what I had to say about what was happening in the text, is what made it so difficult and painful.

What you have are layers of erasure to which I will add this final one: Benway Series is a bilingual press, and all their works so far have appeared in bilingual editions, with one exception: *Holocaust* by Charles

Reznikoff, which came with a fulsome explanation as to why the original English was not published alongside the Italian. *Zong!* is the second-ever Benway Series publication to appear only in Italian, but there is no explanation for the absence of the original English. There is the erasure of me as the author by all the parties, including Wesleyan, who sold the translation rights for $150 and went ahead with a translation of my work without telling me; the erasure of the full meaning of the text; the further erasure in refusing to listen to my explanations about why the translation was unacceptable, and failure to present at least an explanation for the absence of the English, yet again another form of erasure.

The Charter of the International Federation of Translators states quite clearly that the translator "being a 'secondary' author...is required to accept special obligations with respect to the author of the original work." That was not how the translator interacted with me—she had her own ideas:

> [T]housands of lives [are] lost to the blind politics of the European Union and to the fascist sentiments periodically resurging in Italy. I would lie if I said that this translation was done without having them in mind, keeping always in mind their obliterated conversations with history, the survivors' plea for human civil rights, and their children's call for citizenship. I think the dotted line I have traced between them and the victims of the Zong massacre does not erase the voices of your book, rather it makes them resonate further. This is just my perspective, neither formally nor ethically unfounded though.

At no time did the translator ever acknowledge, let alone accept the validity of what I was saying regarding the formal properties of the work.

The publishers, Benway Series, were dismissive, as is clear from the quotation above; and Wesleyan insisted that the versions were the same until I said I was going to make the entire situation public, at which point they got on board, acknowledged the differences, agreed that the translated text was not the same as the original and joined me in calling for the books to be destroyed. It's still painful when I think of what happened, and I can still feel a bodily reaction to the whole experience, even as I talk about it now because it's such a blatant and overdetermined example of how much contempt they have for me. Even as they speak admiringly about the book and how wonderful it is, I sense them thinking I should be grateful for the fact they thought the book worthy of translation, so what was my problem? I do not believe I would have been treated the same way if I were a white male poet. What I see in my mind's eye when I think of it are the doors being closed in Black people's faces, in my face, of Black people being told, "No, we're not renting the place any longer." All of the many and different ways in which Black people's presence, our being human, is met with this implacable kind of rejection, even as our creations, our cultural products, and our very labor are appropriated. And in that respect, I say that this is an example of the articulation and performance of whiteness—a certain Eurocentric whiteness that leads with a nurtured, carefully cultivated innocence about Italy's role in the machinations of colonialism and racism. I don't know how else to explain it. Whiteness, arrogance, European arrogance, all those things.

Barbara Ofosu-Somuah: I've heard people, particularly white folks, express frustration about *Zong!*. They could not understand it and felt it was not meant for them. Your response in those instances was simply, "Well, it's not for you." There is power in those moments, particularly for me as a young Black woman who has spent a lot of my life shaping and shifting myself to be palatable. Can you speak to the tension or expectation to be palatable? Have you also felt that? When did you begin saying, "No, this is who I am. This is the work I create. You meet the work where it is, and it's not going to meet you where you are?"

M. NourbeSe Philip: The question you raise around palatability finds its best answer in what Glissant refers to as the right to opacity, which on the street takes the form of, "it's a Black thing, you won't understand." As scholars, writers and thinkers, we want our ideas to be disseminated and engaged with by a wide readership. Still, we must all contend with the historical reality of our subjugated cultures in a white supremacist, capitalist system, which has meant theft and appropriation of resources, cultural expressions, and products. We have seldom been able to protect ourselves from the rapacious acts of such a system, let alone our creative expressivities, our inner lives, or our psyches. As

Black and African-descended people, we will naturally respond differently to the idea that a non-Black person has an inherent right to our cultural products. They don't. The non-Black person, if they are interested and willing to make changes, will not approach in that manner. Someone declaring *Zong!* a masterpiece, for instance, as happened at REVRRB/ORAshuns[6], and saying that other people have a "right" to access it leaves me unmoved. I acknowledge here how many works I have read in translation and for which I am grateful. There is no "right" to translation, particularly as it relates to Black and African-descended people. Let us not forget that it was through the translation of the Bible into indigenous languages in Africa, for instance, that cultures were diminished and even destroyed. It was how people were made afraid of their own indigenous belief systems and came to see them as expressions of the devil. So, translation has a checkered history in all subjugated cultures. And for me, the declaration of it being a masterpiece ranks lower than if I have a sense that the ancestors are happy with the work the text is doing, which is first and foremost laying those souls to rest.

What runs through this entire debacle, the sense I have, is that those involved believe I don't know the "value" of the work or are not interested in how I hold the work. They believe that they can best bestow meaning, their meaning, on the work. They clearly don't know my work enough to know that everything in *Zong!* was laid down in my two previous publications, *She Tries Her Tongue; Her Silence Softly Breaks* and *Looking for Livingstone: An Odyssey of Silence.* In the former, I was working with the idea of taking up space on the page and fragmentation and disjuncture, and in the latter, I explored the concept of silence within the colonial context. It's almost as if they perceive the work to be the product of someone who doesn't know what they're doing—that it hasn't been thought through deeply and rigorously. They don't know, for instance, that *Zong!*, while perfectly accessible to being seen as a modern work, working with the idea of the fragment and bricolage, is also within the millennia-old Nigerian Yoruba oral tradition of Oriki.[7] That there is a formal strength and rigor to the text [which is] necessary to meet the ferocity of the cataclysm that was the Maafa. You can't meet what that experience meant and survive it without having inner and societal structures to meet it. That strength in the text is reflected in the organizing principle of the fragments seeking to breathe into the space above.

When I left the practice of law many years ago, I remember thinking and writing that it was going to be our griots, our storytellers, our writers, our artists, our musicians who would be the ones to really help us to get over, to integrate this—I don't even have a word for it sometimes, this state into which we've been cast. I am happy the work can shore up people like yourself even in its indecipherability and in my acknowledgment of its opacity. When I wrote *Zong!*, one of the ideas I was working with was how to make meaning [out] of this atrocity, that you can take people, consider them things and throw them overboard, and then try to collect insurance money for them because they weren't considered people. One of the justices who sat on the appeal in Gregson vs. Gilbert[8] actually said it was no different from throwing animals overboard. And so, meaning and absence of meaning and failure of meaning are woven into my engagement with the story. My question is, should we, as beings who are human, understand what happened? Should we even try? How is it possible to understand such an act?

Barbara Ofosu-Somuah: As we wrap up, I'm wondering two things, is *Zong!* translatable, and who gets to translate *Zong!*?

M. NourbeSe Philip: I have said in the "Notanda" that *Zong!* is already a translation on one level, and the idea of translation is woven throughout the work. For instance, you have a word that means something in French or English, and that same word will mean something else in Ewe or Yoruba or any other language I was using. So, on that level, *Zong!* is already working with translation. The scholar Richard Douglass-Chin wrote in an email to me: "the work is a translation (Latin trans + latere, to carry) of the bones of the dead." (Sep 8, 2021).

Translation requires that the translator know both the language of the original text and the text into which the work is being translated. As we know, language is never simply just words. I want to argue two things here related to language. In an earlier essay, I raise the issue of "whether the absence of certain words in a language make understanding an experience impossible. If those words do not exist, how do speakers of that language understand that for which no word exists, or what they cannot or refuse to perceive. English and the languages in which colonialism happened do not have the words for what happened to us."[9] Still, I want to take this further and ask—of myself, of you, and of others—what if the "language" in which it is written comprises more than the words and more than the weight of inference and resonance than words already carry? What if that is what I'm gesturing towards when I talk about the placement of the words on the page being linked to the events of the massacre—the drownings? And further, what if the "more than words" is actually akin to the opacity that Glissant talks of and insists that we have a right to? What if that opacity, that I think is more than the sum of its parts, is untranslatable?

It's not about making ourselves palatable. There's a sense in which I think while the system exists, we will never be palatable. Doesn't matter what we do. While the system exists. So, we may as well please ourselves.

I think the task we have before us—even me at this advanced age—is working deeply, sometimes quietly, sometimes strenuously, sometimes gently, sometimes not so gently, bit by bit, and being honest with and to ourselves and our truths. The necessary changes will not happen overnight, and we always need to keep in mind that we're playing the long game. This system did not mean us any good. Indeed, it intended our destruction—and unfortunately, we have to function in it and enjoy our lives within it and even the perks it offers—we are, after all, human. Still, I believe we also have to be aware that we're trying to develop another way of being, another way of living together; to quote the groundbreaking scholar, Dr. Sylvia Wynter, we can find new ways to be "human as praxis," through ceremonies that she insists must be found "post humanism." Given our diversity, we need many ceremonies, and I believe *Zong!* to be a code, a palimpsest for one such small enactment of what she calls for and which we need in this particular extended moment we inhabit.

ENDNOTES

1. Barone, Linda & Masone, Roberto. (2014). Marlene NourbeSe Philip's *Zong!*: There Is No Telling This Story, it Must Be Translated. Testi e Linguaggi. 217-230.
2. All correspondence between NourbeSe and the parties can be found at the Set Speaks blog on www.nourbese.com
3. Maafa, a Kiswahili word meaning a great disaster. I use it to refer to the forced removal and enslavement and murder of millions of Africans in the Americas, the Caribbean, and in Arab countries. I first heard the word used in this respect by the late scholar, Dr. Barbara Christian.
4. Édouard Glissant, Poetics of Relations, transl. Betsy Wing, The University of Michigan Press, Ann Arbor, Michigan, 1997
5. M. NourbeSe Philip, *Zong!*, Wesleyan University Press, Middleton, p. 203, 2008
6. REVRRB/ORAshuns—24-hour online event hosted by M. NourbeSe Philip, featuring poets, artists, writers, scholars held on December 10, 2021.
7. Oriki is an oral art form of the Yoruba people. It is usually translated as praise poetry. The similarity with *Zong!* lies in the fact that it is disjunctive, fragmented and coded and requires completion by the listener.
8. Gregson vs. Gilbert is the case that dealt with the massacre on board the Zong.
9. M. NourbeSe Philip, "Jammin' Still," BlanK: Essays and Interviews, book*hug, Toronto, 2017.

21. NOT A GOOD FIT

Madhu H. Kaza

For most of my school years beginning in the second grade I studied French. By the time I reached college, I was reading novels and writing papers in the language, error-ridden though my essays were. A decade after I had stopped studying it, I used French for the first time outside of the classroom, making a trip to Paris when I was nearly thirty years old. I missed quite a lot of the Parisian slang, but on a research trip years later to Chamonix in southeast France I found that I was able to navigate interviews and archives comfortably. I'm not fluent, but the grammar is imprinted in me after all those years of drills. Still, I've used French so little in my life. I'm not sure – as the schoolgirl might ask – what it's for.

I studied Spanish formally for three weeks in Mexico the summer before I began a Ph.D. program in comparative literature. All those years spent in submission to the rules of French, it turned out, did serve a purpose: learning Spanish was easy. I make many mistakes, but despite the three weeks versus twelve years of study, I am more at ease in Spanish than in French. Italian, I studied for one semester, sitting in on an intensive beginner's class in order to take a proficiency exam, which I passed six weeks into the term. I enjoyed speaking Italian, its drawn out vowels in particular. I only learned the basics, enough to talk to a bus driver in Rome or read a magazine. Two summers ago I spent a few weeks working on Portuguese on the Duolingo App. I had just published an essay about Clarice Lispector and I wanted more intimacy with her work than reading her in English (and in Spanish translation) allowed. After I breezed through the exercises on my subway commute for two weeks, the app told me that I was 40 percent fluent in Brazilian Portuguese, but I understood that I was simply 40 percent fluent in

Duolingo. I can't hear Portuguese at all. In college I had also studied Hindi for two semesters, which means I can read and write the script, but my vocabulary is so limited I mostly tell people, "Hindi nahi aati" – I don't know Hindi. I got half way through a semester of Danish, until I got kicked out of the class because auditors were not allowed. I continued for a few months to study it on my own.

I enjoy languages. I'm good at learning them and don't fret as much as I might about my lack of mastery. I can imagine translating from French or Spanish and, with much greater effort, Italian. Recently an acquaintance and colleague approached me about collaborating on a translation of essays by Inger Christensen. Though I am not proficient in Danish, my answer was a quixotic, yes. The language that I cannot imagine translating from is Telugu. Though English is the language of my greatest fluency, Telugu is my first language. In the last decade I have translated contemporary Telugu fiction into English, and yet it remains improbable to think of myself as a translator from this language. I have never been able to articulate the difficulties of this work, tied as they are to my status as an immigrant and to problems of cultural difference.

Literary translation requires considerable skill and attention, of course. I don't mean to sound cavalier about the real challenges of any translation task, and don't claim that translating from European languages is easy. When I say I can imagine translating from French and Spanish or Italian or even Danish, I'm not assuming that I would be a great translator from any of these languages. I have, in fact, translated some poetry from Spanish, which I struggled with for all the usual reasons that translating poetry is difficult. I mean, instead, to emphasize the word "imagine." Translating from world-dominant languages is imaginable, apart from the issue of one's skill, precisely because of their dominance and circulation in the world.

So I want to talk about something other than individual skill. Questions of skill, considerations of all the technical fault lines of translation, take up so much space in discussions of literary translation in the U.S. that they obscure other kinds of problems we might also address. Issues that are less often named, for instance, include questions of literary values and their connection to culture and power. In thinking about my own experience of translating from Telugu, the problem of skill gives way to questions of access (how does one acquire and strengthen skills) and cultural difference (what gets recognized as skill in writing in English, and in Telugu?). At stake is not merely diversity or inclusion, but the kinds of literary cultures we want to participate in and build.

* * *

I translate because I am an immigrant. I write and think and dream in a language distant from my origins, but a language that has become a home. I was brought to the U.S. by my parents when I was five years old. They had immigrated a few years earlier and sent for me when they were sufficiently settled. It's not an unusual immigration story. On my fifth birthday, I left my home, my school, friends, neighbors, extended family, my language, a climate, a whole world and way of life as well as my grandmother and grandfather who had parented me up until then. I lost a life and traveled towards a new one. If translation is the "afterlife" of a text, as Walter Benjamin first argued, I think of all of my life in the U.S. and in English as the afterlife of a child who was raised in a small town in coastal Andhra Pradesh, India. I am living out a translated life. Like many child immigrants I wonder about the person I would have become if I had not left home, the girl whom I had abandoned.

The difficulties with translation from Telugu began, then, with a split in my self. Or to put that statement in reverse: the very knot of identity for me is connected to problems of translation, of what can and cannot be transmitted across borders. If assimilation were easy, if one life and one identity could be converted smoothly into another, I would not need to translate. But the different parts of my self sit in jagged, disproportionate relation inside me, and Telugu and English are two languages that almost never meet in my current North American life. Virtually no Telugu literature in translation has been published in the U.S. Because Telugu is a vernacular rather than national language, English translations circulate primarily on the Indian subcontinent itself.

I didn't come to translation from a love of a particular Telugu writer or a general interest in Telugu literature. I wanted very badly as a young adult to be returned to something that had been disappeared from my life, to find a way to carry the language I had left behind with me. I felt the desire for the language of my infancy, what Dante understood as the emotional call of the language of the cradle. Because it includes the intimacy created with first words, it is a deeply felt yearning, but one difficult to describe, and it's far from literary. When I was growing up in the American Midwest in the 1980s it not only seemed as if Telugu had been voided in me, but also as if the language itself was obscure and dying in the world. It was spoken within the Telugu community in the U.S., but most people outside that community didn't even know that the language existed. To not have the language recognized meant I had to bury that essential, original part of my self. I didn't think I could ever get close to the language again. Once my Telugu speaking relatives died, I imagined it would die out in me as well.

There was a book in my parents' house called *The History of the Kammas*, which is the caste I belong to. Although the cover was titled in English, the book itself was written in Telugu. I recall looking through the book many times, lamenting that I would never be able to crack open knowledge of this history because I could not read the script. I think it was that book that first made me want to try to learn to read Telugu. My first attempt at study was the summer after I graduated from high school. I spent a month at my aunt's house in India, and she arranged to have her friend, a teacher, give me Telugu lessons one hour a day at 7am. There was no pedagogy for teaching Telugu as a foreign language, and his antiquated schoolteacher style meant that I mostly repeated syllables and words without comprehending what I was saying. Nothing came of it.

In college at the University of Michigan, I perused books in the graduate library on the history of Andhra Pradesh and Telugu. The library held books written in Telugu, but I couldn't read them. There were a significant number of students from Telugu-speaking families at Michigan and so, in my second year of college I spoke to the head of the South Asian Studies program asking what it might take to get Telugu language classes started at the university. At that time the only university offering courses in Telugu in the U.S. was the University of Wisconsin in Madison, where Telugu scholar V. Narayana Rao taught. I was told that I would need to raise at least a million dollars for the university to set up an endowed chair or I'd need to raise thirty thousand dollars for a contingent instructor for a year. I decided to try to raise thirty thousand dollars from the Telugu community of southeastern Michigan. I drew up a list of people who said they would be interested in taking a class if it were offered and spent a few months on a fundraising campaign. But I was an unconvincing nineteen year old, and the people with the deepest pockets in the community were professionals who wanted their own children to get professional degrees. They were unsentimental about their language and saw no prospects or future in it. I abandoned my naïve campaign and made a plan to spend a summer learning to read and write Telugu in Wisconsin. It was a revelation that summer to move from orality to literacy as an adult. I discovered that I knew how to make statements or ask questions in Telugu but I didn't always know the component words in a speech act. I was far from being skilled enough to do translation, but I had gained a rudimentary literacy. This, I realized, allowed me to grow out of my childlike relation to the language; to be able to navigate traffic signs or read a newspaper strengthened my sense of belonging to a contemporary culture. What opened up was the possibility of engaging Telugu in greater complexity, of moving from an intimate and emotional personal connection to the language to the consideration of a wider cultural discourse through the writing of others.

The following year, I spent two months in India, and during this time I set up Telugu lessons with a retired professor in Hyderabad. Now that I could read, I was aware of how stunted my vocabulary was and I wanted to build my range of expression. I had to arrange for a car and driver to take me from one end of Hyderabad to his home in Secunderabad, an hour's drive. The professor was a warm and learned man, but he was clearly dismayed by my lack of sophistication. My lexicon was limited to the diction of day-to-day life and I read very slowly. On more than one occasion, when I arrived at his house his wife informed me that he was out on an errand or having coffee with his friends. She would bring me a cool drink and fruit and urge me to wait until he returned. In the Indian manner she told me that he'd be back any minute, which meant eventually. On those occasions, I'd wait for a little while to be polite and then leave. In those two months, I learned a few dozen new words and my reading level remained unchanged. All through these years, I attended a number of Telugu literary events and conferences in the U.S. organized by local Telugu community organizations. I was, without exception, the only young person at these events. I understood very little of what I heard because the texts being discussed were written in a formal, literary Telugu, whereas I only understood the demotic, and because I didn't know the literary history and culture. While the elders were vaguely pleased that I was interested in Telugu literature, they didn't want to interrupt their conversations to break the text or the conversation down to my level. I was still much too slow to gain entry into these groups and so, again, learned very little. The turning point for me came in 2005, thirteen years after I first attempted to study Telugu, when Sitaram Ari, a translator and friend of my parents, asked me to collaborate on translating a book of contemporary Telugu short stories. It was the bridge I needed.

I relate this sad history because I want to be clear that for many years my attempts to improve my Telugu were charged with futility, a constant, chronic feeling of failure. This failure, I recognize only now, was not about my potential talent for or sensitivity to the language, nor was it about my abilities as a writer. I simply didn't have a way. Literary translation is always the result of enormous labor; that labor includes years of study and reading that precedes any particular translation project. And that labor requires either pre-existing privilege and knowledge or access to resources and an infrastructure to support the study of foreign languages. With French, Spanish or any number of other languages I would certainly have had to work hard to gain fluency, but I understood that there were paths: the college courses, the study abroad, the grants and mentorship, graduate school and so on.

My lack of access to Telugu was structural, not an accident of individual circumstances; nor was it an indicator of actual Telugu literary production. Though few people in the U.S. have heard of it, Telugu is not obscure. It is a major language, with over 80 million speakers worldwide, one of the top fifteen languages spoken in the world and the fastest growing language in the U.S. And the dearth of translation from Telugu is not due to an underdeveloped written culture. Telugu has a longstanding literary tradition which includes a Sanskritized classical language and a vibrant modern literary culture in the contemporary demotic. But it's far easier in the U.S. to find literature translated from Dutch or Italian or Hungarian, for example, than from Telugu (or other South Asian languages for that matter). Given that Telugu is more widely spoken than Dutch, Italian or Hungarian, and given its long and active literary tradition, what accounts for the disproportionate difficulty of accessing Telugu? What accounts for the absence of Telugu literature in English translation outside of India? The answers are complex, but I think they are neither strictly aesthetic nor geographical, but about how aesthetics carry politics and history.

* * *

When I began translating from Telugu I ran into a major difficulty: a clash of literary cultures. I could see that it would not be easy to get the work I had begun to read published in the U.S. Telugu literature is quite different in sensibility from contemporary American writing. I could imagine editors in the U.S. receiving Telugu texts and saying (and they did), "It's just not a good fit for us." This phrase is one that many of us have heard in our lives in contexts where decisions around inclusion are being weighed, for instance in the arenas of publishing and employment. It's a phrase that's been directed at me and one I've heard on the other side as a member of hiring and academic search committees. It's not difficult to recognize this lazy phrase as a cover for unexamined bias. What does it mean? What is the phrase doing as a speech act other than closing the door with a feigned politeness and no explanation? I'm not arguing here that people are owed detailed explanations of rejection. Rather, I'm interested in how such a phrase short-circuits the possibility of self-reflection among cultural gatekeepers. It would be easy to simply call people or institutions out as racist or imperialist. But I'm looking for a way to think beyond the impasse of saying that something or someone is not a good fit. One way to do this is to examine more closely what we find ill-fitting, not only by articulating what a work of art is doing, and the values that launch the work, but also naming our own aesthetic values and situating them in the context of a particular time and place.

Translation is an obvious site to think through difference because there's no way around problems of incompatibility, whether it's the incompatibility of words and idioms in different languages or differences in literary traditions and cultural values. What translation opens us up to is not only the wider world that we are a small part of but also the possibility of seeing our own culture more clearly and considering how the languages and literatures of others might expand and alter our own traditions. In *This Little Art*, Kate Briggs argues that translation might be viewed not as the transmission from one language to another of the translator's expert knowledge of a text that's already understood, but as "productive of *new* knowledge." Translation leads us to an "as yet un-acquired, un-grounded, knowledge of the world – of experiences and stories, ideas and things, people and places, tastes and smells, rhythms and sounds." I think this new knowledge of other places, people, things, ideas, creates an opportunity to re-encounter what we already know – the people, places, rhythms, ideas of our own culture – and makes space for strands of thought not yet present or possible. Ultimately, I think it's limiting to maintain an assimilationist, domesticizing stance that translation shows us that other people are just like us. If we need others to be just like us, then our idea of the human is a problem. Beyond identifying with others, it's important to respect the "opacity" of the other, to use Édouard Glissant's term, and to create bridges across points of disidentification. Translation can show us that people are different – they think and write and organize their lives differently than we do. One thing that emerges from recognition of this difference is the opportunity to see our own lives in new ways and to energize our own literary culture. Exposure to other literatures creates unexpected possibilities for Anglophone writing. One question, though, is what gets through? How much difference and what kinds of difference do we allow?

As is the case in many world literatures, the figure of the writer in Telugu culture is connected with the role of the intellectual. The writer is recognized as a thinker of public and moral standing and very likely a partisan. Telugu fiction doesn't eschew politics. Writers may identify as Dalit, Marxist, feminist practitioners. Individual sensibilities certainly come through, but writing is directly connected to social and political worlds. Much of contemporary Telugu fiction arises from a social realist aesthetic. It doesn't lean towards a Western or global reader; it's a literature for its people.

When I first started reading Telugu, I didn't immediately love the stories I was translating. They were feminist stories of women coming to awakening in a deeply misogynist society, but I found the stories somewhat didactic, overly sociological. I didn't think they were all that good. But I knew that I would have to think through this first judgment. I couldn't dismiss the quality of the work without further interrogation, nor could I assume my reaction was an innocent matter of taste. To reject the work outright because it didn't meet my expectations would be to re-enact a colonial violence. In 1835 Lord Macauley delivered his famous "Minute on Indian Education" in which he claimed that "a single shelf of a good European library was worth the whole native literature of India and Arabia." This inane but calculated assessment served as explicit justification for a colonial project of English education that intended to create "a class of persons, Indian in blood and colour, but English in taste, in opinions, in morals, and in intellect." Such a class was formed to strengthen British hegemony in order to control the colony. In a contemporary context, the rejection of a vernacular literature which doesn't align with American aesthetics or a global style, can reinforce neo-imperialist, market driven demands for more easily translatable and easily consumable global fiction.

We could perhaps embrace work that fails to meet our aesthetic expectations on anthropological grounds. In the spirit of inclusion we might acknowledge, for instance, that contemporary Telugu fiction reflects its culture and read it primarily for cultural information. This anthropological approach presents its own problems. At best it is patronizing, at worst another form of cultural violence. The Iraqi-born writer and translator Sinan Antoon has written about the neo-colonial approaches to Arabic literature after the 9/11 terrorist attacks, in which it is read and translated not as literature, but for its "forensic interest," which treats it "as anthropology or ethnology or getting into the Arab mind." Here, translation serves a dubious tactical project, the cultural equivalent of intelligence gathering. Even in a less charged context, for example with the case of Telugu, it is a form of cultural condescension to disregard the fact that the texts of another culture are constructed as *literature*, that they are made with aesthetic choices in mind. I think it's imperative to greet other literatures with questions that are beyond sociological, by engaging the literary values that inspire the work.

If we recognize, for instance, that Telugu literature is grounded in different literary values than American fiction, we might note that in Telugu, literature is more directly valued for its role in social exchange. Telugu respects telling as much as showing. Such differences, though, lead us back towards something else: a consideration of our own values. Many American writers tend to think of themselves as not ideologically marked. But like white privilege or male privilege that idea signals a kind of blinkered thinking. (It's not surprising that the Telugu writers I've met are mostly interested in African-American writing in the U.S.) The dominant American style of fiction is one in which the writer takes care *not* to reveal commitments. It is considered a defect if a work contains sociological elements. The writer should focus on showing and not telling, image not exposition. The writing is anti-intellectual. But we know that these attitudes are themselves a result of cold-war ideology. The CIA was directly involved in channeling artists and writers towards non-political work that reinforced American individualism and capitalism. The CIA funding of important institutions such as the *Paris Review* and the Iowa Writers Program is well documented.

I'm not arguing that we need to abandon our aesthetic values and ideals. Rather, I'm hoping for more awareness of those values and a recognition that those values are historical constructions as opposed to universal measurements of excellence. As John Keene remarks in an essay, "Elements of Literary Style": "No style stands outside the history in which it emerges, or outside the political, social and cultural context in which the author deploys it." He writes:

> a sociocultural asynchrony with the dominant styles in the Anglophone world can present challenges, making the work sound stilted and out of fashion, even though it was written just yesterday and rings with a freshness in its own local context. The easier any literary

> style is to carry over into English, the more likely it is to be read globally, and perhaps translated into other languages from English.... Yet what about English-language writers themselves, or those writers in other languages who see the unique resources of their native tongues and their national and cultural literary and oral traditions as a source of strength, artistry, and innovation, as well as the fount of their distinctive styles?

Among the latter, those writing out of the resources of their own local traditions rather than in a dominant Anglophone style, are Telugu writers. Because their work defies Anglophone literary values it will be less widely read and readily dismissed as failing to meet American standards of excellence and taste. It will not be a good fit.

But it is precisely in this moment of democratic crisis in the U.S. that other literatures with their ill-fitting aesthetics and divergent styles might be most necessary for us to encounter. It's a moment when we need to ask ourselves what function our literary forms serve in our culture and what other purposes they might serve. If I found myself uncomfortable with the committed writing that I first stumbled upon in Telugu, I was also discouraged when I was in India in 2014 and I was asked why, after the U.S. had been at war for more than ten years, the war didn't show up in American writing. Why are people still writing about suburban ennui, someone asked me? Why doesn't your literature reflect upon the terrible upheaval your country has created in the world? These were excellent questions, and I had no answer.

These days I ask myself and others, what can writers in the U.S. do with their words to reflect an era in which language is being used as an instrument of unreality? I think one way of seeing what writers *might* do is to read more texts in translation, to read work that *does* think through social and political issues, and literatures in which writers have a tradition of deploying irony, contorting language or stressing silence to respond to censorship and authoritarianism. Literature in translation, especially literature that is at odds with our own dominant literary culture, can point us to our areas of ignorance; by engaging radical difference we may discover paths – not one but many – that writers have blazed through difficult times.

★ ★ ★

In the end I believe that a tolerance for incongruence is itself of value both in life and in art. As an immigrant I know that the different languages, ideas, ways of perceiving and being in the world that have formed me don't add up to a harmonious whole. There are strands of my identity that will never fit well together. The ability to hold divergent and even contradictory ways of looking at a word, a concept, or an attitude, however, can give rise, I think, to a useful skepticism of smug cultural certainties, a mode of thinking that Edward Said described as "contrapuntal." I don't have a comforting resolution for the conflicting values in American and Telugu literature, but the conflict allows me to look at both aesthetic pleasure and literary ethics in each culture more clearly.

When we bring together incongruent works, or allow ourselves to be receptive to work that doesn't immediately abide with our conventions, some other way of seeing ourselves or a new form of knowledge can come into being. I recently co-translated short fiction by the feminist Telugu writer, Vimala. After working through the short story "The Dark Girl's Laughter," the story became connected in my mind with Marguerite Duras's novella *The Square.* I don't make the comparison with marketing slogans in mind. I don't mean to say, "If you like Marguerite Duras, try Vimala" or "Vimala is the Marguerite Duras of India." The mention of the French writer is not meant to add legitimacy to the Telugu writer. Besides, their styles are distinct. It's that one work made me think of the other. Vimala's story is steeped in specific caste, gender, class and cultural concerns of South India, and Duras' story has a particularly European existential despair. But both "The Dark Girl's Laughter," and *The Square*, provide insight into the lives of dispossessed young women who stubbornly cling to hope when they have no good reason to do so. Both stories lack conventional narrative drive and work instead through a circular and repetitive conversation between two strangers. Each, in a different manner, says something about the lives of marginalized young women. When I look at Vimala's story in this way, further connections – to Clarice Lispector, Mercè Rodoreda, Nawal El Saadawi – come to mind. In reading across distances what we gain is not simply more company, but an opening for solidarity.

ACKNOWLEDGEMENTS

Shushan Avagyan I wish to thank my editors, Kavita Bhanot and Jeremy Tiang, whose practical assistance and moral support defy description. They stood by me during a difficult time, and I am grateful to them for their trust and boundless care. I also wish to thank Deborah Smith for her vision and commitment.

Khairani Barokka Thank you to my family, friends, and partner, to Cok Sawitri, and to the other artists and writers in the piece whose work inspired me. Thank you *Poetry Review* and editor Emily Berry, for first publishing part of this essay in a different form. Thank you editors Jeremy Tiang and Kavita Bhanot, and Tilted Axis.

Lúcia Collischonn I would like to thank all of my fellow mongrel mutt translators, some of whom I interviewed for my thesis, who gave me energy and inspiration to go forth with researching a type of translation that goes against the norm. Special thanks to the editors, Jeremy and Kavita, for their timely and considerate feedback, to the other contributors, specially Anton Hur, who has always been a champion of my work and an extremely quotable genius. I would like to also thank my supervisors Chantal Wright and Will Amos, as well as my friend Rhiannon for pointing out that I do not need to sound like an angry academic on Twitter.

Onaiza Drabu This essay is a product of two years of conversation with my partner, Ali. Nuances in my words were generously teased out by Sila Ulucay, Muqeet Drabu, Muizz Drabu and Kavita Bhanot, patiently, over months.

Kaiama L. Glover This article originally appeared in a special issue of Esprit Créateur [59.2 (summer 2019): 25-41] titled "Race and the Aesthetic in French and Francophone Cultures".

Eluned Gramich I would like to thank Sian Northey, Elin Haf Gruffydd Jones, Alexandra Büchler, Alys Conran and – most importantly – Katie Gramich (also known as Mam) for their support and inspirational work in the world of Welsh writing and translation. Diolch o galon!

Anton Hur I would like to thank BITNA.

Sawad Hussain I would like to thank Eugene Adogla for his tremendous support throughout my career.

Layla Benitez-James Thank you to John Keene whose work first inspired the seeds of this essay, and special thanks to the community of the ever-growing Patchwork Project for inspiration and support. Deep gratitude to the Tilted Axis team for putting together this collection and to editors Jeremy Tiang and Kavita Bhanot.

Madhu Kaza Thanks to Emily Wolahan, who first commissioned this piece for *Two Lines*, and to Sitaramayya Ari for inviting me into the world of translation.

Eric Fishman Thank you to Monchoachi and Mireille Jean-Gilles for their guidance, to Lisa Nam for her wisdom, and to my family for their support.

Barbara Ofosu-Somuah Thank you to M. NourbeSe Philip for making space for mourning, honoring, and defending the ancestors with her work.

Gitanjali Patel & **Nariman Youssef** Our first thanks go to Yew Leong who gave our piece its first home at Asymptote Journal. We are so grateful to Kavita and Jeremy for giving it a new life in this anthology.

Sofia Rehman Special thanks to Mustapha Sheikh for his insights and foresight, to Kavita Bhanot for probing and pushing my essay into its best version with wisdom, and to all the Tilted Axis team for their efforts.

Aaron Robertson For Bettie Robertson.

Hamid Roslan is deeply grateful to Jeremy and Kavita for providing the space for this essay to emerge.

Elisa Taber Thank you for telling me stories, Miguelángel.

Sandra Tamele To Ingamo and Cina, the gentle souls that saw the early spark and kindled it with their loving hands, thank you from the bottom of my heart.

Kavita Bhanot & **Jeremy Tiang** This anthology draws from the work of far too many translators, thinkers and writers to name them all individually here — we are grateful to all who have initiated and continued these difficult conversations, and to those who will continue having them in the future. We could not have done this alone, and would like to thank the many people who guided, inspired and advised us, particularly Ayesha Manazir Siddiqi, Alice Frecknall, Kristen Alfaro, Hana Sandhu, Alyea Canada, and Julia Sanches. Much love to Abbas Jaffary for this wonderful layout and to Amandine Forest for the brilliant cover design. We are also thankful for the support of Kate Griffin and all at the National Centre for Writing, Anna Goode and all at the British Centre for Literary Translation, and above all Deborah Smith and all at Tilted Axis Press.

ABOUT THE CONTRIBUTORS

Shushan Avagyan is the translator of *Energy of Delusion: A Book on Plot, Bowstring: On the Dissimilarity of the Similar, A Hunt for Optimism, The Hamburg Score,* and *On the Theory of Prose* by Viktor Shklovsky (Dalkey Archive), *Art and Production* by Boris Arvatov (Pluto), and *I Want to Live: Poems of Shushanik Kurghinian* (AIWA). Her articles and translations have appeared in numerous publications, including *The Review of Contemporary Fiction, CONTEXT, Asymptote, Contemporary Women's Writing, Music & Literature,* and *The Los Angeles Review of Books.* She teaches at the American University of Armenia.

Khairani Barokka is a Minang-Javanese writer and artist from Jakarta, whose work has been presented widely internationally, and centres disability justice as anticolonial praxis. Among her honours, she has been *Modern Poetry in Translation*'s Inaugural Poet-in-Residence, a UNFPA Indonesian Young Leader Driving Social Change, an *Artforum* Must-See, UK Associate Artist at Delfina Foundation, and Associate Artist at the National Centre for Writing (UK). Okka is the author-illustrator of *Indigenous Species* (Tilted Axis), author of *Rope* (Nine Arches), and co-editor of *Stairs and Whispers: D/deaf and Disabled Poets Write Back* (Nine Arches). Her latest book is *Ultimatum Orangutan* (Nine Arches), shortlisted for the Barbellion Prize.

Lúcia Collischonn is a Brazilian-German translator and PhD candidate in Translation Studies at the University of Warwick. She specialises in Exophony in creative writing and translation, that is, writing literature in a foreign language and translation into and out of one's mother tongue, the theme of both her Master's dissertation and her current

PhD research. She has special interest in the works of Yoko Tawada, having translated, among others, the novel *Etüden im Schnee* (2016) which was published in Brazil in 2019. Lúcia translates from Portuguese, German and Spanish and her PhD focuses on investigating linguistic gatekeeping practices in literary translation. Research interests include: translation theory and practice, multilingualism, postcolonialism, contemporary and world literature, transnational literature and adaptation studies. Apart from her translation and academic work, she likes to lift weights and play bass guitar in her spare time.

Onaiza Drabu is a Kashmiri anthropologist and writer. She co-curates a newsletter called *Daak*, on South Asian literature and art. Her first book, *The Legend of Himal and Nagrai - Greatest Kashmiri Folktales* was published by Speaking Tiger Books in 2019.

Eric Fishman is an educator, writer, and translator. His most recent translation is *Outside: Poetry and Prose by André du Bouchet* (Bitter Oleander Press). He is currently translating a selected volume of poetry by Monchoachi, forthcoming from Phoneme Media/Deep Vellum. Fishman is also a founding editor of *Young Radish*, a magazine of poetry and art by kids and teens.

Kaiama L. Glover is Ann Whitney Olin Professor of French and Africana Studies and Faculty Director of the Digital Humanities Center at Barnard College, Columbia University. She has written extensively about Caribbean literature in such works as *A Regarded Self: Caribbean Womanhood and the Ethics of Disorderly Being* (2021) and *Haiti Unbound: A Spiralist Challenge to the Postcolonial Canon* (2010), and she is the prize-winning translator of several works of prose fiction and non-fiction. Her current project, an intellectual biography titled "For the Love of Revolution: René Depestre and the Poetics of a Radical Life," has been supported by fellowships at the Columbia Institute for Ideas and Imagination in Paris and the New York Public Library Cullman Center. She has also been awarded grants from the PEN/Heim Foundation, the National Endowment for the Arts, the National Endowment for the Humanities, and the Mellon Foundation. She is a regular contributor to the *New York Times Book Review* and is the co-host of WRITING HOME | American Voices from the Caribbean.

Eluned Gramich is a Welsh-German writer and translator. Her memoir of her time in Hokkaido, Japan, *Woman Who Brings the Rain*, won the inaugural New Welsh Writing Award in 2015 and was shortlisted for Wales Book of the Year in 2016. Her most recent publication, *Sleep Training*, is a lockdown ghost story which won The Ghastling Novella Prize 2020. She lives in Aberystwyth with her partner and 2-year-old daughter.

Anton Hur has won PEN translation grants transatlantically. His book translations include *The Court Dancer, Violets,* and *I Went to See My Father* by Kyung-Sook Shin, *The Prisoner* by Hwang Sok-yong, *Cursed Bunny* by Bora Chung, and *Love in the Big City* by Sang Young Park. He graduated from the Korea University College of Law and Seoul National University Graduate School and currently resides in Seoul.

Sawad Hussain is a translator from the Arabic whose work has been recognised by English PEN, the Anglo-Omani Society, and the Saif Ghobash Banipal Prize for Arabic Literary Translation, among others. She is a judge for the Palestine Books Awards. Her recent translations include *Passage to the Plaza* by Sahar Khalifeh and *A Bed for the King's Daughter* by Shahla Ujayli. She has run workshops introducing translation to students and adults under the auspices of Shadow Heroes, Africa Writes and Shubbak Festival. She is the 2022 translator in residence at the British Centre for Literary Translation. She tweets @sawadhussain.

Layla Benitez-James is a 2022 NEA literary fellow in translation and the author of *God Suspected My Heart Was a Geode but He Had to Make Sure*, selected by Major Jackson for Cave Canem's 2017 Toi Derricotte & Cornelius Eady Chapbook Prize and published by Jai-Alai Books in Miami. Layla has served as the Director of Literary Outreach for the Unamuno Author Series in Madrid and is the editor of its poetry festival anthology, Desperate Literature. Poems and essays can be found at

Black Femme Collective, Virginia Quarterly Review, Latino Book Review, Poetry London, Acentos Review, Hinchas de Poesia, and World Literature Today. Audio essays about translation are available at Asymptote Journal and book reviews of contemporary poetry collections can be found at Poetry Foundation's Harriet Books.

Mona Kareem is the author of three poetry collections. She is a recipient of a 2021 NEA literary grant, and a fellow at Center for the Humanities at Tufts University. She held fellowships and residencies with Princeton University, Poetry International, Arab-American National Museum, Writers' Centre Norwich, and Forum Transregionale Studien. Her most recent publication *Femme Ghosts* is a trilingual chapbook published by Publication Studio in Fall 2019. Her work has been translated into nine languages, and appears in *LitHub, The Common, Brooklyn Rail, Michigan Quarterly, Fence, Ambit, Poetry London, The Los Angeles Review of Books, Asymptote, Words Without Borders, Poetry International, English PEN, Modern Poetry in Translation, Two Lines,* and *Specimen.* Kareem holds a PhD in Comparative Literature from the State University of New York at Binghamton. She has taught at Princeton, Tufts, University of Maryland College Park, SUNY Binghamton, Rutgers, and Bronx Community College. Her translations include Ashraf Fayadh's *Instructions Within* (nominated for a BTBA award), Ra'ad Abdulqadir's *Except for this Unseen Thread* (nominated for the Ghobash Banipal prize), and Octavia Butler's *Kindred.*

Madhu Kaza was born in Andhra Pradesh, India, and works as a writer, translator, artist, and educator based in New York City. A translator of Telugu women writers, including Volga and Vimala, her own writing has appeared in the *Los Angeles Review of Books, The Yale Review, Guernica, EcoTheo Review, Chimurenga, Two Lines* and more. She is the editor of *Kitchen Table Translation,* a volume that explores connections between migration and translation and which features immigrant, diasporic, and poc translators. More recently, she guest-curated a feature on writing from less-translated languages for the Summer/Fall 2022 issue of *Gulf Coast,* and in 2021 she served as a juror for the National Book Award in translated literature. She works as the Associate Director for

Microcollege Programs for the Bard Prison Initiative and also teaches in the MFA program at Columbia University.

Monchoachi was born in 1946, in Martinique. His writing is marked by the astonishing character of the Creole language, a language rich in its very poverty, having preserved a speech unaltered by Western rationality, which is reflected in particular in its articulations and the constant play that inhabits it with the invisible. There Monchoachi finds a resource from which to draw: listening to what the word has to say about our relation to the world, a world obstructed and deafened by its present course. Following a period of bilingual publication, Monchoachi transported Creole into the body of a writing that presents a French surface — and there Creole makes its own mark.

Yogesh Maitreya is a poet, translator and writer. He's the founder of Panther's Paw Publication, an anticaste English publishing house. His books are blueprints of his existence in this vast world.

Barbara Ofosu-Somuah is an educational equity researcher, writer, and emerging Italian-to-English translator, from Accra, Ghana, and the Bronx, New York. As a translator, she attempts to bring the works of contemporary Afro-Italian writers to English-speaking audiences. She has received both Thomas J. Watson and Fulbright research fellowships to investigate the racialized lived experiences of Black people, primarily womxn, across the African diaspora. During her Fulbright year, she collaborated with various Black Italian organizations/collectives as they unpacked the reality of concurrently embodying Blackness and Italianness in a culture that perceives both identities as incompatible. Ofosu-Somuah has a bachelor of arts in sociology, psychology, and Italian, from Middlebury College.

Gitanjali Patel is an award-winning researcher and a Wolfson postgraduate scholar at the University of Birmingham, where her research focusses on translation as a critical pedagogy. She is also the director of Shadow Heroes, an organisation that supports young people in embracing all sides of their linguistic and cultural heritages through creative translation workshops, and a Renaissance One Associate Artist.

M. NourbeSe Philip was born in Tobago, and is an unembedded poet, essayist, novelist, playwright, and independent scholar who lives in the space-time of the City of Toronto where she practiced law for seven years before becoming a poet and writer. Among her published works are the seminal *She Tries Her Tongue, Her Silence Softly Breaks*; the speculative prose poem, *Looking for Livingston: An Odyssey of Silence*; the young adult novel, *Harriet's Daughter*; the play, *Coups and Calypsos*; and four collections of essays including her most recent collection, *BlanK*. Her book-length poem, *Zong!*, is a conceptually innovative, genre-breaking epic, which explodes the legal archive as it relates to slavery. *Zong!* was named the 2021 winner of *World Literature Today's (WLT)* 21 Books for the 21st Century. Among her awards are numerous Canada Council and Ontario Arts Council grants, including the prestigious Chalmers Award (Ontario Arts Council) and the Canada Council's Victor Martyn Lynch-Staunton Award (Outstanding mid-career artist), as well as the Pushcart Prize (USA), the Casa de las Americas Prize (Cuba), the Lawrence Foundation Prize (USA), the Arts Foundation of Toronto Writing and Publishing Award (Toronto), and Dora Award finalist (Drama). Her fellowships include Guggenheim, McDowell, and Rockefeller (Bellagio). She is an awardee of both the YWCA Woman of Distinction (Arts) and the Elizabeth Fry Rebels for a Cause awards. She has been Writer-in-Residence at several universities and a guest at writers' retreats. M. NourbeSe Philip is the 2020 recipient of PEN/Nabokov Award for Achievement in International Literature. She is also the 2021 recipient of the Canada Council for the Arts' lifetime achievement award, the Molson Prize, for her "invaluable contributions to literature."

Dr. Sofia Rehman is an independent scholar specialising in Islam and Gender, an author, and educator. When she is not reading books for research, she is reading them for pleasure. She is the founder of Leeds Lit Book Club which is now in its 8th year. During the global pandemic she launched the Islam and Gender read alongs in which she facilitates readings of academic texts penned by Muslim female scholars in conversation with a global virtual audience and has recently been featured by both Vogue Arabia and Refinery29. She is a contributor to Mapping Faith: Theologies of Migration edited by Lia Shimada and to Cut From the Same Cloth? edited by Sabeena Akhtar. She has publications of her own due out with Oxford University Press and Kube Publications. You can connect with her on her Instagram @Sofia_reading where she talks about all things related to books, faith and academia.

Aaron Robertson is a writer, translator, and editor at Spiegel & Grau. His translation of Igiaba Scego's novel *Beyond Babylon* (Two Lines Press) was shortlisted for the 2019 PEN Translation Prize and National Translation Award. In 2021, he received a National Endowment for the Arts grant in translation. Aaron's work has appeared in *The New York Times, The Nation, Foreign Policy, n+1, The Point,* and elsewhere. His first book, *The Black Utopians*, is forthcoming from Farrar, Straus, and Giroux in 2023.

Hamid Roslan is the author of *parsetreeforestfire* (Ethos Books, 2019). His other work can be found in the *Asian American Writers Workshop, Asymptote, minarets*, the *Practice Research & Tangential Activities (PR&TA) Journal, The Volta, Of Zoos*, and the *Quarterly Literary Review Singapore*, among others. He is currently pursuing a Masters of Fine Arts in Writing at Pratt Institute.

Ayesha Manazir Siddiqi is a writer and editor. Her essays and reviews have appeared in publications including the *Independent, CeaseFire Magazine, The Theatre Times, Wasafiri, Media Diversified*, the *Express Tribune*, and *Burnt Roti*. Her fiction has been published in anthologies by Peepal Tree Press, Oberon Books, Influx Press, and EMC. Her plays and monologues have had rehearsed readings and stagings at venues including the Rich Mix, Theatre 503 and the Tristan Bates theatre in London, and the Impact Hub in Birmingham, and she's also written for *BBC Radio 4*. Recently, Ayesha was contributing editor for the *Serial/New York Times* podcast, *The Trojan Horse Affair*, and her debut novel *The Centre* is being published by Picador next year. Ayesha is from Karachi and lives in London.

Elisa Taber is a doctoral candidate at McGill University. She writes and translates herself into an absent presence. *An Archipelago in a Landlocked Country* is her first book.

Sandra Tamele, BArch, CIOL DipTrans, the first Mozambican to publish literature in translation (2007), founder member of the Mozambican Translators Association (2016), founder member of the Mozambican Publishers Association (2022). In 2015 Sandra designed and has since sponsored/organized 7 consecutive editions of the annual literary translation competition that led to the establishment of Editora Trinta Zero Nove (2018), the first Mozambican Publisher dedicated to Literary Translation. The initiative was awarded the LBF International Excellence Award in 2021. Sandra's start-up is spearheading the publication of audiobooks in the country, growing its catalogue from three titles and one language in 2019 to over fifty titles and 7 languages now, and is a trailblazer in the PALOP with a growing distribution network, and the only Publisher in the region with presence in the Bologna, Cairo, Frankfurt, London, and Sharjah International Book Fairs. Sandra translated 17 books (poetry, short stories and novels) from English and Italian.

Nariman Youssef is a Cairo-born literary translator and translation consultant based in London. She has translated numerous works of poetry and fiction from Arabic, and has led curated translation workshops with Shadow Heroes, Shubbak Festival and Africa Writes. She also works in the arts and heritage sector and, since 2013, has managed and an in-house translation team at the British Library. She holds a master's degree in translation studies from the University of Edinburgh.

ABOUT THE EDITORS

Kavita Bhanot is ECR Leverhulme Fellow at Leicester University. She wrote the landmark essay 'Decolonise not Diversify' in 2015. She has edited three short-story collections, including *Too Asian, not Asian Enough* and *Book of Birmingham,* and co-founded the Literature Must Fall collective and festival, with whom she organises reading groups and events. She is an editor with Media Diversified, for whom she curates essays under Literature Must Fall. Kavita is writing a book with Pluto Press on Literature Must Fall as a new paradigm for reading and writing. Her translation of short stories by Anjali Kajal won a 2021 Pen Translates award and will be published by Comma Press (2022). She won third prize in the 2018 SI Leeds Literary Prize. For the last ten years she has been a reader and mentor with The Literary Consultancy, with whom she runs workshops with publishers on political/ethical editing.

Jeremy Tiang has translated over twenty books from Chinese, including Yan Ge's *Strange Beasts of China* for Tilted Axis Press, as well as novels by Yeng Pway Ngon, Zhang Yueran, Shuang Xuetao, Chan Ho-Kei, Lo Yi-Chin, Geling Yan and Liu Xinwu. He also writes and translates plays, and won the Singapore Literature Prize in 2018 for his novel *State of Emergency*. Originally from Singapore, he now lives in New York City.

Copyright © Shushan Avagyan, Khairani Barokka, Kavita Bhanot, Lúcia Collischonn, Onaiza Drabu, Eric Fishman, Kaiama L. Glover, Eluned Gramich, Anton Hur, Sawad Hussain, Layla Benitez-James, Mona Kareem, Madhu Kaza, Yogesh Maitreya, Monchoachi, Barbara Ofosu-Somuah, Gitanjali Patel, M. NourbeSe Philip, Sofia Rehman, Aaron Robertson, Hamid Roslan, Ayesha Manazir Siddiqi, Elisa Taber, Sandra Tamele, Jeremy Tiang, Nariman Youssef 2022

Monchoachi translation copyright © Eric Fishman 2022

"All the Violence It May Carry on its Back: A Conversation about Diversity and Literary Translation" was originally published in July 2021 as a special feature in *Asymptote Journal.*

"'Blackness' in French: On Translation, Haiti, and the Matter of Race" was originally published in a special issue of *Esprit Créateur* [59.2 (summer 2019): 25-41] as "Race and the Aesthetic in French and Francophone Cultures".

An earlier version of this "Western Poets Kidnap Your Poems and Call Them Translation: On the Colonial Phenomenon of Rendition as Translation" appeared in issue 7 of *Poetry Birmingham Literary Journal.*

"Entre crié et écrit" was originally published in *Éloge de la servilité,* ed. Monchoachi. Vauclin: Lakouzémi, 2007.

An earlier version of "Not a Good Fit", titled "Engaging the New Knowledge", was originally published in *Two Lines* (Spring 2019).

All rights reserved.

tiltedaxispress.com

The rights of Shushan Avagyan, Khairani Barokka, Kavita Bhanot, Lúcia Collischonn, Onaiza Drabu, Eric Fishman, Kaiama L. Glover, Eluned Gramich, Anton Hur, Sawad Hussain, Layla Benitez-James, Mona Kareem, Madhu Kaza, Yogesh Maitreya, Monchoachi, Barbara Ofosu-Somuah, Gitanjali Patel, M. NourbeSe Philip, Sofia Rehman, Aaron Robertson, Hamid Roslan, Ayesha Manazir Siddiqi, Elisa Taber, Sandra Tamele, Jeremy Tiang, Nariman Youssef to be identified as the authors and Eric Fishman as a translator of this work have been asserted in accordance with Section 77 of the Copyright, Designs and Patent Act 1988.

ISBN (paperback) 9781911284789

ISBN (ebook) 9781911284772

A catalogue record for this book is available from the British Library.

Cover art: Amandine Forest

Typesetting and ebook production: Abbas Jaffary

Edited by: Kavita Bhanot and Jeremy Tiang

Publicity: Hana Sandhu

Community Manager: Tice Cin

Foreign Rights Director: Julia Sanches

Publisher: Kristen Vida Alfaro

Print edition made with Affinity Publisher

Printed and bound by Clays Ltd, Elcograf S.p.A.

ABOUT TILTED AXIS PRESS

Tilted Axis is a non-profit press publishing mainly work by Asian writers, translated into a variety of Englishes. This is an artistic project, for the benefit of readers who would not otherwise have access to the work – including ourselves. We publish what we find personally compelling.

Founded in 2015, we are based in the UK, a state whose former and current imperialism severely impacts writers in the majority world. This position, and those of our individual members, informs our practice, which is also an ongoing exploration into alternatives – to the hierarchisation of certain languages and forms, including forms of translation; to the monoculture of globalisation; to cultural, narrative, and visual stereotypes; to the commercialisation and celebrification of literature and literary translation.

We value the work of translation and translators through fair, transparent pay, public acknowledgement, and respectful communication. We are dedicated to improving access to the industry, through translator mentorships, paid publishing internships, open calls and guest curation.

Our publishing is a work in progress – we are always open to feedback, including constructive criticism, and suggestions for collaborations. We are particularly keen to connect with Black and indigenous translators of Asian languages.

tiltedaxispress.com
@TiltedAxisPress